.

One Nation Indivisible

★ ★ ★

HOW ETHNIC SEPARATISM THREATENS AMERICA

J. Harvie Wilkinson, III

▲▼ *Addison-Wesley Publishing Company, Inc.*

Reading, Massachusetts   Menlo Park, California   New York
Don Mills, Ontario   Harlow, England   Amsterdam   Bonn
Sydney   Singapore   Tokyo   Madrid   San Juan
Paris   Seoul   Milan   Mexico City   Taipei

Library of Congress Cataloging-in-Publication Data
Wilkinson, J. Harvie, 1944–
    One nation indivisible : how ethnic separatism threatens America / J. Harvie Wilkinson, III.
        p.   cm.
    Includes bibliographical references and index.
    ISBN 0-201-18072-3
    1. Pluralism (Social sciences)—United States.   2. United States—Ethnic relations.   3. Multiculturalism—United States.   I. Title.
HM276.W497   1997
305.8′00973—dc21   96-39225
                                                                         CIP

Jacket design by Suzanne Heiser
Text design by Diane Levy
Set in 11-point Caslon 540 by Shepard Poorman Communications Corporation

1 2 3 4 5 6 7 8 9-DOH-0100999897
First printing, April 1997

Addison-Wesley books are available at special discounts for bulk purchases. For more information about how to make such purchases in the U.S., please contact the Corporate, Government, and Special Sales Department at Addison-Wesley Publishing Company, One Jacob Way, Reading, MA 01867, or call (800) 238-9682.

To
Nelson and Porter

Contents

Preface

*T*his is a book about national unity. About how the *United* States can live up to its name. About how a place of many races can remain a single country. About America meaning something special to Americans no matter what their race or ethnic origin may be.

No one doubts the increasing diversity of America. Legal immigrants from around the world arrive in this country by the hundreds of thousands every year. American cities today present an extraordinary array of ethnic cultures—Indian, Ethiopian, Korean, Haitian, Lebanese, Vietnamese, and many others—a mosaic found nowhere else on earth. We have also awoken to the contributions of African Americans, Latinos, and other ethnic groups that have helped build America over the centuries. Many argue now about whether to restrict immigration and about how to return America to what she used to be. Some deplore the loss of the old homogeneity and fear the new future of ethnic diversity.

New America is here, however. It is a fact. It should be a glorious fact too, but that will depend on what we do.

At present, we are not doing well. Our civil rights laws are courting racial separation at the very moment we should be seeking national unity. We have started down the road of ethnic division just as our multicultural future is taking shape.

We are pursuing separatist politics, dispensing separatist entitlements, offering separatist education, and constructing separatist modes of thought and speech. Americans of all races and backgrounds have forgotten who we are and to what we belong.

As the United States becomes a multicultural nation, we must consider what form that multiculturalism will take. Whether we will become a nation of interethnic union or a nation of separate ethnic enclaves is unclear. Whether ethnic diversity will become our deepest reservoir of national strength or the cause of our undoing is uncertain. America may be a stronger nation by 2100 or it may no longer be one nation at all. It should now be apparent that the question of union was not settled when Grant and Lee left Appomattox. The question of race tore our national fabric once before, and it can do so again.

This book not surprisingly reflects my professional outlook and background. Since 1984, I have served as a federal judge. Before that, I taught law at the University of Virginia. I recognize that the separatist threat to our country is larger than the law alone. And yet I believe that law can affect our behavior—that it can bridge differences or it can open chasms that we cannot close. Americans have the potential for profound racial fellowship *and* for intense racial animosity. The law will have much to say about which side of our country's personality prevails.

We stand now at a critical juncture in our race relations— one every bit as important as that of 1860 or 1954. I explore in this book the threat of separatism to American society. I ask what has caused us to drift apart and what may bring us back together. Chapter 1 shows how dramatically America has changed in recent years. Chapter 2 asks how all this change should affect our outlook on civil rights.

The middle section of the book explores two competing views of our country—the integrationist vision of America and the separatist one. As we shall see, it is the separatist vision that is gaining ground.

The final section addresses actual separatist practices in different areas of American life—in our politics, entitlements, education and speech. In each of these areas, we face choices that will bring us closer together or drive us further apart. The choices before us are not easy. How we make them will affect our future—even our existence—as a nation. That is what is at stake.

Part One

NEW AMERICA

— *1* —

The Medley of America

$\mathcal{A}$merica has transformed itself again. Our country has always been a remarkable mélange of ancestries. As Walter Lippmann observed in 1914, "The great social adventure of America is no longer the conquest of the wilderness, but the absorption of fifty different peoples." But today's America is more diverse than at any time in our history. The most recent ten-year accounting of ourselves revealed that, for the first time, more Americans are descended from the forty-eight million who immigrated to the United States since 1790 than from those who lived in the United States before 1790.

But eighteenth-century comparisons are not necessary to underscore the change in America. Today a decade is a demographic century. In 1990, Efrian Nava was sixteen years old. If she had been born ten or twenty years before, she would have been one of the few Latino faces in her high school. Ten years earlier her Los Angeles high school was 90 percent black, and twenty years earlier it was 90 percent white. Instead of being twenty-six or thirty-six years old, though, Efrian was a teenager and part of a Latino population that comprised almost half of Inglewood High School.

Efrian's school mirrors the changing snapshot of California, where America is recasting itself more quickly than anywhere else. In 1980, California was 76 percent white. By 1991, the Hispanic community had grown almost 70 percent, the Asian community 127 percent. The 1990 census showed that California was 57 percent white. Inland Fresno was the site of the state's most dramatic change: its Asian American population increased by an extraordinary 626 percent in the 1980s. Nearly one in four Californians is foreign born. And in 1996, state experts reported that only one in two Californians was Anglo. Thirty percent of the population was Latino, over 10 percent Asian, and 7 percent African American.

Though no other state approaches California's diversity, the rest of our country has changed as well. The 1990 census catalogued a fivefold increase from twenty years ago in the number of foreign-born Americans—twenty-one million Americans, almost nine million of whom entered the United States in the 1980s. Today's America has a record number of Asian and Hispanic Americans. The Asian population has grown to 3.4 percent of the population, up from 1.6 percent in 1980; and the Hispanic population has jumped from 6.4 percent of the population to 9.8 percent. Hispanic Americans may surpass African Americans as the largest minority before the year 2010.

The future holds more ethnic diversity in store. By the turn of the century, Hispanic, black, and Asian children will constitute close to a majority of American children. Already, 27 percent of Americans between the ages of five and fourteen are black or Hispanic, and nearly 4 percent are Asian. And if present trends continue, these racial groups will compose close to half the entire U.S. population by the year 2050. Anglo Americans will then become the largest American minority group, at least for a while.

Racial and ethnic classifications have real drawbacks. Invariably, they oversimplify. The catchall categories of Asian and Hispanic mask endless differences. An astonishing sixty countries sent an annual average of over one thousand immigrants to the United States from 1971 to 1985. Even immigrants from one country cannot easily be grouped together. Ethiopians in San Francisco speak at least six different languages. Some are Christian, some are Jewish, and others are Muslim. Chinese and Filipinos constitute the largest number of Asian Americans (both roughly approximating the number of Native Americans), but a multiplicity of places of ancestry comprise the category "Asian": from India to the countries and islands of the Southeast Asian peninsula to Hawaii and Samoa. In 1992, for example, mainland China, India, the Philippines and Vietnam provided the bulk of Asian immigrants. But five other countries also sent over ten thousand immigrants to the U.S. that year: Japan, Korea, Iran, Pakistan, and Taiwan. Mexican Americans are the predominant immigrant group from those countries to the south of us. Other Americans, however, claim Puerto Rico, Cuba, El Salvador and even the tiny islands of St. Lucia, St. Kitts, and Montserrat as their ancestry. Aside from Mexico, at least ten thousand immigrants came from Cuba, the Dominican Republic, Haiti, Jamaica, El Salvador, Guatemala, and Colombia in 1992.

Since World War II the United States has welcomed more permanent immigrants than any other country—and today America remains the preferred destination for immigrants. Immigration to the United States increased substantially in the decades following the passage of landmark legislation in 1965. In fact, the 1980s was one of only four decades in our history in which immigration accounted for at least 30 percent of the nation's growth. The state of California, by itself, accepts more immigrants than any other nation. Nearly one million new permanent residents now enter the United States each year, and fully 80 percent of these immigrants arrive from Asia, the Pacific Islands, and Latin America.

As arresting as these statistics are, they do not capture New America. The numbers do not by themselves reveal what they have forged: a profoundly different nation. Political life reflects these changes. Elected bodies increasingly mirror the ethnic diversity of the country. Political interest groups have organized to represent each of the varied ethnic groups in America. Groups involved in immigration reform include the Irish Immigration Reform Movement, the Japanese American Citizens League, the Pacific Leadership Conference, and the National Council of La Raza, to name just a few. President Clinton heralded an effort to make his cabinet "look like America." Office seekers compete for new combinations of voters. One contestant for the school board in Queens courted supporters by speaking English and two dialects of Chinese. Candidates who compete for votes in Washington, D.C.'s First Ward face a dauntingly multilingual constituency: the voters speak over twenty-four different languages. Our history is becoming as diverse as our politics: Martin Luther King Day is a national holiday, and in the Black Hills of South Dakota, a statue of Sioux chief Crazy Horse is being carved that will dwarf the four presidents memorialized on Mount Rushmore.

Political America is not, however, where the developing snapshot of the nation is most evident. Literally every corner of public space showcases a changing country. Our new diversity is present in shops and on streets, where entrepreneurs hawk Afghani cotton pouches, Malian mudcloth hats, and Japanese yukata. And it is unmistakable in airports, where the chatter of some 148 of the world's 208 language groups represented in the United States may be heard. Spanish-only radio and television crowd on the dial with other distinctive language stations. Even the toys we select for our children reflect our new nation. Black, Asian, and Hispanic dolls, in addition to Anglo ones, now inhabit Fisher-Price dollhouses.

Sometimes New America makes me want to be a child again. I should love to be young and feel the vitality of our new nation in my veins. But New America has plenty to tempt a fifty-two-year-old too. The dizzying assortment of ethnic cuisine is my middle-aged feast. Vendors of ethnic foods preside over a multibillion-dollar industry that encompasses everything from Indian grocers to frozen burritos to specialty Thai spices. At Biba in Boston, diners choose from the foods of ten nations or more, including grits with crab, tandoori lamb, and Chinese pork rump. Street concessions now peddle far more than hot dogs and pretzels: falafel, Asian noodles, gyros, and sushi stands saturate the streets and food courts of America's cities. And the trend is not confined to urban centers on the two coasts. Birmingham, Alabama, is home to over sixty Chinese restaurants, nearly ten times the number it had in 1980.

The variety of cultural expression is staggering. More than seventeen hundred arts organizations in the United States are ethnically oriented. Their missions are as mixed as the ancestries they celebrate: acclaimed flamenco dancer Jose Greco seeks to preserve Spanish dances and styles; traditional storytellers in Tucson educate Native American children about their history; and community-based artists in Alaska work to promote the art of Alaska's seven native cultural groups.

Along one block in Queens, passersby may encounter a Chinese-owned bakery, a Korean-run stationery store, and a Bangladeshi-owned grocery. Of course, New York's ethnic enclaves are nothing new, but today they have a fresh face: Albanians in Belmont and Bedford Park in the Bronx;

Dominicans in Manhattan's Washington Heights and Spanish Harlem; Haitians and West Indians in Brooklyn's Flatbush. New York's Chinatown, like its Asian population, is exploding, edging its way into neighboring Little Italy. Customers of New York Telephone can expect repair service in 140 languages, including Fiji, French, Russian, Sioux, Swahili, and Twi. But it is not just our largest cities that are changing. Suburban sprawl, too, is being reshaped by a new ethnic and cultural diversity. Nearly half—43 percent—of Hispanic Americans are suburbanites. Asian Americans, too, mostly live in suburbs, making their mark on places like Filipino Daly City, Chinese Monterey Park, and Little Saigon of Westminster, Orange County.

Though the degree of today's diversity is new, our tradition of blending cultures has not faded. Today's analogue to the Louisiana Cajuns or Pennsylvania Dutch may be our mingled foods. A Franco-Oriental restaurant in Chicago, French-Chinese nouvelle cuisine in San Francisco, or a sampling of lime-cilantro-jalapeno ice cream in Los Angeles typify our New America. And, in perhaps the ultimate test of interaction, our ancestries are mixing through marriage as well. The 1990 census disclosed that 56 percent of unions among Caucasian Americans are between those whose ethnic backgrounds do not overlap at all.

Just over a quarter century after the Supreme Court invalidated antimiscegenation statutes, the number of marriages across racial and ethnic boundaries remains small. Only 2 percent of marriages by Anglos are with non-Anglo partners, and just 4 percent of African Americans marry non-African Americans. Intermarriage for Hispanic and Asian Americans is somewhat greater. Younger people, though, intermarry at a higher rate. Twice as many young white Americans, compared with the white population as a whole, and nearly 10 percent of young African American men, intermarry. And, one survey reported, 40 percent of native-born American Puerto Ricans are married to Anglo Americans.

New Americans encounter each other in the schoolyard and workplace. Students in Arlington, Virginia's, public schools speak fifty-nine different languages, including Farsi and Khmer. Half of the teenagers entering the job market in Los Angeles are Latino, 12 percent are Asian, and 11 percent are black. Employers and educators face upcoming generations with vastly different experiences and practices from their own. Teachers and supervisors instruct across a cultural divide.

Sometimes New America only adds to my gray hair. Is there any longer an America? Or is it only just New? What does the future hold? Will our young folks come through? Young Americans are coming of age with this new nation already upon us. It remains to be seen, however, whether this fact will lead to interracial harmony. In some cases, younger generations can form the bridge between older generations who face difficulty understanding each other. Police officers in Dallas's most ethnically diverse neighborhood, for instance, protect residents who speak twenty-seven different languages. The children are named Vajin, Karwan, Sasha, Hong, and Luo Fei. The languages they speak are as varied as their names: Chinese, Kurdish, Somali, Ido, Cambodian, Farsi, Bengali, Russian, Urdu, Spanish, and English. Not surprisingly, the children are often pressed into service as interpreters for the adults.

There is reason to hope that younger generations will thrive in multicultural America. At the University of California at Berkeley, where there is no ethnic majority, the bulk of freshmen report that they were attracted to the school because of its cultural variety. We must beware, however, of sweet prophecies about future generations, which have been uttered before. The American civil rights movement rested its hopes on the young people of America. Thirty years later, however, racial conflict in the high schools refuses to subside. Most ominously, hate crimes are committed increasingly by younger perpetrators.

Today's signals about the future of America are difficult to read. Those who come of age in New America may lead us through the obstacle course that is before us. They may also, however, falter in their attempts to grapple with our old antagonist of race. What is clear, however, is that America itself will never be the same. At some point in the twenty-first century—"*Time* guesses that it will be the year 2056—the 'average' American will be someone whose origins are in Asia, Africa, Arabia, the Hispanic world, or the Pacific Islands." Or, more probably, America will be so diverse that it will make little sense to speak of an "average" American at all.

Each of us will relate to the rapid change in America in intensely personal ways. Often I catch myself comparing New America with the land of my boyhood. It seems to me now that growing up in America after World War II was much like gazing into a reflecting pool. Everything seemed the image of everything else. The houses and the hairstyles were all pretty much the same. The few TV shows featured white middle-class family life, and the first-grade textbooks featured Dick and Jane. The president was a war hero with a winning grin. Wheaties really was the Breakfast of Champions and the drug of choice was indeed bubble gum. As a young boy in Richmond, Virginia, I went to Saint Christopher's, a small school in tall pines that taught fair play. My father was a bank president, and our family attended the midtown Episcopal church, Saint James's.

My childhood was as distant from multicultural America as any childhood could possibly be. Although there have been attempts to portray the 1950s as an era where "many people were already beginning to question the purpose of their lives," people were not on the whole receptive to new ideas or unorthodox beliefs. As a youngster, I was troubled by the thought that communists and socialists might sneak into my beloved Virginia. I was sent away to boarding school for watching the subversive Bob Cummings show. I never had a black schoolmate until I went to college. Worse still, I never really raised a protest. Conformity was so comfortable for those of us in the majority that discrimination against the minority became a subject of indifference and neglect. Life was as bountiful to me as it was difficult on others. Nostalgia does not seem in order for a decade when segregation reigned by law in the South and by custom almost everywhere else.

It is easy to throw off on those square, corny, stolid years. Their sameness could even be too much for children. I did not warm quickly to the gestures of patriotism. I was embarrassed to place my hand on my heart during "The Star-Spangled Banner," for fear my friends might see. I mumbled "America, the Beautiful" for fear of being caught off-key. The Pledge, the flag, the salutes, the songs, the entire Rotarian eternity of it all, either bored me stiff or made me ill at ease. It took me a long time to understand that affection for a country, no less than for a child, is no cause for embarrassment. I did not come quickly to the realization that national symbols are more than skin-deep. My childhood gaze did not comprehend the feeling for America that existed all around me. That those Americans of my childhood really did live and breathe their country's virtues. That they were never ashamed to show the world the home of the brave and the land of the free.

★　★　★

The years of my childhood may have more in common with the conformity of earlier centuries than with the America of today. The country Alexis de Tocqueville described in 1835 was composed mostly of "the peoples of Europe." The early days of the Republic were marked by relative homogeneity. "Providence," wrote John Jay, "has been pleased to give this one connected country to one united people—a people descended from the same ancestors, speaking the same language, professing the same religion, attached to the same principles of government, very similar in their manners and customs." Moreover, it was a society explicitly devoted to assimilating newcomers: John Quincy Adams once exhorted all immigrants to "cast off the European skin" and embrace American culture. If an Irishman could "cast off his European skin," an African could not—his skin marked him as different. So while European immigrants melded into early American civil society with comparative ease, black slaves and Native Americans were pushed to the margin, unassimilated and unacknowledged.

The relative homogeneity of European immigrants undoubtedly facilitated their early integration. Since those early times, one of America's defining characteristics has been its increasingly varied and diverse influx of immigrants. New trends in immigration at the beginning of the twentieth century changed the face of America. Between 1880 and 1920, over twenty-three million people came to America, many from southern and eastern Europe. Notwithstanding this new diversity, the goal of assimilation continued to predominate, despite the emergence of some early "cultural pluralism" theories. James Bryce in 1888 remarked upon "the amazing solvent power which American institutions, habits, and ideas exercise upon newcomers of all races." But blacks were excluded from Bryce's observation, just as they continued to be excluded from American life by Jim Crow laws enacted in many Southern and border states at the turn of the century.

The demographics of the United States in the 1950s might have surprised de Tocqueville only mildly. In perhaps the most important development, African Americans began a massive migration out of the South. At the turn of the century, blacks made up about 47 percent of the population of the five Deep South states; by 1970 blacks comprised 25 percent of those states. As the black population moved north and west in search of industrial jobs during World War II and other economic opportunities in the 1950s, African Americans began to acquire a greater measure of influence in Northeastern and midwestern states. This demographic shift was one of the underlying forces behind the fledgling civil rights movement.

During the same period that African Americans were migrating out of the South, new immigration patterns began to lay the foundations for our modern diversity, though progress at first was slow and piecemeal. Although in 1950 immigration quotas severely restricted immigration from many non-European countries, by 1965 the most restrictive rules had been gradually changed to permit truly worldwide immigration.

The 1965 Immigration and Nationality Act represented a bold shift in immigration policy. Congress abolished the old national-origin quota system, which allocated visas according to numerical targets for each country. This quota system favored northern and western European immigrants while disfavoring other regions. After 1965, immigration policy provided preferences to immigrants based on family relationships and occupational qualifications. The family-preference policy was crucial to the new immigration strategy: it awarded immigrant visas to those who had close familial connections to United States citizens or permanent residents. The resulting wave of immigrants differed dramatically from its predecessors. European immigration dwindled as Latin America and Asia became the primary sources of new American immigrants.

The 1980s probably saw the greatest numerical influx of total immigrants, legal and illegal, in the nation's history—roughly ten million people.

Today, a virtual cottage industry of commentary ponders the consequences of immigration. The commentators themselves draw two starkly different visions of the future. Both visions are, ironically, steeped in nostalgia. Those disenchanted by the changing demographics of America summon a homogeneous American identity that they claim will be subverted by the flow of Asian and Latin American immigrants. Pundits on the other side dismiss any questions about the path we are taking; their dreamy invocation of Ellis Island imagery slights the challenges we face today. Neither the optimists nor the pessimists adequately address the serious questions that confront New America.

The optimists and the pessimists agree on nothing. It is hard to believe that they inhabit the same land. The pessimists preach that American culture as we know it is on the brink of destruction, mainly as a result of our immigration policies. Lawrence Auster alleges that the continuing flow of immigrants from "Third World countries" is "feeding a host of cultural ills that may well prove incurable," including

> the loss of a common language, common literature, and common national identity; the dismantling of the common American citizenship in favor of group rights and quotas based on race; the decline of skill levels and the development of a permanent two-tier society . . . the overwhelming of basic social institutions . . . the effective loss of U.S. sovereignty to foreign-based criminal gangs . . . [and] murderous interracial conflict in the major cities.

In short, he says, our "American national identity and way of life are being delegitimized and submerged by the continuing Third-World invasion of this country."

Peter Brimelow's broadside against current immigration policies in the 1995 book *Alien Nation: Common Sense about America's Immigration Disaster* sounds many of the same themes. He claims that today's immigrants are less skilled and less educated than previous immigrants, more divergent from the American majority, more prone than past immigrants to crime, and more eager to launch an ethnic and racial transformation of this country. There is no breathing space, he argues, to foster integration of these new immigrants because of the steady increase in immigration since 1965.

A real rub for Brimelow seems to be that the new arrivals are not from Europe. They are "from completely different, and arguably incompatible, cultural traditions." Brimelow insists that "the American nation has always had a specific ethnic core. And that core has been white." Auster decries "the steady decline of Americans of European descent from majority toward minority status." One statistic roars again and again: European Americans may be approaching minority position in the next century.

The pessimists subtly seek to define Americans by the color of their skin. They would deny this country the vast potential contributions that persons of divergent backgrounds have to make. They would leave America a largely white island in an increasingly interconnected and interracial world. Moreover, they yearn for a past that never was. Indeed, a lower percentage of Americans are foreign born today than in the early part of this century.

What critics see today as an undistinguished mass of European stock was not what our predecessors saw. Each successive whitecap of Irish, Germans, Italians, or Poles was greeted with the same howls we hear now. Opposition to immigration was a central theme of the Know-Nothing movement. The "new" southern and eastern European immigrants of the late nineteenth century were seen as threatening because they were Catholics, did not speak English, were not craftsmen or farmers, were physically different from earlier immigrants, and crowded together in cities. Catholic birthrates would overwhelm the Anglo-Saxon population; the Italians would never assimilate. At each interval, previous waves of immigrants are viewed favorably; it is the present generation of immigrants who are seen to pose a threat. In short, today's pessimistic view of New America sounds an old—much refuted—refrain.

The weakness of the gloom and doom position about multiethnic America has a parallel, however, in its optimistic opposite. Those who glibly dismiss the challenges of multicultural America are wearing blinders. Their view is obstructed by a rendition of our immigrant past, one they see as not essentially different from today. If one side of the debate is tainted by pessimism, the other is marred by utopian visions of happy togetherness.

The romantic notion of New America starts with our past, our "nation of immigrants" past. "Of all the political experiments in mankind's history," effuses Kansas City columnist Jerry Heaster, "this nation has been unique in its willingness to provide a refuge for foreigners seeking a better life. . . . The practical result of America's willingness to accommodate myriad ethnic and cultural influences has been its ascent to power and greatness." Often the immigrant is portrayed as more in tune with America than those who were born here. "In an era of crass materialism and widespread, growing cynicism, immigrants help renew, enrich, and rediscover the values of America," writes Sanford Ungar in his book *Fresh Blood: The New American Immigrants*. The immigrants "remind us of ideals too often forgotten, except in empty political dialogue, in America today: the value of family, respect and care for our elders, kindness and compassion for a larger community of interest."

The optimists assume that the future will be just like the past. As a historical matter, they point out, immigration has been a positive force for national growth. It has brought not only economic benefits, but also new ideas, new strengths, and new energy. The immigrant, invariably, is a heroic character: "[Immigrants] are strong, adventuresome, brave—the best. They will go where the bread and dignity of work is to be found, no matter the law or barbed wire, always have, always will." The list of individual immigrants who have made valuable contributions to our country is endless: John Paul Jones, Albert Einstein, Martina Navratilova, John Shalikashvili, Vladimir Horowitz, and Hakeem Olajuwon, to name but a few. "Just as they always have been," continues Ungar, the immigrants "are the valedictorians of today, the concert pianists and rocket scientists of tomorrow, the writers, poets, and musicians working at the frontiers of creativity."

The United States, the optimists assert, has an endless capacity to welcome newcomers. This is so because our democratic political system and our capitalist economy draw on individual strengths by maximizing individual choices. When immigrants become citizens, they are assimilated into the American political system, but in a way that preserves their freedom of political choice. Likewise, when new immigrants enter the American market, they are free to pursue their personal goals and interests in the most productive manner. In this way, our political and economic freedoms have always allowed us to make fruitful use of our differences. The contributions of every American, regardless of race or ethnic group, potentially enrich our culture, art, politics, science, and economy.

The optimists gloss merrily over the dilemmas of multicultural conflict. Controversy over immigration is said to result simply from a "loss of courage" on the part of Americans. One commentator even suggests that citizenship and voting should not be paired; aliens should be permitted to vote. Julian Simon, an economist who finds no basis for limitations on immigration, asserts that "there's no reason whatsoever to think that there's more conflict in the United States now than there was in the past." Thus, the difficult questions that unprecedented diversity poses are, in reality, nothing new. The optimists refuse to recognize the danger that New America may produce interminable racial conflict and possess no national core.

Both the optimists and pessimists see only part of the picture of New America. Clutching to a rosy memory, each ignores the challenges of a new country in a new century. New America is fundamentally different from the nation we have known, and it will present dangers and opportunities that we are not now prepared to meet.

The debate over immigration itself is a sign of the shoals ahead. It is surely legitimate to ask whether a society can accommodate all the "roughly 1 million legal immigrants who take up permanent residence each year." It is legitimate also to examine "concerns about organized crime, welfare, big government, family values, civil liberties, population growth, economic competitiveness, [and] the protection of American workers," all of which are part of immigration policy. Yet the way we are debating the immigration issue has the potential to permanently divide New America. The debate has not just been waged by extremists either. Both Brimelow (the pessimist author of *Alien Nation*) and Ungar (the optimist author of *Fresh Blood*) are respectable figures. Brimelow is a senior editor of *Forbes* and *National Review*, while Ungar is dean of the

School of Communication at American University. Yet Brimelow astonishingly sees in present immigration policies nothing less than "Adolph Hitler's posthumous revenge on America," while Ungar sees in the opponents of those policies nothing more than "self-proclaimed 'real' Americans" and "obsequious super-patriots." " 'There has never been any real basis for opposing immigration but racism, in one form or another,' " reads the concluding quotation from Ungar's book.

The white American as nativist; the immigrant as alien. If these degrading stereotypes were employed in a discussion on domestic race relations, we would be quick to denounce them. Yet somehow they have become staples of the immigration debate. It is true that immigration issues have always been supercharged—us versus them, Old Americans versus New Americans and the like. While we may have had the luxury of this heated crossfire in times past, we no longer do. Today, assaults on Anglo Americans as mean-spirited nativists will only increase the hostility of those populations toward our newest citizens. In multicultural America, moreover, immigrants will share to an increasing extent the characteristics of *American* minorities. Raw arguments against immigration will thus strike many Asian and Hispanic Americans, for example, as raw dislike of *them*. Whatever the merits of Proposition 187, which denied illegal immigrants in California access to most public benefits, it was not exactly a unifying event. "At pro-187 meetings and rallies," notes Gregory Rodriguez of Pacific News Service, "proponents demonized Mexicans as violent and parasitic. As a result, even second- and third-generation Latino-Americans, many of whom themselves favored curbing illegal immigration, feared the Prop 187-inspired hysteria would lead to discrimination against all Latinos." What the school segregation conflagrations were to the 1950s and 1960s, the immigration issue may become to New

America. This is because we have lost the capacity to conduct debate on any subject without resort to the rhetoric of race.

So how to remove race from preoccupying everything we do? How to adapt those old values of national self-esteem to New America? This will require that Americans like each other more and understand each other better than we presently do. I would not want my son and daughter, to whom this book is dedicated, to inherit the too homogeneous nation I grew up in. I do want them, however, to live in a strong and unified America. Unfortunately, the evidence is mounting that this may not be their destiny. The clouds of racial separatism gather—ones that are more menacing than those that shadowed American life in the years after World War II. If we ignore the storm clouds of separatism, we deprive our children of a country that is both diverse and indivisible. Indeed, they may not make the acquaintance of America at all.

"The proof of a poet," Walt Whitman wrote in the 1855 preface to *Leaves of Grass*, "is that his country absorbs him as affectionately as he has absorbed it." Will there be fewer poetic visions of America? Will fewer citizens be willing to absorb it? As the debate over immigration demonstrates, the future of our country remains a question mark. We are indeed on the verge of a new frontier, although it is no longer one of broad plains and rugged mountains. Instead, it is a frontier of peoples and of cultures. One wonders whether we shall create the great nation from our frontier that our nineteenth-century forebears created from theirs. And what mistakes we'll make, as they surely did, along the way.

This book is an attempt to address the difficulties that now confront us—especially those pertaining to the law of civil rights. It adopts neither the optimistic nor the pessimistic picture of America's multicultural future, because that future depends on what course we now undertake. The choice that confronts America is between ethnic separatism and national oneness. The road ahead may be one of debilitating racial discord, or of singular, unprecedented national strength. It's our future, not someone else's. What we make of New America is up to us.

— 2 —

Making the Medley Work

New America requires new thinking on civil rights. Policies that were viable in the bipolar world of black and white will no longer work in a multicultural setting. The civil rights policies we have followed since the 1970s are not only outmoded; they serve to separate us as well. It is not merely quaint, therefore, but dangerous, to take Model T civil rights law onto the multicultural superhighway. If we do not change course, our hopes for national unity shall be overtaken by the reality of racial division.

There are several civil rights policies we must reexamine in multicultural America. First, the model of discrimination in biracial America makes less and less sense in a multicultural setting. The snapshot of racial discrimination that still dominates debate is drawn from the epic civil rights battles of the 1950s and 1960s. We still see in our mind's eye the defiant gestures of intransigent segregationists, their lines in the dust and their fists in the air. The malignity of the George Wallaces and the Bull Connors lingers in the national psyche still. So do the Great Marches—on Washington in 1963 and from Selma to Montgomery in 1965. Both the heroes and villains of America's civil rights years were so vivid that they are permanently etched in our collective memory. As well they should be, given the magnitude of injustice that existed and the magnitude of prejudice that must be remedied still.

Nonetheless, this midcentury model of discrimination—one where a white majority suppresses a black minority—will not explain events in a multicultural society. The standoffs at the schoolhouse door and the urban race riots of the 1960s revealed the tensions between black and white America. The old order of race relations was, at its worst, characterized by a sharp duality of antagonisms, much like two pugilists in a ring. This duality of antagonisms was most evident in black-white relations, but it was not confined to them. Anglos and Hispanics in the Southwest and whites and Asians in the West experienced tensions as well. In each case, a white majority oppressed an American minority of color.

This old order of race relations is changing rapidly. In recent decades, advances in transportation, migration into and across the country, and the call of economic opportunity have brought minorities not just into contact with the white majority but into increasing contact with one another. Thus the new order of race relations is kaleidoscopic, with antagonisms and alliances shifting every which way. Multicultural America boasts more combinations of racial combatants, and it is becoming increasingly difficult to predict who the combatants will be. Where once an "us" versus "them" mentality often characterized the relationship between black and white Americans, now the same sentiment describes hostilities between minority races. Conflicts between African Americans and Korean Americans in New York and Los Angeles, and between Hispanic Americans and African Americans in Miami and Washington, D.C., have generated national attention. Racial perspectives of all sorts have become badly oversimplified. A politically active Hispanic American in northern

Virginia, lamenting divisiveness within the Hispanic population, "admire[s] the Orientals, because they're close-knit"; while an Asian American political activist, lamenting that Asian Americans "are so fragmented," believes that Asians "have not learned the true process, like . . . Hispanics."

A bipolar perspective on race relations is thus badly oversimplified. The transition from the biracial conflict of old to the multicultural conflict of today can be captured by comparing the 1965 and 1992 race riots in Los Angeles. The 1965 riot in Watts reflected hostilities between black and white Americans. The 1992 uprising, following the verdict in the Rodney King case, exhibited a host of racial subplots, not just black versus white. Its racial ingredients included conflicts between African Americans and Korean Americans, between African Americans and Hispanic Americans, and between groups often thought of as within the same racial classification, Chicanos and Salvadorans. Following the riot, another videotape of a police beating further aggravated racial tensions—this time the beating was of a Hispanic youth by an African American police officer.

Not only has the variety of racial antagonisms proliferated in multicultural America, but their geographic scope has expanded as well. Racial conflict in midcentury America tended to involve, first, the Deep South and then the urban centers of the Midwest and North. Soon, however, the potential for conflict will lack any predictable locus. Americans are a mobile people. Racial and ethnic diversity is coming to communities at an ever accelerating pace. It is no longer accurate to think, for example, of the Hispanic American population as one that resides exclusively in Florida and in the rim states of the Southwest. There are substantial Hispanic American communities in Chicago, Denver, Hartford, Connecticut, and Springfield, Massachusetts. The growth of large Asian

American communities in Washington, D.C., and its Virginia and Maryland suburbs belies any perception that Asian populations are confined solely to the three states on America's West Coast. Not only does the Washington metropolitan area now contain Asian supermarkets, barbershops, cleaners, and churches, but Asian Americans are fast becoming an important political force. Diversity has also pierced America's heartland. In Garden City, Kansas, roughly the geographic center of the continental United States, immigrants have transformed the landscape. Over 20 percent of Garden City's citizens were born abroad, and 40 percent are nonwhite. The town boasts a weekly Spanish newspaper, a Laotian market that distributes Thai videos, a Vietnamese-language mass at a local church, and a Buddhist temple. The patterns of multicultural mobility will have much the same impact as the migration of black Americans into northern and midwestern cities in the 1920s and 1930s. All Americans will face the renewed challenge of racial tolerance even as they confront the renewed potential for racial conflict.

In short, the old midcentury model of racial discrimination is woefully incomplete. It tended to view racism as indigenous to whites alone. But as the novelist Neil Bissoondath has noted: racism is a universal curse, "as American as apple pie, as French as croissants, as Indian as curry, as Jamaican as Akee, as Russian as vodka. . . . It's an item on every nation's menu. Racism, an aspect of human virulence, is exclusive to no race, no country, no culture, no civilization." If the universalism of racial prejudice was obscured by the civil rights battles of the 1950s and 1960s, it is a fact that multiethnic America will have to confront. For Anglo Americans are a diminishing demographic force. Interminority racial conflict is a steadily rising phenomenon. In many jurisdictions, minorities have become the majority, and the potential perpetrators and victims of discrimination in America now boast national origins in more than eighty different countries.

What difference will all this make? Will the lack of predictable white/black antagonists make racial conflict in twenty-first-century America any less virulent? It is possible, of course, that an America of shifting racial alliances will manage to mute racial differences better than it did in the old biracial world of black and white. Any scenario of racial conflict, however—whites and Asians versus Hispanics and blacks, or Cuban Americans versus Chinese Americans, or whomever versus whomever—is an ugly one. The fact that the rash of racial conflict can now break out in so many forms ought to redouble our resolve to be rid of it. Indeed, as long as pervasive racial consciousness persists in this country, multiracial America may look on the simplicity of biracial conflict with something akin to nostalgia.

For all their nastiness, biracial issues have not, at least since the Civil War, threatened the very concept of nationhood. Multicultural racial conflict, however, does just that. Race conflict by definition accentuates race consciousness. The very pervasiveness of that conflict increases the desire of each racial group to withdraw into itself. From behind its own walls and barriers, each race comes to believe that New America has slighted it. Racial leaders increasingly indulge the rhetoric of racial haves and racial have-nots. A racial ranking system is also taking hold—in their book, *The Bell Curve: Intelligence and Class Structure in American Life*, Richard Herrnstein and Charles Murray rate the races in terms of intelligence. In such an atmosphere of racial consciousness, it becomes increasingly difficult to construct any national identity. The civil rights struggle of the 1950s and 1960s sought to realize the best of American ideals. The multiracial conflict of the 1990s has no such animating end.

New America cannot withstand these separatist trends. Recent levels of immigration have already made the task of forging common values uncommonly challenging. And with the passing of the Cold War, an American identity can no longer be forged from the need to face a formidable adversary. Without an international mission or nemesis, the American mystique may vanish in the mists. Some academics now decry "the evil of a shared national identity" altogether. The forces pulling Americans apart are powerful. What may be weakening is our will to resist.

Charles Johnson, a professor of American literature at the University of Washington, proclaims the 1990s "the most intensely race-conscious decade [of] the century." Unfortunately, our preoccupation with race in the twenty-first century threatens to become even more powerful. This is so for many reasons: the role of race in American history, the continuing presence of racial and ethnic divisions on the international stage, and the security of racial solidarity as a rallying cry for those threatened by the bewildering pace of modern change. This last development should not be understated. As technologies render adjustments difficult and skills obsolete, and as the international economy brings prodigious dislocation to the domestic workforce, there will be a temptation to see it all in terms of race.

This temptation will manifest itself in several ways. Anglo Americans may perceive new immigrants as part of a conspiracy to take away their jobs. Discussion surrounding the North American Free Trade Agreement (NAFTA) manifested such sentiments. Opponents of NAFTA feared the "giant sucking sound" of American workers losing their jobs to Mexican laborers, and NAFTA thus "became a lightning rod for anger over lost jobs [and] illegal immigration." The debate over California's adoption of Proposition 187 in 1994 (the so-called

Save Our State initiative) is also illustrative. The law, which denies to illegal immigrants a host of public services including health care and schooling, was proposed at a time when California was suffering a prolonged recession, several successive budget deficits, a loss of jobs, and general economic hardship.

Anglo Americans will not be the only ones, however, to seize the racial explanation for economic misfortune. African Americans may blame Hispanic Americans for the declining numbers of jobs in urban centers. This has already occurred in Miami, Washington, D.C., and Los Angeles. In Los Angeles, for instance, a conflict arose between African Americans and Hispanics over jobs at a hospital in Watts. Constructed after the 1965 riots and named the Martin Luther King Hospital, it is considered by black Americans to be symbolic of their historic struggles for racial justice in Los Angeles. Indeed, blacks regard employment at the hospital almost as a matter of right. Now, however, almost 90 percent of the babies born at the hospital are Hispanic, and Hispanics seek more jobs at the facility to reflect their growing presence in the community. Asian Americans have also entered California's multicultural fray, pointing to racially based admissions and employment policies as barriers to their success. Chinese Americans, for example, recently protested a San Francisco high school's admissions policy, alleging that it valued racial balance over academic merit.

The nature of ethnic friction in New America will be more than just economic, however. It will be more complex even than school admissions controversies or job disputes between Hispanics and blacks. Consider the case of West Indian Americans. There are now more than half a million in the New York area alone, and they make "substantially more money than American blacks. They live in better neighborhoods." In fact, they "fare about as well as Chinese and Korean immigrants."

The relative success of the West Indians (or many Asian Americans, for that matter) raises the risk of prejudice in two ways. First, notes Malcolm Gladwell in *The New Yorker,* "the example of West Indians as 'good' blacks makes the old blanket prejudice against American blacks all the easier to express. The manager can tell black Americans to get off their butts without fear of sounding in his own ears, like a racist, because he has simultaneously celebrated island blacks for their work ethic." Second, the danger exists that West Indian Americans (or successful Asian Americans) will look down on other minorities as lower rungs on America's racial ladder. In multiethnic America, the danger is that racial hierarchies and pecking orders will develop, and that prejudices will coalesce around them.

In New America, therefore, politicians of all persuasions will be tempted to energize their followings with both subtle and obvious appeals to race. Leaders of the Right will suggest that racial alienation stems from the injustices of affirmative action. Leaders of the Left will imply that the vestiges of white racism account for the setbacks suffered by minorities. Either way, the convenient course will be to reduce political issues to race. That way, the victims become "us" and the perpetrators become "them." One's own predicament becomes the product of the racial discrimination by or the racial preference given someone else. "It's because I'm brown"; "It's because he's black"—it's so easy to repeat the racial refrain. In New America, with each person a potential victim or perpetrator of discrimination, the opportunities to offer racial explanations for misfortunes multiply exponentially. Racial politics of both the Right and Left could thus make of New America nothing other than a perpetual racial stew.

Faced with such prospects, our perspectives on civil rights must at least be up to date. The old biracial model of discrimination was right for its time. Segregative laws and customs governed much of America. The country was morally obligated at midcentury to be preoccupied with race. In New America, with racial antagonisms increasing in variety and racial appeals increasing in number, we are equally obligated to rise above race. Clinging to the old biracial model of white majority/black minority discrimination under the radically altered racial circumstances of New America makes little sense. It is not just that the midcentury model fails to account for America's changing racial landscape. Its statement about America is also deeply separatist. Under the old model, discrimination is the deed of whites alone, and each minority group becomes nothing more than the newest candidate for Anglo prejudice. The model thus posits a permanent division in our national life between white Americans and Americans of color. It impedes an ecumenical definition of American citizenship, where discrimination is equally condemned, irrespective of the racial identity of those who practice it. The Jim Crows of the twenty-first century could be white, or they could be brown, or black, or yellow. The search for an America dedicated to the common precepts of citizenship must recognize that members of *all* races share a propensity for prejudice, just as all share the potential to rise above it.

★   ★   ★

New America is rapidly becoming a self-segregated nation. As segregation becomes the way of life for multiple American minorities, the goal of One Nation Indivisible will gradually disappear. Indeed, this is already happening. The desire of the races to be left alone is growing. *Washington Post* columnist Juan Williams says succinctly: "Self-segregation is in."

Earlham College president Richard Wood, an active partici-
pant in the civil rights movement of the 1960s, notes that
"You hardly ever hear the word [integration] anymore, except
in a derisive way." Instead, there is now "a real struggle about
whether we all want to be participants in a common American
culture with some variety, or if we want to emphasize our
differences."

Whether it is the formal creation of a congressional district
or the informal gathering of students in a schoolyard, segregated preferences are gaining ground. The rise in segregative
sentiment among blacks is especially disheartening because
African Americans were once the foremost champions of an
integrated nation. "In the short run," wrote Justice Thurgood
Marshall in 1974, "it may seem to be the easier course to allow our great metropolitan areas to be divided up each into
two cities—one white, the other black—but it is a course, I
predict, our people will ultimately regret." Now, it seems,
that course has become an increasingly popular one. One recent survey showed 56 percent of African American respon-
dents believing that blacks should participate in black-only
organizations and 50 percent believing that blacks should
form a separate political party. Four decades after *Brown v.
Board of Education*, reports *The Wall Street Journal*, "a weary
Kansas City [school] district seems inclined to accept a half-
victory that would, in practice, embody elements of the old
'separate but equal' era." This time, however, the segregative
arrangements appear to have increasing support within the
black community itself. "There is no inherent academic benefit in black kids mixing with white kids," argued Edward J.
Newsome, a black school-board member. "I think it's just
natural for people to seek out people like themselves. . . . I
don't see anything wrong with that," declared Suzetta Parks,
an African American businesswoman.

The new segregation traverses all regions of the country. One-third of America's black public school students in 1996 attended schools whose minority enrollment was 90 to 100 percent. One-half of all black students attended such schools in the nation's most segregated region—the Northeast. Self-segregating tendencies also transcend the boundaries of class. Indeed, writes Glenn Loury, "ambivalence about integration is at least as strong among blacks as among whites, and operates as powerfully in the black upper and middle classes as in its lower classes." Part of the explanation for the trend is pure resignation. Says NAACP Legal Defense Fund leader Ted Shaw: "My sense is a lot of people are saying, 'We're tired of chasing white folks. It's not worth the price we have to pay.'" The reemergence of segregation has brought a resurgence of racial pride. "With a Eurocentric curriculum, it appears one race is superior over the others," claims Audrey Bullard, principal of the J. S. Chick Elementary School in Kansas City, whose enrollment is 98 percent black. "The African-centered curriculum makes [students] feel 'I'm a part of this. I'm not on the outside looking in.'"

Because of the black community's long experience with civil rights issues, other minorities in multiethnic America may follow its lead. And because African Americans led the way to racial integration, any significant shift in their sentiments will have a huge effect. Perhaps that is why the verdict of acquittal in the O. J. Simpson murder trial hit the nation with such stunning impact—it was seen by many whites as a decidedly separatist statement more than forty years after *Brown v. Board of Education* declared integration to be the law of the land. It was sad enough that the trial, the verdict, and the reaction to the verdict all came to be discussed so prominently in terms of race. The media regaled us with stories of black viewers breaking into applause and whites staring in glum silence as the verdict was announced, and the polls rushed to confirm a racial divide—"eight in ten blacks say justice was done in the Simpson case—and two out of three whites disagree."

As a judge, I must confess, the Simpson trial had hit me hard. Judges, like most Americans, aspire to live by the principle that one's conduct matters in a courtroom, not one's status. Either the evidence holds up or it does not, and the government must prove all elements of a criminal offense beyond a reasonable doubt. Judges recognize that juries can acquit, notwithstanding the law or the facts, but most of us shudder at the prospect of "jury nullification," and think acquittals—or convictions—on the basis of race to be America's most nightmarish prospect. To this day, I do not know whether the Simpson verdict was a racial statement. I am torn between my belief that juries generally go about their duties with enormous care and my knowledge that racial issues and appeals saturated this most publicized of trials.

Where has the Simpson verdict left the *American* ideal— Equal Justice Under Law? The Simpson case was, for all its hype, still supposed to be *a trial*—the American system of criminal justice on display before the world in that most American arena, the courtroom, where justice is forever blindfolded and racial identities are ideally set aside. Yet, step by step, the case came to represent the kind of proceeding that many devoutly hoped they would never witness again. It became in the end an event of deep racial estrangement, with seemingly different racial perceptions of reality, and with the races seemingly rooting for different sides. For many African Americans, the stark racism of Mark Fuhrman and the LAPD meant that the historic injustices would never be cured. For many whites, the closing argument of Johnnie Cochran meant that the historical scores would never be settled. "The result," wrote Harvard professor Henry Louis Gates, "is that race politics becomes a court of the imagination wherein blacks seek to punish whites for their misdeeds and whites seek to punish blacks for theirs. . . . And so an empty vessel like O. J. Simpson becomes filled with meaning, and more meaning—more meaning than any of us can bear." The "meaning," in fact, ultimately operated to exalt racial interpretations of current events and to diminish through racial acrimony the allegiance to yet one more American institution. The law, the courts, the Constitution, the very system of justice that embodies a nation's high hopes and fond ideals, had somehow become enduringly enmeshed in race.

Thirteen days after the Simpson verdict came the Million Man March, making October 1995 one of the most separatist months in American history. The march struck many Americans, black and white, with profound ambivalence. Its message was supposedly one of personal accountability and pride—a chance for young black men "to straighten their backs." However, the chief messenger, Louis Farrakhan, harbored a long list of intractable hatreds—for Jews, for whites, and for gays. Women, who accounted for a tiny fraction of the crowd of half a million, had largely honored Farrakhan's request to stay away. More than three decades earlier, Martin Luther King graced the Washington Mall with a dream of racial harmony and brotherhood. Louis Farrakhan had a dream also, but of racial supremacy and separateness: "I don't need to be in any mainstream," he declared. "There is no way that we can integrate into white supremacy and hold our dignity as human beings. . . . White folks are having heart attacks today because their world is coming down."

Almost one year after the Million Man March, thousands of Latinos staged their first march on Washington, protesting anti-immigration sentiment, urging amnesty for illegal immigrants and education for their children, and demanding that politicians not take them for granted. Indeed, one of the poignant footnotes to the Simpson verdict and the Farrakhan march was the comments of Hispanic and Asian Americans, who felt left out of America's new racial conversation. "It's all black, white, black, white," said Jorge Aguilera, a freelance photographer who is black and Puerto Rican. "If I were to listen to the media, only half of me exists. Where the hell is my Latino side to these people?" It was a sad irony, to say the least, that members of America's "other" minorities felt less than American because their racial viewpoint was not solicited by the press. "Latinos [soon] will be the largest minority group in America, and yet to the media, we still don't exist," declared Jorge Klor de Alva, a Latino anthropologist at the University of California at Berkeley. "Racism comes in all forms, against all people," warned David Chang, whose parents' grocery store on Chicago's North Side had been robbed three times. "What's worse for us [as Asian Americans], we don't even have a voice in the media or in politics. It's not fair." In a multicultural environment, however, racial "fairness" is the most elusive quality of all. America's most race-conscious conversations, it seems, will always be insufficiently race conscious in our new multicultural world.

The Simpson verdict and the Million Man March only sharpened trends toward self-segregation within the black community, the implications of which are grim for all Americans. In the days before *Brown*, both blacks and whites understood, from their very different perspectives, that separate meant unequal. The litigation of the pre-*Brown* era attests amply to that. Segregation may be more voluntary now, but whether it can ever be more equal remains much in doubt. Notwithstanding the legal, political, and economic progress made by black America since *Brown*, the basic infirmity of separatism lingers. The more separate a minority is, the less significant it becomes to the larger majority of Americans, who see in its separatism an easy excuse for neglect. Michael Kelly in *The New Yorker* draws a telling analogy between Farrakhan's racially segregated mass demonstration and that of a Ku Klux Klan rally seventy years before:

> The men who marched on Washington in 1925 and 1995 meant to show America the power of an idea of segregation—the power of standing unified and apart from the integrated muddle of democracy. . . . The poor and working class whites of 1925 figured that in their separate oneness they could wield power far beyond their numbers and their wealth, and they believed that the people who ran the country would be properly impressed. But the people who ran the country then—like those who run the country now—tended to reward political minorities who wanted to stand alone by granting them their desire.

Somehow the old nostrum of self-segregation is becoming the guiding maxim of a multiethnic nation. The tendency of the races to look inward is rising just as New America requires us to reach outward. More and more Americans seem to believe that there is an inalienable right of the races to remain apart—that there is some natural right of racial privacy to parallel the individual right to free association. We now suppose that we can find in separatism some form of racial coexistence. When we absolutely have to come together, we will. But when we have any choice about the matter, we shall stay apart. In other words, there is to be at best racial sufferance of a sort, but no real prospect of racial understanding. If this is our view, it is a tragic one. To set mere "toleration" or "coexistence" as a goal of national race relations is to surrender to a separatist vision of America. Martin Luther

King's view of black nationalism in the 1960s applies with equal force to modern separatist movements of all races: they are "made up of people who have lost faith in America." For each race to go its own way means that there is no common way, no American path.

The distinction between acceptance and toleration is a crucial one. Toleration is a mere putting up with. A racially tolerant society is far preferable to a racially antagonistic one, but it offers no prescription for a unified nation. An accepting society is something different altogether. Acceptance, in the words of Bissoondath, "requires true understanding, recognition over time that the obvious differences—the accent, the skin colour, the crossed eyes, the large nose—are mere decoration on the person beneath. It is a meeting of peoples that delves under the surface to a knowledge of the full humanity of the other." For America to become a racially accepting nation will require racial integration.

It seems downright dreamy these days to cheer for racial integration. It seems naive to promote it as the wave of the future, not a relic of the past. But if understanding, not mere coexistence, is our goal, then racial integration will be indispensable to achieving it. We will never understand one another if we never interact. A lack of understanding may shed some light on the recurring spate of conflicts between black and Korean Americans. African Americans may have mistaken traditional Korean mannerisms for signs of rudeness. "When a customer complains about prices being too high, our reaction is to smile. And here that smile is often misunderstood," Hwanhee Kim, a Korean American social worker, told the *Washington Post,* adding that the "American custom of looking another person in the eye while talking is considered rude in Korea." Conversely, Koreans may not be aware of the historic sacrifices made by African Americans on behalf of all minorities. As one Korean American observed, "The Koreans who have just gotten here are not aware of the civil rights movement. They don't realize that the reason they can send their children to the best schools is that blacks died for the right."

This is more than a matter of misunderstanding in a convenience store. The threat to eighteenth- and nineteenth-century America lay in the doctrines of sectional self-determination. The threat to twenty-first-century America lies in the creed of racial self-segregation. Without racial integration, we will lose a sense of shared aims and linked destinies. Civil rights law must thus regard racial separatism not simply as a moral wrong but as a barrier to togetherness. In removing the wrong of race discrimination, civil rights law not coincidentally promotes the goal of national unity. It reaffirms that racial integration is good for Americans—in our jobs, in our neighborhoods, in our schools, and in our politics. More than just a good, however, integration is the preeminent condition for cohesion in our multicultural country.

That national unity will not survive without racial integration should be self evident. Think, for a moment, of a Chinese American, Mexican American, or African American looking at the dome of the Capitol or the portico of the White House. The symbols of America can be meaningful to minority citizens or they can be alienating. Which they become will depend on the sum of these citizens' relationships with their fellow Americans. If racial and ethnic minorities experience a sense of welcome and considerateness, then national symbols will become sources of pride. If minority citizens sense that they are shunned and avoided by the majority of their countrymen, then racial symbolism will begin to substitute for national allegiance.

I recognize, of course, that the proximity brought by racial integration has led to its share of nasty incidents. I understand that when a black church is burned to the ground, the cause of racial interaction becomes buried in mistrust. Still, as a society, we must persist. Integration, no matter how painstakingly slow to achieve, is far preferable to voluntary segregation, "an idea that the very worst racists would be all too happy to live with." With integration, we take our chances on an unpredictable admixture of racial conflict and harmony. But without integration, there will be no possibility of interracial dialogue, no prospect for interracial friendship, and no potential for interracial understanding. Without racial integration, Americans will be left to sulk in a long separatist silence.

The ways in which law works to promote racial integration must be adapted to contemporary conditions. The early decades of the civil rights struggle witnessed a sharp clash of moral values. In the 1950s and 1960s the force of law was necessary to storm the fortress of de jure segregation. In the 1960s and 1970s, the Supreme Court also vested federal district judges with sweeping powers to achieve integration in the schoolyard and the workplace. To impose anything less than a numerical blueprint for substantial integration of the races was seen as a concession to the forces of reaction.

The 1990s are a grayer period in which the justifications for judicial action are much harder to come by. Discrimination itself is more subtle and complex today, and separatist sentiments more likely represent a mutual preference. In a multicultural setting, moreover, it is not only more difficult to get the racial numbers "right"; it is also more hazardous to predict the responses of disparate racial communities to integration. In earlier decades, white flight to suburban school districts and private schools thwarted many an ambitious school desegregation plan. Today, a retreat into racial and ethnic isolation would confound an overzealous judicial decree.

The biggest danger, however, is that our confused 1990s will cause law to forfeit its unifying, integrative function. Our national goal must remain one of racial integration. Wisdom, though, is a matter of degree. Law should act as a facilitator of integration, not as a bludgeon for it. When the law remedies discrimination, it acts as a facilitator of integration. When it imposes quotas, it becomes a bludgeon. When school attendance zones are drawn to maximize integration, the law is a facilitator. When cross-town student busing is employed to achieve the same result, the law becomes a club. As one shifts from racial intent to racial effect in judging public acts, one moves as well from facilitation to coercion. The old school freedom of choice plans acquired an ugly name because black pupils in the South were intimidated against selecting predominantly white schools. Today, however, such rights of minority choice and opportunity are less subject to majority abuse. Kweisi Mfume, the new head of the NAACP, insists "that young people deserve the right to have an ability to matriculate with others of different races and different religions, not necessarily through busing but through the opportunity to at least attend the same schools. . . . There is a great deal of value and worth in that, because the real world looks like that." Admittedly, the lines are hazy—not all will agree on when facilitation ends and bludgeoning begins. In subsequent chapters I express my view of the proper role of law in particular areas. But the general point is clear. Law must lead Americans to integration; it cannot march them there.

★   ★   ★

*T*he ability to achieve racial integration is limited by powerful forces, which have deep roots in American history. To begin with, there is a realm of private choice that the law should not presume to touch. People will choose their friends: the most the law can hope is that creating a climate of public understanding will discourage people from exercising private prejudice. Freedom of association is not confined to personal friendship. Neighborhoods exhibit ethnic and racial solidarity, in part from self selection. There are the barrios and the enclaves; there are the Chinatowns and Little Italys. The cities of America often seem collections of ethnic villages. Indeed, noted Justice Antonin Scalia, "the history of the populating of North America is in no small measure the story of groups of people sharing a common religious and cultural heritage striking out to form their own communities."

When we speak of the black community or the Greek community, we acknowledge that America is really a country of communities. When a group of Americans has suffered a common history of oppression, the story of overcoming that oppression is naturally a source of shared pride. Communalism, then, is not just something we accept in America; it is something we celebrate. Ethnic festivities and holidays honor revered traditions and beloved figures of the past. The several city-sanctioned ethnic parades in New York City include not only the Saint Patrick's Day and Chinese National Day parades, but also the Philippine Independence, Norwegian American Day, West Indian Carnival, Korean Day, Nigerian, Sikh, Hindu, Steuben Day, and Pulaski Day parades. Chinese New Year is celebrated throughout the country; the San Francisco parade draws half a million spectators as well as a television audience stretching into Hong Kong. As a nation of immigrants, Americans have relatives, childhood memories, and stories from grandparents that kindle pride in their distinctive national and ethnic origins. Of Cinco de Mayo, which commemorates a ragtag Mexican cavalry's astonishing defeat of the French army in 1862, an instructor in a Latin American studies program says, "Is Cinco de Mayo really just a celebration? I don't think so. It keeps reaffirming our rights, heritage and history. . . . It's a symbol of identity." Being an American does not mean shedding oneself of all other identities. Being an American is not inconsistent with being an Arizonan or a South Carolinian. Neither should it be incompatible with being a Greek American or a Korean American. One may be a loyal and patriotic citizen and still harbor the multiple sentiments and affections of the human heart.

The centrality of communalism in America is most evident in the area of religion. In fact, the Constitution affirmatively sanctions the right to religious separatism in that clause of the First Amendment guaranteeing the free exercise of religion. The right of religious communities to remain apart has also been blessed by the Supreme Court. The 1972 case of *Wisconsin v. Yoder* makes it clear that the right to religious community means much more than the right to attend religious services with other members of one's faith on a designated day of worship.

The Old Order Amish in Green County, Wisconsin, were about as separate a religious community as it is possible to be. The Amish renounced modern life in all its forms. They rejected telephones, automobiles, radios, and television. "They sought," said the Supreme Court in *Yoder,* "to return to the early, simple, Christian life de-emphasizing material success, rejecting the competitive spirit, and seeking to insulate themselves from the modern world." Out of a belief that "salvation requires life in a church community separate and apart from the world and worldly influence," the Amish refused to send their children to public or private high school. "The high school," according to Amish belief, only tended

> to emphasize intellectual and scientific accomplishments, self-distinction, competitiveness, worldly success, and social life

with other students. Amish society emphasizes informal learn-ing-through-doing; a life of "goodness," rather than a life of intellect; wisdom, rather than technical knowledge; community welfare, rather than competition; and separation from, rather than integration with, contemporary worldly society.

When Wisconsin sought to enforce its compulsory school attendance law against members of the Amish faith, the Supreme Court sided emphatically with the Amish. Chief Justice Warren Burger wrote an opinion applauding Amish life, and reminding readers that the values of Western civili-zation had been preserved during the Middle Ages "by mem-bers of religious orders who isolated themselves from all worldly influences against great obstacles." There was a dan-ger, he warned, in succumbing to the forces of conformity. "There can be no assumption that today's majority is 'right' and the Amish and others like them are 'wrong.' A way of life that is odd or even erratic but interferes with no rights or interests of others is not to be condemned because it is different."

The *Yoder* decision was a great victory for the principle of communalism. One need only read the Supreme Court's de-scription of Amish life to understand why racial, ethnic, and religious communalism all have real appeal. Communalism can instill a sense of individual stability in a world of dizzying change. It can nurture a sense of belonging in a society of bewildering impersonality. Because claims of ethnic tradition and community are legitimate, they are also seductive. Their very seductiveness, however, should give us pause. Commu-nalism can divide groups from one another on the basis of race or ethnicity, and it can sever distinctive racial subgroups from society as a whole. In New America, moreover, claims of communalism will arise with increasing frequency because there are so many more communities to assert them. Therein lies the danger. Do courts exempt the Amish from compliance with school attendance laws only because the Amish are perceived as good? By what criteria are judges supposed to distinguish "worthy" religious communities from "unworthy" ones? If ethnic group A or racial group B establishes a claim to separate treatment from the state, then it becomes that much harder to deny the claim to C. If, as a matter of its own traditions, one racial or ethnic group succeeds in establishing its separate institutions, how do we deny that right to any other?

Where does communalism end and separatism begin? The question is much more troubling in a multicultural nation than in a relatively homogeneous one. The question confronted the Supreme Court, once again in the context of a religious community, in the case of *Board of Education of Kiryas Joel v. Grumet*. The claim of religious communalism in *Kiryas Joel* went well beyond that in *Wisconsin v. Yoder.* In *Kiryas Joel*, a New York statute had actually carved out a special public school district for the religious enclave of Satmar Hasidim, practitioners of a strict form of Judaism. Notwithstanding the fact that the Constitution discourages racial classifications and encourages the free exercise of religion, the basic conflict between the impulses of nationalism and separatism was very much in evidence. There was a powerful argument to be made in *Kiryas Joel* for the recognition of the Satmars' communal claim:

> The Satmars' way of life, which springs out of their strict religious beliefs, conflicts in many respects with mainstream American culture. They do not watch television or listen to radio; they speak Yiddish in their homes and do not read English-language publications; and they have a distinctive hairstyle and dress. Attending the Monroe-Woodbury public

schools, where they were exposed to much different ways of life, caused the handicapped Satmar children understandable anxiety and distress.

The Supreme Court, however, found the creation of the special school district violated that clause of the First Amendment forbidding government to establish religion. But Justice David Souter's lead opinion did not focus on the role of law in preserving a nation, seemingly the natural and obvious response to the claims of communities for separate treatment. The creation of the special school district, Justice Souter said, was unconstitutional only because other religious communities seeking school districts of their own might not receive them. That, however, was the wrong argument. The law's defect was not that it failed to promise further fragmentation. Justice Anthony Kennedy in a concurring opinion was left to address the argument for unification. The special school district was unconstitutional, he said, because government had sought to draw "political boundaries on the basis of religion." In his view, "the danger of stigma and stirred animosities is no less acute for religious line-drawing than for racial." The divisive effect of drawing school or legislative districts on the basis of race or religion was too obvious to overlook.

The *Kiryas Joel* case was one of the Supreme Court's most contentious. Many will be tempted to agree with Justice Antonin Scalia, whose dissent framed the issue as one of tolerance for a tiny religious sect whose Grand Rebbe had journeyed to America's shores in search of religious freedom. And if it were just a question of this one school district, in this one state, for this one sect, no one would raise objection. Where, however, does it end? Does every race and every religion that seeks its own political and educational boundaries get them? If so, we shall have willed ourselves a future that features routine public favoritism on a racial and religious basis.

The *Yoder* and *Kiryas Joel* decisions underscore one thing: the practical impact of the Amish and Satmars' claims may seem small, but the principle underlying those claims was one of huge significance. The rise of communalism on a large scale may portend the descent of national identity. The law of civil rights must come to grips with that prospect. In biracial America, civil rights law was free to emphasize equality. In multicultural America, it must emphasize national unity as well. It is impossible to overstate the importance of this new dimension to our civil rights debate. Although calls for black solidarity arose sporadically during the late 1960s, the chief emphasis of the civil rights movement remained that of overcoming the barriers to first-class citizenship for black Americans. Today, however, the civil rights debate has suddenly acquired profound nationalist and separatist implications. Whether racial solidarity or national unity becomes the dominant mode of discourse, whether separation or integration becomes the prevalent American condition, will depend in large part on our approach to civil rights. Civil rights law can exacerbate the tensions among racial and ethnic groups or it can help to heal them. It can enhance our appreciation of American citizenship or it can cause us to lose sight of it. It can bring different groups of Americans into closer contact or it can ensure they stay apart. At midcentury, we were discussing racial inequality. At century's end, we must debate not only the promise of equality but also the meaning of nationhood.

It may help to remind ourselves just why our sense of national unity remains so important. The first reason speaks to America's obligation to the world community. This country, for all its flaws, represents more to the world than most of its citizens will ever recognize. It remains a beacon of hope; an exemplar of democracy; a symbol of freedom; and a showcase of economic and technological innovation. In all of these areas, the United States is expected to set an example. As regional conflicts of a racial nature intensify around the world, it becomes all the more important that America not slide into racial disarray. Or else, as Ralph Waldo Emerson said of America, "the inventions [will be] excellent, but the inventors one [will be] sometimes ashamed of."

Unfortunately, the American example in race relations has often been a poor one. With the advent of a multicultural nation, it seems almost as if providence has handed us a second chance. Multiculturalism affords America a new opportunity to set a standard of racial acceptance, one that can in time become as much of an achievement as our political and economic systems.

One of the things I enjoy most as a judge is attending naturalization ceremonies. It's a welcome break from deciding cases, and it reminds me how lucky I am to be a citizen of this country. Each Fourth of July, I drive the wooded road to Monticello. That beautiful building somehow reminds me that the ugly institution of Jefferson's day has perished and that his great ideals live on. On Independence Day 1995, people from many different countries have arrived to be naturalized on the lawn of Thomas Jefferson's home. Julia Dawn Abbinante has come from the United Kingdom; Malik Hafiz Abu-Ghazalah from Jordan; Christopher Fru Achua from Cameroon; Mithlesh Kumari Agarwal from India; Rosalina Bandola Alacaraz from the Philippines; and so on. The municipal band plays "America, the Beautiful," and Boy and Girl Scouts lead us in the Pledge of Allegiance. The immigrants take the oath of citizenship, many with tiny American flags in their hands. We judges speak to them on the meaning of citizenship, of jury duty and the right to vote, and of the importance of bringing their distinctive contributions to America, even as they accept ours in return. At the end of the ceremony, the new citizens express their own thoughts. Many say, with tears in their eyes, how they have waited all their lives for this day. The corners of the globe from which they come have seen too much of racial hatred. Surely we owe them a land where race and ethnicity is subordinate to the citizenship they have waited so long to achieve. Surely we owe countries and regions torn by race the belief that such discord is not humankind's inevitable way.

It is not just to the world community that we owe the example of a nation not beset by racial strife. It is to ourselves. We deserve better than to go about our lives in an atmosphere of racial cacophony. Racial recriminations pollute a country's environment as surely as the most toxic chemical. Racial tensions sow mistrust in personal relationships and consume personal energies in unproductive antagonisms. They make public progress of all sorts more difficult to come by, and they divert the nation's focus from common goals. In large national enterprises and in small daily occurrences, race relations set the tone. In fact, our quality of life will be affected by the quality of race relations as much as by the consumer price index and the growth of the GNP.

It is not only to ourselves that we owe a commitment to national unity as against racial separatism. It is to generations of Americans that preceded us and to those that will follow. Americans fought the Revolution and held the Constitutional Convention to create a new nation. When Americans died at Antietam Creek, it was in part for union. Those who fought at D-Day did so in the name of America. Military sacrifice, however, is only the most dramatic manifestation of the contribution citizens make to nationhood. The men and women who devoted their lives to the cause of racial equality in the civil rights movement did so in the belief that they were making this a better and a more unified nation. One could go on forever with tales of personal patriotism. Suffice it to say that in ways great and small our forebears created an America that is ours to change and improve, but not to lose.

★ ★ ★

*H*ow then does civil rights law promote the goal of national unity? The search for unity amid the diversity of New America must change our thinking. One change involves the usefulness of affirmative action. Simply put, the advent of multiculturalism makes the argument for affirmative action more difficult to sustain.

Whatever the merits or demerits of affirmative action in a biracial society, it is the most dangerous of policy prescriptions for a multiethnic nation. Recall for a moment what the basic rationales of affirmative action are. Affirmative action programs, it is said, will (1) bring the benefits of racial diversity to the school and to the workplace; (2) remedy past histories of discrimination against members of racial minorities; and (3) ensure that no racial group suffers significant underrepresentation in the business, professional, and governmental councils of modern America.

Even the most ardent advocates of affirmative action recognize, however, that "no other group compares to African Americans in the confluence of the characteristics that argue for inclusion in affirmative action programs." When Dean Paul Brest of the Stanford Law School canvassed the claims of Native Americans, Latinos, and Asian Americans for inclusion in a multicultural affirmative action program, he was stymied. In view of "the vast number of groups and subgroups that are arguable candidates" for multicultural affirmative action programs, he concluded, "policymakers may reasonably come to different conclusions about which groups to include, and that different institutions may appropriately decide to include different groups." Of course, he cautioned, the failure to include "a particular group in an affirmative action program does not entail complacency about its members' circumstances."

Dean Brest's difficulties are understandable. In a multiethnic nation, there is no theory of group preference that will not create hard feelings. Although black Americans have suffered most acutely from discrimination in this country, an affirmative action plan premised on that fact faces problems. Harry Pachon, president of the Tomas Rivera Center in Claremont, California, laments the fact that "the debate over affirmative action has been put largely in the context of gender or black-white relations in American society. Yet the ethnic group [Latinos] that constitutes one out of eleven Americans is not heard from, much less seen, at the roundtables and in the discussion that has so polarized American society."

Pachon then proceeds to make the case for inclusion of Latinos in affirmative action programs. "Latinos," he notes, have been a major part of "our nation since at least 1848. Since that time, Hispanic citizens have faced inequities in employment, housing, and education." Even today, Latinos face discrimination. For one thing, they "are disproportionately concentrated in the Southwest (half of all Latinos live in California and Texas) and thus are not adequately represented in the New York–D.C. power corridor that influences national policy making."

Even the seeming gains that Latinos have made, contends Pachon, can be misleading. The higher employment rate of Latinos at the Department of Justice "merely reflects its need for border patrol agents and undercover operatives, which has led the agency to reach aggressively into Hispanic communities for appropriate candidates." The failure to include a group in an affirmative action plan, suggests Pachon, may deny that group its rightful place in the American sun. "As far as fighting in World War II and Vietnam goes, Hispanics have won more Congressional Medals of Honor than any other ethnic group (thirty-eight), and they constitute 35% of those named on the Vietnam Memorial."

Suppose, then, that we heed Professor Pachon and resolve to include Hispanic Americans as well as African Americans in most affirmative action programs. That too presents problems. Some Asian Americans, for example, see themselves as victims of a model minority myth in which they "are depicted as champion entrepreneurs and college whiz kids, the immigrant parents working as urban greengrocers as their American children win the annual Westinghouse Science Talent Search." The model minority myth, lawyers Theodore Wang and Frank Wu say, obscures certain facts—that "Asian-American men earn between 10 and 17% less than their white counterparts" or that "more than 44% of Chinese-Americans who live in California are not fluent in English." But "perhaps the most damaging impact of the model minority myth is that policy makers regularly assume that Asian-Americans do not need affirmative action and automatically exclude this group without any analysis."

Indeed, when the Stanford Law School failed to include Asian Americans in the school's affirmative action program, the Stanford Asian and Pacific Islander Law Students Association raised questions about the appropriateness of lumping Asian Americans together in a single, nonpreferred category. Pacific Islanders, Filipinos, and Southeast Asians, it was suggested, presented a stronger case for inclusion than Japanese, Chinese, and Korean Americans, because Pacific Island and Southeast Asian immigrants suffer special "disadvantages based on language barriers, lack of educational and occupational status and low income." "The Law School," therefore, "should consider some Asian and Pacific Islander ethnicities as a positive factor in admissions decisions."

Even this solution has its problems, however. Within the various subgroups of the Asian American population, "immigrants arriving at different times from the same country of origin" are culturally, economically, and linguistically distinct. Thus, "third generation Chinese and Japanese Americans say they have more in common with each other than they do with Japanese from Japan or recent Chinese immigrants." So the question arises whether an affirmative action program should favor only recent immigrants in a given minority group on the grounds that they are likely to be less well off and the target of more prejudice than those who have been in America for several generations.

The more one fine-tunes a multicultural affirmative action program, the more resentments one creates. It will always be possible to construct a plausible case for the inclusion of this or that particular ethnic group. But what of the whole of America? The theories of inclusion will always seem underinclusive to those left out. And the theories will always be based on slippery, treacherous generalizations about someone's ethnicity or race. In this sense, multiethnic affirmative action becomes a celebration of differences in a country that needs nothing so badly as a sense of togetherness.

With the participation of more racial minorities in public programs, it becomes that much easier to engender racial suspicions. The jobs, funds, and contracts that go to one racial group will allegedly do so at another's expense. The admission slots reserved for students of race A will assertedly exclude seats that should be occupied by students of race B. Thus one race comes to view another as its natural competitor and adversary. Government, so it seems, becomes an endless racial roundtable. In Washington, D.C., there are now recommendations that the largely African American city government adopt affirmative action policies on behalf of Hispanics. In Miami, African Americans feel that Cuban immigrants own a disproportionate share of jobs. And in Compton, California, blacks complain that they are refused employment because they fail to satisfy a recently emerging job criteria—the ability to speak Spanish.

With a more complex pool of racial claimants, public decision makers are saddled with the dreadful task of distributing racial shares. It is difficult to imagine a more depressing preoccupation for America at this point in its history. At the precise moment that the United States is emerging as a multiethnic nation, it is counterproductive, to say the least, to dispute which minority in which jurisdiction deserves Most Favored Victim status. Such a debate will descend into destructive racial stereotypes, elicit endless rhetoric of racial deprivation, engender lasting racial enmities, and generally diminish all who are involved in it.

Racial feuding will also drum into the national psyche the poisonous notion that it is one's race that matters most. In time, it will become difficult to disassociate any issue from the specter of race. Racial statistics will be scrutinized for every workforce, for every admissions policy, for every public distribution of benefits in order to determine whether each race did or did not receive its due allotment. Of course, what constitutes a fair racial share will be the continually unsettled question. The more racial groups dispute their racial shares, the firmer the grip of race consciousness over society becomes. Group thinking leads ineluctably to a view of group entitlements, and to the perception that individual qualifications must always be advanced against the ubiquitous backdrop of one's race. Ultimately, the acrimony of competing racial claims threatens to subsume the search for common national bonds: the worst civics lesson we could give to New Americans is that their rights as citizens henceforth depend upon their race.

We must reflect just a moment on the consequences of viewing America through the lens of race. One such consequence involves our connection with our heritage. New America has brought a struggle for the soul of American history, with each race often seeking to claim racial credit and assess racial blame. When two UCLA history professors unveiled their first set of standards for the teaching of American history, the United States Senate resolved to oppose those standards by a vote of 99 to 1. The charge, it seems, was that the standards upgraded the role of race, ethnicity, and gender in American historical consciousness and downgraded the contribution to political freedom and scientific progress made by white males. "Under these standards, Paul Revere and his midnight ride will never capture the imagination of our children," contended Senator Slade Gorton of Washington. "Our children will not learn of Thomas Edison, Alexander Graham Bell, the Wright brothers, or Albert Einstein."

A more racially inclusive look at American history is long overdue. But the contribution of one need not imply the disparagement of another. If the question becomes, as the columnist George Will fears, whether American history is no more than "a gloomy manifestation of the disease called Western civilization," then our past, no less than our present and future, will be a racial battleground for years to come. It is important that the glorious moments of American history be ones in which *all* citizens can take pride. It is critical that the shortcomings of the American story be seen by *all* for what they were. If, however, race becomes the focal point, then does the Declaration of Independence become a proclamation for whites only, because its signatories were uniformly Caucasian? Does the Civil War become insignificant for Hispanic and Asian Americans, because they were neither its chief combatants nor its direct beneficiaries? Does Jackie Robinson cease to be an American hero, even as George Washington becomes a patron saint for whites?

The visit of Nelson Mandela to Miami in 1990 brought such questions to the fore. The changes in South Africa are ones which Americans should applaud; they mirrored America's emergence from its own sad experience with racial oppression. Mandela is a person whom America should embrace; his struggles for the cause of freedom reflect values at the core of American ideals. Yet Miami's largely Cuban American city administration refused to welcome Mandela officially, protesting his relationship with Fidel Castro, who had supported Mandela's African National Congress. Instead, city officials issued a statement proclaiming Mandela's visit "unacceptable," predictably sparking another series of clashes between African and Hispanic Americans. The rest of Mandela's American tour was triumphant; but for a moment in Miami, racial divisions marred his visit. If Cuban Americans cannot identify with a Nelson Mandela, and if Anglo Americans cannot identify with a Martin Luther King, then we have traded our national heritage for mere racial history.

It is important to see in American history a story that is marred by race, but is in the end something much larger than race. There is value in recognizing the distinctive contributions made by racial and ethnic minorities to American history, but that is because those contributions benefited all Americans, not just the members of a single race. Our postage stamps proclaim with just pride the achievements of racial minorities in every area of endeavor. The ultimate source of that pride, however, is not racial, but the knowledge that this country would not be what it is without the contributions that countless *individuals* had to make.

Four trends will make it difficult for New America to remain one strong country. With the old midcentury model of discrimination and the more recent allure of affirmative action, we've been talking about ways of thinking about prejudice. With communalism and voluntary self-segregation, we've been discussing ways of living and associating in America. Some things about these trends seem legitimate; others not. The trends, however, all have one thing in common. They exalt the race over the citizen, the part over the whole, the things that divide us over those that unite. Will our children walk down their twenty-first-century streets and see fellow Americans or only someone who is black or brown or yellow or white?

The first step in making sure Americans on the street in the year 2050 don't see each other through racial lenses is for the law not to impose those lenses today. For that reason, the month of June 1995 was a remarkable one at the Supreme Court. In a trio of cases, each decided by a vote of 5 to 4, the Court disapproved race-based rationales for public decision making. In *Miller v. Johnson,* the Court took up the hot coals of legislative redistricting, holding unconstitutional a Georgia congressional district that was drawn predominantly for reasons of race. In *Adarand Constructors v. Peña,* the Court applied its strictest level of scrutiny to minority set-asides in government contracting, condemning racial classifications in federal programs as well as state ones, whether for benign or malignant purposes. Finally, in *Missouri v. Jenkins,* the Court restricted the ability of district judges to order race-based relief in school desegregation plans. The proper goal of desegregation decrees was not to impose racial balance for its own sake, but to "restor[e] the victims of discriminatory conduct to the position they would have occupied in the absence of that conduct."

One observer called it the Color-Blind Court. However, one term at the Supreme Court does not make a trend. The majorities for race neutrality were tenuous, and even those justices in the majority were not in lockstep. One thing only is certain—the debate over race consciousness in New America is far from concluded. It is impossible now to escape the impact of that debate upon our nation's future. Indeed, the justices themselves recognized the stakes. "In the eyes of government, we are just one race here. It is American," wrote Justice Antonin Scalia in the *Adarand* case. The Supreme Court, however, sits high above the tensions that tear at our Republic. Even as the justice penned his words, the evidence was mounting to undermine his statement. Unless we change course, the one American race of which he spoke will be no longer.

Part Two

THE LEGACY OF *BROWN*

— 3 —

The Integrative Ideal

We must always remember that the odious part of the *Plessy v. Ferguson* formulation "separate but equal" was the word "separate." In the midcentury South, separate restrooms and water fountains were marked for whites and blacks. There were no signs on the schools, but everyone knew they were separate too. The indignities of that regime would seem too searing a historical experience ever to be forgotten. Of course, no one today advocates the return of legally enforced apartheid. Yet the lines of racial separatism are reemerging in a subtler form. Now, at century's end, we are in danger of squandering the legacies of Abraham Lincoln, who gave us union, and of Thurgood Marshall and Earl Warren, who gave us *Brown*.

It is disquieting that the legacy of *Brown v. Board of Education* should be in doubt just as America emerges as a multicultural nation. This country's diversity is, on the one hand, a source of enormous hope. It is also a development fraught with prodigious dangers of racial fragmentation and ethnic strife. In these uncertain times, *Brown* reminds us that the whole of America remains greater than its separate parts. The relevance of that decision only grows with the new challenges of pluralism.

The premise of *Brown* was simple: Racial integration, or at least the end of racial segregation, would overcome the invidious failures of separatism. Though *Brown* did not mandate the means of desegregation, it clearly envisioned a much greater degree of racial interaction. It did this for three reasons. First, the justices hoped that racial prejudice would fade with propinquity and that generations that shared the same classrooms, sports teams, and school activities would abandon the misconceptions of their forebears. Second, genuine equality seemed increasingly impossible under conditions of separation. The Court's statement that "separate educational facilities are inherently unequal" reflected the fact that, in a separatist culture, public resources and energies would be lavished disproportionately on the majority race. Third, integration was not viewed as a change that would benefit only blacks. Rather, the Court seemed to appreciate that both races would profit from racial interaction and that this greater understanding could only serve to strengthen the social fabric.

Brown loosened our tongues and opened our eyes. It allowed us to talk about segregation more freely and to see segregation more clearly. Amid all the consternation at our unveiled apartheid, there was hope. "I am watching the comings and goings of the Baptists," wrote the author Willie Morris in 1971 on his return to Mississippi. They "are meeting in state convention assembled across the street at the First Baptist Church, strolling across the capitol grounds with an air of such sweet and satiated and omnipresent piety that my Methodist wellsprings turn a little sour. Two small Negro children walk past, pointing upward at the spreading magnolias that never lose their leaves even in the winter. Do you think they sense, these are *our* magnolias now too?"

Racial integration was not just legally required at the time of *Brown*. It was *morally* compelled. Perhaps never in the history of our jurisprudence has a constitutional clause—the Equal Protection Clause—assumed so great a measure of moral content. The sit-ins, marches, boycotts, and demonstrations which ended in landmark civil rights cases were morally inspired. At the time, biblical injunctions were as important as court-ordered ones. *Brown*'s moral message was that separatism was incompatible with beliefs in the innate equality of human worth. Dr. Martin Luther King Jr.'s appeals were likewise ecumenical in character. His words during the Montgomery bus boycott were not addressed solely to the Holt Street Baptist Church congregation, or to the members of King's own race or religion, but to the conscience of the entire country. Likewise, it was imperative that our laws not fragment the body politic but rather embody broad and inclusive concepts of humanity and citizenship.

The federal judiciary has played a unique role in implementing the integrative ideal. Because of *Brown*'s extreme unpopularity in the region that it most affected, its enforcement first fell to that part of government least subject to voter sentiment. For fulfilling that responsibility, federal judges in the South sometimes paid an enormous personal price; two accounts of this period are appropriately titled *Unlikely Heroes* and *Fifty-Eight Lonely Men*. Although the "unlikely heroes" included Fifth Circuit judges John Brown, Richard Rives, Elbert Tuttle, and John Wisdom, it was the federal district judges who were left to implement *Brown*'s principles initially, and who felt most keenly the sting of community displeasure. "By the end of 1960," writes Jack Bass,

Skelly Wright had become the most hated man in New Orleans. Pairs of federal marshals alternated in eight-hour shifts at his home to ensure his physical safety, and they escorted him to and from work. With few exceptions, old friends would step across the street to avoid speaking to him.

Those of us on the federal bench today cherish the extraordinary role our predecessors played in promoting a unified view of American citizenship—a view in which the law transcends divisions of race. *Brown*'s integrative ideal became a special mission of the inferior federal courts, whose members labored, sometimes brick by brick, to bring the walls of separatism down.

In the end, of course, black citizens themselves made the greatest contribution toward the integrative ideal. Whether they were motivated by the shining promise of an integrated society or the rank injustice of a segregated one is not crucial. In the days following *Brown*, such distinctions were different sides of the same coin. As important as the contributions of the civil rights leaders were, we feel most inspired by unheralded moments of individual courage. It now seems difficult to believe that in 1961, John Hardy, a black college student, was beaten over the head with a gun by a white registrar when he sought nothing more than to register two black residents of Walthall County, Mississippi, to vote. It now seems inconceivable that Southern blacks faced dogs, hoses, billy sticks, and paddy wagons for claiming their lawful rights. The first blacks to enter a formerly segregated school or college, to sit in a "white" seat at the lunch counter or on the bus, to seek a home in the "white section" of town, or to apply before a white registrar in a black belt county exhibited extraordinary fortitude. Why would young students endure the hissing, shouting, jeering, spitting, and nearly omnipresent threats of personal and mob violence to enter Little Rock High School in the fall of 1957? Why would parents allow their children to undergo any such experience? Much of the explanation must lie in the lure of entering the mainstream of American life after many long years of being locked out. These common dreams, born in the hearts of the long oppressed, inspired small acts of personal courage and perseverance on the order of that found at Valley Forge.

★　★　★

How much the civil rights movement accomplished on foot—black Americans walking miles to work rather than riding Montgomery's segregated buses; trodding arm in arm from Selma to Montgomery; standing in line before the registrar in Macon County; and, of course, marching gloriously and triumphantly on Washington. The physical fatigue brought spiritual peace. "Yes friend, my feet is real tired," said one elderly lady during the Montgomery bus boycott, "but my soul is rested."

It is clear that the integrative ideal lived in the hearts of most black Americans in the 1950s and 1960s. The more difficult question is whether it ever took root in the hearts of whites. While black Americans sought integration as an everyday reality, many whites supported it only in theory or at a distance. Yet it is not fair to white Americans—not to white legislators who cast courageous votes for civil rights, not to white civil rights workers who risked and in some cases gave their lives for equality—to charge it all up to hypocrisy. The real story is more complex.

In Virginia, the real story begins with a tragic tale called "massive resistance." Massive resistance was the war cry of Senator Harry F. Byrd, one which meant to tell the "rest of the country" that "racial integration is not going to be accepted in the South." Virginia would resist the *Brown* decision at every step. On integration, "I am not a gradualist. I am a neverist," declared Byrd loyalist and congressman William

Munford Tuck. The governor of Virginia, J. Lindsay Almond, was no less strident. "We will oppose," proclaimed his 1957 campaign platform, "with every faculty at our command, and with every ounce of our energy, the attempt to mix white and Negro races in our classrooms. Let there be no misunderstanding, no weasel words, on this point. . . . We will not yield as long as a single avenue of resistance remains unexplored."

Other Virginians were scrambling to lend legitimacy to this lawlessness. A country lawyer by the name of William W. Olds exhumed John C. Calhoun's antebellum doctrine of Nullification and presented it to the editor of the *Richmond News Leader*, James J. Kilpatrick. Kilpatrick renamed the doctrine Interposition and waged a remarkably successful editorial campaign on its behalf. Under this doctrine, the state could interpose its sovereignty to annul what the state deemed to be an unconstitutional federal ruling. The newspaper even drafted an interposition resolution declaring the *Brown* decision "null, void, and of no effect."

My own recollections of *Brown* begin with conversations in the family den. I was old enough to be allowed to listen, but too young to be permitted to speak. What I gathered was that some court wanted to put blacks and whites together in school. The politicians had rebelled and shut down public schools where black children were about to walk in. So kids went to school in churches, museums, and private homes or sometimes received no education at all. Senator Byrd was said to want the governor to go to jail rather than "give in."

This troubled my dad, who night after night turned it over with his friends. Father's closest friends in Richmond were lifelong Virginians. To a young boy, there was something reassuring about them; they offered stone to build a self around, character that would not crumble. They talked, they listened, they paused and touched a finger to the chin. They were Lewis Powell, Virginius Dabney, George Gibson—gentlemen in the true sense of being gentle men. They wanted to integrate the schools, the theaters, the parks, and the playgrounds. They sought to raise funds for black colleges, sponsor projects in black history, support black candidates for city council. They also revered peace and order in their own dens. Father and his friends were patient with the pace of progress. They felt Richmond needed to be educated, not startled by a sit-in.

Each of Father's friends did his own soul-searching during that difficult period. Virginius Dabney was the Pulitzer Prize–winning editor of the *Richmond Times-Dispatch*. Dabney's history was that of a Southern liberal. His call for a federal anti-lynching law was, said Walter White of the NAACP, "one of the most significant positions taken by an American newspaper since the Civil War." In 1943, Roy Wilkins of the NAACP had praised Dabney's editorials opposing racial segregation on streetcars and other common carriers. Yet in the period after the *Brown* decision, the editorial voice of the *Times-Dispatch* fell mostly silent, neither championing massive resistance to school integration nor condemning it. Dabney's liberal friends wondered where their erstwhile supporter was; his conservative bosses were dismayed that Dabney refused to follow the fiery leadership of James J. Kilpatrick. For Dabney himself, the years after *Brown* were pure misery. What editorials there were endorsing massive resistance had to be written by someone else. Dabney himself was too hesitant to embrace the integrative ideal. But this also must be said—when faced with the daily temptation to please his superiors on the paper with segregationist manifestos, Virginius Dabney did not give in.

Lewis F. Powell Jr. is best known as a voice of decency and moderation on the United States Supreme Court. But the years after *Brown v. Board of Education* were among the most difficult of his life. His personal journey paralleled that of Virginius Dabney. Like Dabney, Powell served in a critical position in the post-*Brown* years—he was chairman of the Richmond School Board. In part because segregationists on the Richmond City Council controlled the school board's budget and in part because the state of Virginia controlled racially sensitive pupil assignments, minimal progress toward integration took place during Powell's school board tenure. Indeed, when Powell resigned from the school board in the spring of 1961 to accept an appointment to the State Board of Education, "only two of Richmond's 23,000 black children attended school with whites."

Like Dabney, Powell did not raise his voice on behalf of racial integration. "The central interpretative problem of Powell's years in state and local education," writes his biographer John C. Jeffries Jr., "is his steadfast silence on desegregation." The silence reflected not only Powell's own deeply private nature but also the fact that real influence in the Richmond of the 1950s was not perceived as a vulgar public commodity. A powerful unwritten code prevailed that the establishment arranged the affairs of the community within its own ranks. So Powell worked behind the scenes—he emphasized the lawlessness of Interposition in a debate with James J. Kilpatrick before the august Forum Club; he visited Senator Byrd in a futile effort to turn the old patriarch away from massive resistance; he helped orchestrate a gathering of Virginia's business leaders to impress upon Governor Almond "that massive resistance was the greatest single obstacle to industrial development"; he stood up for the right of black leaders to speak at meetings when angry whites would have shouted them down. And he fought to keep the Richmond schools open. "On desegregation," writes Jeffries, "[Powell] did no more than the law required, but when forced to choose between segregation and education, he always chose education."

The absence of public statements from Richmond's most prominent citizens on the moral imperative of integration is disturbing. Eventually, with the help of quiet influence, economic pressures, and court orders, Virginia's long ordeal of massive resistance came to an end. Eventually, black schoolchildren began to enter schools with whites. The troubling thing is that it took so much time. Looked at from the denial of the right of black and white schoolchildren in the 1950s to attend desegregated schools, the judgment on the Powell record might be severe. Looking at the human being, the judgment would be far more generous. Like Dabney, there is not in Powell's past a trace of race-baiting or demagoguery. They were men who worked within the milieu of their time and in the manner of their time to do what good they could.

As one of Virginia's foremost bankers, my own father did not storm any gates during that period. He did, however, help to organize the group of business executives who urged Governor Almond to bring massive resistance to an end. For a long time, I tended to see the travails of Father and his friends as something unique to Richmond, Virginia, and as an atypical slice of national life. I came to a different view when I read in law school that the Supreme Court had in 1955 ordered desegregation to proceed "with all deliberate speed." In "deliberate speed," that old phrase that gives on the one hand and takes with the other, I saw all the ambivalence of my father's den. What black America had gained in *Brown I*, white America tempered a year later in *Brown II*. As troubling as the pace of deliberate speed was the implicit assumption that integration was of benefit only to black citizens and that desegregation would proceed according to white terms.

The best that can be said of deliberate speed is that it was better than that other famous phrase of civil rights jurisprudence—"separate but equal." "Deliberate speed" was not a perfect phrase, but like the talk in my dad's den, it was better by far than what had gone on before. Progress in Richmond, Virginia, in the 1950s was figuratively on foot, but like the Montgomery bus boycotters, the feet were moving in the right direction. Whether it was the brave step of the black child into a formerly all white school or the long journey of my father's friends from the racial attitudes of their ancestors, something valuable was won. The integrative ideal was the city on the hill, and the climb at least and at last had begun.

★ ★ ★

Perhaps the ideal of integration, like so many other ideals of the post–World War II decades, was destined to fail. Ours is a more jaded time, and the belief in the possibilities of America is sadly not what it was. Although Watergate and the Vietnam War were not primarily racial issues, they somehow dimmed the prospects for racial harmony. Race relations themselves have also gone through an especially troubling period—what with the controversies over student busing to achieve school desegregation in the 1970s, the unraveling of a national civil rights consensus in the 1980s, and the continuing debate over affirmative action proposals of all varieties. Given today's multiracial tensions, it is tempting to say that the ideal of integration is impractical; that it was, alas, a hollow hope; and that forty years after *Brown*, the gulf in racial understanding gapes wider than it ever did. Much objective evidence exists to support the discouragement of persons of all races. The inner city's plight—crime and drugs, joblessness, broken homes, health and housing problems—remains a daily rebuke to our racial hopes of yesteryear. It reminds us that while *Brown* lowered the de jure barriers to racial equality, it left all the de facto obstacles to equal opportunity dreadfully high.

Thus our urge to say that *Brown*, and the integrative ideal, cannot operate as a blueprint for a multiracial society. If the integrative model has fallen short in the bipolar setting of blacks and whites, why not abandon it in the vastly more complex context of multiracial America? Should civil rights law not countenance the desires of different minority groups for separate institutions and identities? If racial controversy and conflict represent the social norm, then should the accommodation of separatism be the preferred path to social peace? Should the law tacitly permit or actively encourage an Asian American school, a Hispanic American public housing unit, an Anglo American public employees union, or an African American township? Should Title VII of the 1964 Civil Rights Act permit an employer to assign its Hispanic American workers and its African American workers to different areas of a plant? Are there not certain plausible concessions to racial realities that twenty-first-century civil rights law must learn to make?

Brown's response to such questions is a proper and resounding no. Although its mandate was threatened with violence many times, the decision was nonetheless upheld, even on those sad occasions requiring the aid of United States marshalls and federal troops. In times of conflict, the short-term expedient was often to let the separate races go their separate ways, but that expedient almost always carried serious long-term costs. A country in which race governs social and political relations eventually loses the ability to summon its citizens to the duties of citizenship. Racial allegiances would come in time to eclipse national ones. *Brown* does not "ask us to reject enriching differences—integration need not flatten diversity—but to fulfill the opinion's promise, we must be able to rise above [race]." *Brown* stands for the premise that race is not the salient characteristic of an American citizen or even a relevant characteristic for public decision making at all.

It is not that *Brown*'s integrative ideal has brought us the ideal society; it has not. It is that the alternative visions are so unbearably grim. While it would be wrong to confuse *Brown* with "Anglo-assimilation," it would be equally wrong to reject the integrative ideal because it has not yet solved all our racial problems. In the 1950s, *Brown*'s opponents attempted a sectional nullification of a national future in which all Americans might play their part. Similarly, the proponents of separatism in the 1990s propose a racial veto over an American vision in which shared purposes, common efforts, and interracial partnerships remain our goal.

— 4 —

The Specter of Separatism

*H*istorical landmarks like *Brown v. Board of Education* should last for centuries. This decision, however, has been endangered after decades. The integrative ideal is no longer one that America shares. It is being overshadowed on all sides by the specter of separatism.

White America first seized the rhetoric of separatism in the aftermath of *Brown v. Board of Education*. This may seem a startling conclusion in view of the 1964 Civil Rights Act, the 1965 Voting Rights Act, and the cascade of court decisions seeking to turn *Brown*'s integrative ideal into an everyday reality. What all the official actions did not—and could not—do, however, was post a sign of racial welcome to black Americans. Indeed, the rhetoric of race in the decades after *Brown* had a mind-your-own-business message. It was not just the bullying cry of the crude segregationist that told African Americans to keep their distance. Rather, it was mainstream political and legal discourse in America that assumed a separatist cast. It is little wonder, then, that many African Americans responded with a separatist philosophy of their own. Together these separatist visions of white and black America make *Brown v. Board of Education* seem a fond but distant memory.

To understand the separatist vocabulary of white America, one must first reflect on the concept of the "code word." A code word is one whose real meaning lies encrypted in its stated wording. A code word sounds benign on the surface, but speaks malignantly beneath. By 1970, several potent code words had entered the American political vocabulary. Each was designed to wink and nod at white Americans, passing the word that the integrationist fever of the 1960s had run its course. The Nixon administration was awash in self-congratulations over this new class of political weaponry—the code word delivered a separatist message, but subtly enough to escape full-scale condemnation of its racial connotations.

The separatist implications of code words were not lost on black Americans. In fact, the most celebrated code phrase of all—"law and order"—depended mightily for its meaning on the listener. To many white Americans, the 1960s had been a decade of unsurpassed turbulence and upheaval. "Law and order" promised a respite from the change that lapped at the very edges of their living rooms. To many black Americans, however, the phrase suggested something quite different. Alabama governor George Wallace had made the crime issue his own, a fact that alone made it suspect in many minority communities. More importantly, the "order" in "law and order" suggested that the status quo would be hammered into place. In the criminal justice system, "order" had been the watchword of all-white police forces, all-white prosecutors, all-white juries, and an all-white bar and bench. The ascendancy of "law and order" as a political rallying cry in the 1970s thus evoked the most exclusionary of racial images—a criminal justice system in which an all-white apparatus determined black fates. "Order" may also have suggested the antithesis of "opportunity," which requires that racially established arrangements be forgone in favor of open ones. A less separatist formulation of "law and order"—"order and opportunity," for example—would have had alliterative balance but absolutely no political bite. "Law and order" thus stood as a separatist fortress, its drawbridge up for blacks, down for whites.

The "Southern strategy" of the Nixon administration, of which law and order was part, was another example of separatist, racially coded speech. The unspoken adjective before the Southern strategy was invariably "white." Black Americans could sense that the success of the Southern strategy did not depend upon their votes. Instead, it seemed the very opposite: "a cynical strategy . . . catering in subtle ways to the segregationist leanings of white Southern voters—yet pretending with high rhetoric that the real aim was simply to treat the South fairly, to let it become part of the nation again." The strategy was successfully parlayed by the administration into a huge 1972 presidential election victory. Its long-term consequences were to turn the South into an even more Republican region, but on ever more separatist terms. The Southern strategy meant that biracial political coalitions would be spurned, that political hegemony would be built on appeals to white voters, that the Republican party would become the white-majority party and the Democrats the black-minority party, and, coincidentally, that racial separatism would be the new soup of the political day.

The new racially coded speech also spread to the subject of judicial nominations. President Nixon, in meeting commitments to Senator Strom Thurmond of South Carolina, promised to name "strict constructionists" to the federal bench, and especially to the Supreme Court. To be sure, "strict constructionist" is a perfectly sensible term. It envisions judges who will follow the intent of lawmakers rather than their own personal predilections. It means jurists who will pay attention to constitutional history and statutory text.

These sober jurisprudential meanings were not, however, all the Nixon administration had in mind. It was impossible to escape the conclusion that strict constructionism was becoming yet another separatist code word—one implying judges who would relax the pressures for Southern school desegregation and tolerate historic segregationist norms. It was a tragedy that one of the finest judges and gentlemen in all the land, Clement F. Haynsworth, got caught in the coded political crossfire and was rejected by the Senate for a seat on the Supreme Court in 1969. It was fortunate, by contrast, that Judge G. Harrold Carswell, the least of whose difficulties was his much celebrated mediocrity, suffered the same fate. "I understand the bitter feeling of millions of Americans who live in the South at the act of regional discrimination that took place in the Senate yesterday," fumed the president, shortly after the Carswell defeat. Those who harbored bitter feelings over Carswell's rejection could not have included Southern blacks, who remembered Carswell's declaration in earlier political life that "I yield to no man in the firm, vigorous belief in the principles of white supremacy," and that "segregation of the races is proper and the only practical and correct way of life in our states."

It would be nice if separatist figures of speech had never invaded the sanctuaries of the courts themselves. The legal discussion of desegregation after *Brown* was, however, dominated by terms that communicated to black Americans the sense that they were unwelcome intruders in newly integrated neighborhoods and schools. The term "de facto segregation" implied that racial separation, if sufficiently subtle, was all right. Phrases such as "white flight" and "tipping

point," which figured in the discussion of school desegregation remedies, conveyed to blacks the length to which whites
would go to avoid their presence. The fear was always of a
massive white exodus if the minority presence became too
evident or the minority enrollment too high. To be sure, the
delicacies of legal discourse sometimes served to disguise the
real stakes involved. The driving principle of Supreme Court
desegregation jurisprudence in the 1970s was that "federal remedial power may be exercised 'only on the basis of a constitutional violation' and, 'as with any equity case, the nature of
the violation determines the scope of the remedy.' " Just as
with political code words, however, this legal terminology
suggested above all the sense that *Brown* had limits. It portrayed profound ambivalence at best in white America's commitment to the ideal of integration.

The conventional wisdom holds that mainstream white
Americans strove mightily to achieve an integrated society in
the wake of the *Brown* decision. Indeed, one may point to a
raft of legislation and court decisions to support that view.
When we examine the vocabulary of race and listen intently
to the American conversation, the integrationist impulse becomes much less clear. Resistance to racial integration was
not confined, as the story has it, to bands of extremists or
even to regional intransigents. Rather, the political and legal
dialogue of America after *Brown* became pointedly exclusionary and profoundly separatist. Even the words chosen to
express admirable ideals—color*blindness*, for example—somehow managed to suggest indifference to the realities of injustice. The return to fashion of minority separatism is a
deplorable development, but it is only fair to note the seman-
tic separatism of white America that preceded it. At least,
then, one may understand how, after listening year upon
year to talk of white flight and Southern strategies, African

Americans came to sense that the separatist impulse in their white fellow citizens still ran deep.

★   ★   ★

*T*he separatist impulse after *Brown* began with white America, but it has not ended there. The most certain characteristic of separatism is its contagious nature—why should Bill care to play with Bob, if Bob disdains to play with Bill? Sadly, such separatism is coming into vogue just as New America is coming into being. Bereft of unifying principles, the different communities of America could easily engage in mutually destructive exercises of racial factionalism. There is a good deal of ugly evidence that this is exactly what is happening. Rather than following the integrative path of our predecessors, the United States may now be traveling the strife-torn road of countries in which the manifestations of racial discord predominate.

Sobering signs of virulent separatism abound in the nation today. Indeed, no racial or ethnic group is immune from them. American separatism manifests itself in three broad categories. First, there is the old form of white Anglo separatism—discrimination against racial minorities. Despite constant efforts to stem its effects, this insidious taint of discrimination remains alive in American culture. Second, there are the efforts of racial minorities themselves to withdraw from the American mainstream. Here, separatism is defined by the rejection of the integrative ideal and the adoption of disassociative forms of "self-segregation." Third, multicultural conflicts can arise where one minority group attempts to separate itself from another. Although interminority friction has always existed in this country, the recent flood of new immigrants has exacerbated latent tensions. This tripar-

tite dynamic of separatism complicates any attempt to restrain racial tensions and to build interracial unity.

Within each of the three versions of modern separatism,
certain underlying themes and motivations appear. Broadly
speaking, these themes could be called the "power" and
"pride" manifestations of separatism. Power separatism is
group identification motivated by the struggle for scarce resources and political power in society. Inspired by past discrimination that preserved some institutions as all-white
enclaves, power separatists seek to turn the tables by guaranteeing representation based on race in economic, political,
and educational realms. Power separatism often appears in
the quest for numerical set-asides in public contracts, in the
allocation of jobs, or in the reservation of spaces in the education admissions process. A slightly different manifestation of
power separatism may exist in redistricting disputes, where
racial bloc voting and the creation of safe "minority seats"
may encourage polarization of politics on the basis of race or
ethnicity. Recent struggles between minority groups for control of various workers' unions is another classic example of
power-motivated separatism. Our most democratic of institutions, juries, are the latest site in the battle for proportional
racial representation in basic institutions of public life.

Pride separatism, in contrast to power separatism, involves
ethnic or racial affiliation with an emphasis on cultural identity. The benign manifestations of pride separatism involve
Italian Americans' Columbus Day festivities, Irish Americans'
Saint Patrick's Day parades, as well as Brooklyn's West Indian
Carnival, the largest street festival in New York City. The
challenge, however, is to make laudable assertions of ethnic
pride compatible with American traditions and ideas. The
direction that pride separatism will take is anything but

clear. Increasingly, minority groups on college campuses are demanding separate facilities, separate curricula, and separate social opportunities. And the very universities that devise affirmative action programs to promote diversity countenance these separatist arrangements once their diverse students have arrived. At Brown University, for instance, students demanded and received dormitories divided by ethnicity. Separatists at the University of Pennsylvania sought similar living arrangements. At Cornell University there is the predominantly black Ujaama dormitory, the Latino Living Center, and Akwe:Kon, an American Indian house. And minority engineering students at Cornell "have separate study lounges." African Americans at Georgia Tech recently sponsored their own separate yearbook. "Multicultural curriculum," a common offering at many colleges, may help inspire interracial understanding or it may foster the rejection of American ideals. Across college campuses, the expression of racial pride threatens to eclipse the search for interracial harmony. *Snapshots of Color*, a student magazine at Dartmouth, reportedly limits its membership to students of color. Even calls for racial secession can be heard: African Americans, according to one college professor, must "go on our own, do for ourselves, build up our own economy, our own lands, to build our own nation. . . . We don't seem to be able to bridge the gap between whites and non-whites."

The phenomenon of pride separatism is not confined to higher education. Forty years after *Brown*, the resegregation of public schools is a real and troubling development. Even in fully integrated public schools, self-segregation limits the benefits of shared classrooms and facilities. As one observer in San Francisco noted, "When the school bell rings for lunch, students fall into ethnic formation. Asians may cluster in one favorite corner, blacks in another, Latinos somewhere else. Many school yards can be mapped by ethnicity alone." Language differences, another aspect of pride separatism, have heightened interminority dissension.

Majorities, of course, can practice pride separatism too. White schoolchildren can cluster on playgrounds and in cafeterias, and white parents can congregate for a hand of bridge or a game of golf at exclusive—and exclusionary—country clubs. Although the country club has been a bastion of white pride separatism (and the downtown business club a separatist power center too), it does not end there. Twenty-five years after the graduation of the first truly integrated class at Petersburg High School in Petersburg, Virginia, the class of 1971 held separate black and white class reunions. Organizers of the black reunion made clear their white classmates were welcome, but the whites chose instead to attend the reunion of the last preintegration class of 1970. The whites protested no racial animus was involved—they simply wanted to celebrate with the people in the class of 1970, who had been their friends since elementary school. Separatism results.

Both power and pride separatism divide us, though they do so in different ways. Power separatism divides us by positing race as the historical instrument of empowerment in America. The allocation of resources based on racial identity undeniably has an American pedigree: from the all-white clubs to Irish American police forces to ethnically based sponsorship in old-school politics, not to mention the long reign of Jim Crow. But though this tradition is one we recognize, it is not one we celebrate; it is one we have sought to escape. Power separatists would escape through a racialism all their own— through remedies with a benign ring. To be sure, notes Justice John Paul Stevens, we can often discern the difference between a race-conscious policy designed to "perpetuate a caste system and one that seeks to eradicate racial subordination." That does not mean, however, that modern power separatism is any less divisive than its discredited forebear. Beneficiaries of power separatism displace people solely because some hold the right race cards and others do not. The inevitable result is racial resentment that a society seeking to rise above race cannot afford.

Power separatism also frames American institutions in terms of race in a way that frustrates an integrative vision. As one commentator observed: "Maintaining important permanent structures based on race posits permanent separation and therefore economically, politically, and intellectually counterproductive isolation." Thus power separatism fosters a permanently divisive political order; its blueprint for society is a racial road map, not a nationalizing vision.

Pride separatism is a more subtle divider. Its attention to racial and ethnic distinctiveness can lead to healthy self-respect or to hostile introversion. An Afrocentric curriculum is, for all its importance, not an Americentric course of study. Taken to extremes, separatist curricula deprive students of the generalists' understanding and seek to emphasize the experience of one race to the exclusion of "rival" cultural traditions. But "traditions are worth teaching because they are good and true, never because they are mine or thine," notes Kwame Anthony Appiah, a Harvard professor of African American studies. If American public schools taught Jewish children Jewish American history, black children African American history, Anglo children Anglo American history, then by "what [constitutional] right would we forbid children from going to the 'wrong' class?"

There is a way to teach cultural values—by "adding voices to the [American] story as they were added to the nation." And there are nonseparatist outlets for cultural pride. It's "Bach *and* James Brown. Sushi *and* fried catfish," writes

Henry Louis Gates Jr. "I want to be black, to know black, to luxuriate in whatever I might be calling blackness at any particular time—but to do so in order to come out the other side, to experience a humanity that is neither colorless nor reducible to color." The pride separatist, by contrast, makes race the sum and substance of human experience, with one's own race becoming the infallible guide.

Different languages, different cultures, and the pride and power struggles that accompany them may be endemic to a multiracial nation. Unfortunately, it is not always easy to tell the good from the bad in New America. Law, however, comes with a unifying obligation in our country. We stand before the law as equals. Its commands speak to the citizen, not to his race. The Anglo American and the Hispanic American pay the same taxes and obey the same speed limits as the Asian American and the African American. If the law were to relinquish its unifying spirit, our hope for One Nation Indivisible would be lost.

★　★　★

It is important to understand just how seductive a separatist vision will seem to New America. To begin with, there are members of some racial groups who simply do not like or respect people of other races. Prejudice remains all too regrettably a part of the human makeup, and it will suit the prejudiced just fine to hold to a minimum their meaningful contacts with members of another race. Separatism may also seem to spare society the prospect of more racial turmoil. Separatists will argue for division in the name of interracial peace—school principals and university presidents, planning commissioners and zoning board members, city councillors and county supervisors, and, of course, state and federal judges will be asked to separate the races to achieve a social truce.

It may also seem more justifiable to accord "separate but equal" treatment to members of two *minority* groups than to segregate a majority and minority race. Suppose that a given separatist solution—one, for example, that assigns Korean Americans to one public housing complex and African Americans to another—accords with the wishes of the overwhelming majorities of both minority groups. Separation of minorities from each other, some may argue, lacks the stigma of segregation in the pre-*Brown* era. Before *Brown*, it was clear that to separate black children "from others of similar age and qualifications solely because of their race generates a feeling of inferiority as to their status in the community that may affect their hearts and minds in a way unlikely ever to be undone." But it is doubtful that segregated public housing arrangements for two consenting minority groups impose a badge of inferiority upon either one. The case for separatism thus appears to presuppose that "separate but equal" retains a place and that *Plessy*, in some transfigured form, remains relevant still.

The rationales for separatist solutions to multiracial problems do not stop here. Often, as we have seen, such rationales will include strong arguments for the maintenance of community cohesion and pride. The rise of black power spokesmen Stokely Carmichael, Eldridge Cleaver, and H. Rap Brown in the late 1960s is partly attributable to the failure of desegregation efforts to respect the distinctive contributions of the African American heritage. Similarly, the rise of neighborhood school associations in opposition to court-ordered busing of the 1970s stemmed partly from the failure of desegregation decrees to respect what Justice Lewis Powell once termed "the deeply felt desire of citizens for a sense of community in their public education." Courts in multicultural America do not have the option of overlooking the communal dimensions of contemporary racial conflict. Prejudice or bigotry toward another will not fuel every multiracial conflict. Many will be motivated by the simple desire to preserve the values that have sustained ethnic communities throughout the centuries. Dismissive charges of parochialism do a disservice to beliefs that, for those who hold them, have stood the test of time.

Such appeals to the right of free association and to the values of cultural heritage are what make issues in multiracial America so vexing. Even when we speak of Anglo Americans, African Americans, Hispanic Americans, Asian Americans, or Native Americans, we acknowledge the balance between ethnic tradition and national identity. It is one thing to acknowledge the delicacy of that balance. It is quite another, however, to allow racial identities to play a pivotal role in public decisions. The danger of establishing racial or ethnic enclaves in education, the workplace, or the political arena is that separatism has the uncanny potential to feed upon itself. The flip side of communalism is a society that has ceased the search for common ground. If, for example, the organizing principle of political life is to be single-race constituencies, the organizing principle of residential life single-race neighborhoods, the organizing principle of the workplace the single-race task force, then what, ultimately, do we have? I suggest we have a society where leaders neglect the need for interracial communication, where groups regard public resources as matters of racial entitlement, and where every minority asserts a special racial experience which others have not had and thus cannot question.

Perhaps the claim of an Inaccessible Racial Experience is the most troubling part of the separatist perspective: the idea that only members of a given racial group can truly understand what it is like to be part of that group. The feeling is said to be beyond the comprehension of those not in the group, who are either too privileged or too uncaring or simply too much on the outside to know. Whites, in particular, have not felt the slings of racial prejudice. They have not shared the alienating experience of coming of age in an America where racial slights, even if unintended, can be daily reminders of differences. Not only whites, however, are judged uncomprehending. The gulf in experience and understanding is said to be as great among minority groups themselves. African Americans are said not to appreciate the language issues unique to the Hispanic population. In turn, Hispanics are said not to grasp the full historic significance of slavery and Jim Crow. The cultural traditions of Asian Americans are perceived as rooted in a different continent from those of African Americans, which in turn are rooted in a different continent from those of Hispanic Americans. The net result is that credibility in America is reduced to a matter of being a racial insider.

Claims to a unique and Inaccessible Racial Experience are used to justify many versions of separatism. In New York City, for example, supporters of all-black schools argue that black children will be more "comfortable" and will perform better when surrounded exclusively by those who "understand" them. There is something "unique" and "special" in the black experience that nonblack teachers cannot transmit. The commonly expressed notion that "it's a black thing—you wouldn't understand" surfaced in Spike Lee's explanation of why any film on the life of Malcolm X had to have a black director. "You needed an African-American who knows what it feels like to be . . . a second-class citizen. You needed someone who knows what it feels like to have a white woman cross the street or clutch her purse when she sees you coming."

It is not only minorities, however, who boast of an Inaccessible Racial Experience—witness the view that blues music is fathomable only to blacks, country music only to whites. Such sentiments also underlay a well-publicized controversy in 1983 at Harvard Law School regarding the selection of Jack Greenberg to teach a seminar on civil rights law. Greenberg was well qualified for the post; he had worked for years at the NAACP Legal Defense Fund, was a central figure in that organization's landmark legal victories, and had taken over the directorship following Thurgood Marshall's departure. Yet African American and other minority student groups organized a boycott of the class. The protest was based significantly on the contention that since Greenberg was a nonminority, he was not an acceptable instructor for a course in civil rights law.

I do not deny the points of difference. Growing up in a ghetto or barrio is profoundly different from growing up in Grosse Point. The differences, however, have as much to do with economic circumstances as with race. Moreover, within Grosse Point or Chicago's South Side, a world of distinct personal experiences abounds. This fact challenges the perception that human differences are a function of nothing more than race. It is impossible, ultimately, for any one person's experience to duplicate any other's. Siblings in the same household often have vastly different formative impressions. Parents often want children to be more like themselves than children want to be. That is no cause for despair. Difference does not mean that people cease talking or listening or assisting one another. The fact of difference can aid as well as impede communication. After all, we would not have much of interest to impart to one another if we were in all respects the same.

The idea that only members of a particular race can understand the experiences of that race involves a questionable corollary: that the persons of that race all possess similar beliefs and opinions. This view is "based on the demeaning notion that members of the defined racial groups ascribe to certain 'minority views' that must be different from those of other citizens." The notion of a racially monolithic mind-set fails to square with reality. African Americans have long held widely disparate opinions on many issues central to the civil rights debate, including the fundamental conflict between integration and separation. Think of the differing philosophies of Martin Luther King Jr. and Malcolm X or those of Booker T. Washington and W. E. B. Du Bois. Consider more recent disputes within the black community regarding the place of historically black colleges and immersion schools for black American youth. One poll shows African Americans splitting 48 to 42 percent in favor of capital punishment. Those who type blacks as liberal should note, among other things, that black American conservatives now anchor radio talk shows in almost twenty cities, including Washington, Denver, and Seattle. Then those who may be tempted to think of black talk show hosts as conservative should tune in to the Pacifica radio network and listen to Julianne Malveaux.

A similar diversity of views characterizes other minority communities. Hispanic American groups disagreed over the desirability of the North American Free Trade Agreement (NAFTA). The Korean American Grocers Association and the Korean American Chamber of Commerce supported different mayoral candidates in a recent election in Washington, D.C. When whites dispute abortion rights, balanced budgets, and public school prayer, it is naive to view American minorities as monolithic. The nomination of Clarence Thomas to the Supreme Court presents a particularly poignant illustration of deep divisions among persons of the same race. Some African Americans who opposed Justice Thomas's nomination suggested that although he was black, his views were not, even calling him a "radical double agent." Such a view carries the notion of the Inaccessible Racial Experience to its most ludicrous extreme: apparently racial experience is inaccessible not only to persons outside the race, but sometimes even to persons within.

It is easy to understand the origins of the Inaccessible Racial Experience. It was, after all, a system of slavery and segregation that contributed to the shared travails of black Americans. We can also understand how prejudice and simple ignorance help to perpetuate the idea that racial experience is unique. Those outside a race often tend to view the members of that race in a simplistic and undifferentiated way. For example, an African American civil servant who grows up in a black neighborhood knows better than anyone else how many personalities, attitudes, talents, and preferences black people exhibit. But the taxi driver who refuses to take that same person home may see only "black." Racial solidarity often arises in response to such daily slights.

Similarly, Asian Americans know their nationalities are quite diverse, but they know also that Europeans have often lumped them together as a single race. In 1982, a Chinese American named Vincent Chin was killed by two Detroit auto workers because they thought he was Japanese. Similarly, bigots have hurled the racial epithet "Chink" at Asians of all national origins. The fact that Asian Americans are quite diverse, therefore, does not prevent others from seeing them as the same.

Understanding the crude categories of prejudice does not mean, however, that we in America give up on seeing one another individually. Nor should we succumb to the notion that race is the impenetrable barrier that the most prejudiced among us would make of it. Indeed, it is the function of the law to punish prejudiced conduct rather than legitimize the barriers that prejudice attempts to create. To understand that history and bigotry have built up walls is one thing. To conduct our national life within those walls is altogether something else.

The idea that racial experiences are mutually inaccessible is affecting all walks of American life. Take, for example, the field of journalism. Editors in multicultural America will be powerfully tempted to match the race of the reporter with the subject of the reportage. Why risk the outcry when a Hispanic news commentator delivers a biting assessment of a black political figure? Why not just recognize that a significant Asian American news source will be more likely to talk to a fellow Asian American reporter? Taking race into account in such assignments will mark a sad turn of events. America will be the poorer, for example, if black reporters are tacitly removed from other beats to cover mainly black events.

The idea that interracial reporting is in jeopardy is anything but theoretical. Consider the case of Paul Teetor, a white reporter for Vermont's *Burlington Free Press*, who was sent to cover a community forum on racism in March 1993. As William McGowan reports in *The Wall Street Journal*:

> During the forum, a white woman trying to defend Vermonters against angry accusations of white racism was cut off at the microphone by the moderator, a black mayoral aide named Rodney Patterson. Mr. Patterson directed that the woman be escorted outside, explaining that the meeting was "specifically designed for people of color" to describe their "ethnic experiences" of living in Vermont.

When reporter Teetor's story defended the ejected woman, minority activists, led by Mr. Patterson, denounced the story as "ugly" and "distorted." They threatened a lawsuit unless an apology was issued and Mr. Teetor was fired. *Free Press* editor Ronald Thornburgh promptly terminated Mr. Teetor "in a 90-second meeting without giving him a chance to defend himself, [without] reviewing a videotape that supported the reporter's account or talking to any officials in attendance (who also confirm what Mr. Teetor reported)." The lesson of the incident seems clear: when a reporter of one race dares to criticize the actions of members of another race, cries of insensitivity and inability to understand will place that reporter's assignment, promotion, or even employment in jeopardy. In the end, if interracial reporting is to be discouraged, the public may reassess the trust it places in journalists' fearless exercise of First Amendment freedoms.

The impact of the Inaccessible Racial Experience upon American journalism does not stop there. Ruth Shalit of *The New Republic* contends that the endemic social problems of the inner-city go underreported, in part because middle-class, majority-white institutions like the *Washington Post* seek to avoid charges that they cannot comprehend the problem. Such ultrasensitivity serves no one. Whether the problem was contaminated meat or dilapidated tenements, social awareness has always been the precursor of political reform. Such awareness will not be possible if interracial comment on deplorable social conditions is no longer legitimate. "In early 1993," reports Shalit, "Metro reporter Sandra Evans spent months following around a Prince George's County social worker, meticulously documenting the neglect and abuse that goes on in the social service system. She told the story from the point of view of the social worker. Unfortunately, the social worker was white, and all the kids were black. When the story got done, her editors [on the *Post*] wouldn't run it. They told her straight out, the problem with this piece is it looks like a white woman imposing her values on the black world."

The notion of the Inaccessible Racial Experience has even penetrated the world of psychotherapy. In an article entitled "Psychiatric Apartheid," Dr. Sally Satel, a consultant on multicultural therapy for the Center for Equal Opportunity in Washington, D.C., explains how race consciousness has affected the counseling professions. The theory of multicultural therapy, she notes, "presumes that if therapist and patient are members of different groups, especially racial groups, they will experience miscommunication and mistrust. The therapist must therefore learn a different set of rules for treating patients of each different race."

In accord with this theory, some hospitals have begun assigning patients to treatment teams that specialize in a specific racial or ethnic group. Viewing race or ethnicity as a "patient's most clinically important attribute" has one problem, says Satel. "The patient is a human being, not a cultural puppet. As any truly competent therapist knows, psychotherapy can never be about celebrating racial diversity. Therapy is not about groups. But it is about individuals and their infinite complexity. Clinical multiculturalism replaces individual analysis with group-based generalizations and spends more energy separating patients into groups than treating them."

To speak of the Inaccessible Racial Experience is to surrender to the somber role of race in human history and to foreclose a future based on the productive potential inherent in individual diversity. The notion of inaccessible racial cultures elevates supposed racial differences in the human persona above all else. It implies that the designation "Asian," "Hispanic," "Anglo," or "African" American is somehow more significant than membership in the human race. That is a profoundly misanthropic view. Whatever divides us as blacks and whites is less important than what unites us, transcendentally, as human beings. "I believe in my bones that the things that separate us make up one percent of who we are, that ninety-nine percent of our lives are similar," says Charles Johnson, author and professor of literature at the University of Washington. "The same planet supports us. We have the same environment. You have two arms and legs and I have the same. We have given so much over the years to that one percent, complexion, it's a travesty. I think it's one of the great tragedies of our species."

To accept the Inaccessibility of Racial Experience is also to deny the value of empathy. Some will question, of course, whether interracial empathy is even possible. They see race relations as inherently oppressive or antipathetic and deny that equal and harmonious arrangements are achievable. On this point, we confront two paradoxical sets of historical facts. For example, although American slaveholders and Jim Crow apologists were indisputably white, the members of Congress who passed the Reconstruction-era civil rights laws and the Civil Rights Act of 1964 were largely white also. The act of 1964 was not a gesture of paternalism, but an attempt to accord equal treatment to persons to whom equality had too long been denied.

The members of Congress who supported that legislation had not experienced personally what it was like to be denied service at a restaurant or rejected for employment only because of their race. Yet they understood the injustice involved; they could empathize. Much of the appeal of the modern civil rights movement lay in the power of interracial empathy. The strategies of nonviolent protest and passive resistance were designed to demonstrate to persons of goodwill everywhere the contrast between the movement's claims for simple justice and the often violent oppression which they met.

It will be hard to sustain an empathetic social order if separatists succeed in circling the wagons around their own races.

It is not just that separatists reject the possibility of interracial understanding. They actively contribute to misunderstandings by attributing paramount importance to racial characteristics and experience. *Brown* sought to discourage us from racial stereotypes. It was treacherous to generalize about race, *Brown* said, both because such generalizations were unfair to individuals and because they involved significant dangers of inaccuracy and distortion. Today's reemphasis on race in multicultural America may regrettably revive patterns of stereotypical thought. Each racial group may, of course, promote a favorable view of itself. But the dangers of that course should be apparent: the temptation for each race to prove its own virtue carries with it the temptation to identify another race's vice.

Such good race/bad race dogma has already been pushed to its depressing extreme by Leonard Jeffries and Michael Levin, both professors at the City College of New York. Jeffries, chairman of the Black Studies Department, theorizes that climate determines racial characteristics, with the races divided into "sun people" and "ice people." Sun people are highly creative, cooperative, and intuitive, and ice people are naturally cruel, aggressive, and materialistic. African Americans belong to the former group, Caucasians to the latter. Levin, a professor of philosophy, espouses opposite, but equally abhorrent, views associating positive and negative attributes with race. He believes that blacks are intellectually inferior to whites, and more prone to criminal misconduct.

In the end, the doctrines of separatism threaten to propel society to a crisis state. If the majority cannot truly understand the plight of the minority, or if the members of one minority culture cannot really perceive what it means to belong to another, then our basic decisions of governance are suspect. Even the simplest public acts will be thrown into doubt. Can, for example, an African American professor grade the performance of an Asian American student whose values and experiences the professor cannot begin to glimpse? The implications of racial separatism for the rule of law are every bit as serious. Can Anglo American jurors render fair verdicts on Hispanic American criminal defendants? Can Asian American judges fairly hear cases involving African American civil rights plaintiffs? When we cease to draw from a common fund of national experience, and instead represent distinct strands of racial experiences, an important premise of public decisions will have been undermined.

This brings me to a final point. Racial separatism represents a serious threat to the concepts of nationhood and citizenship, more serious than any threat the country has faced since the Civil War. Meeting that threat requires balance. On the one hand, it is important to remain sensitive to real manifestations of racial prejudice, which only the naive would contend do not exist. On the other, it is crucial that we not interpret every event through the lens of race. Efforts to revitalize urban America are essential, for example, because fellow Americans suffer the acute consequences of urban decay. But what matters is their deprived state, not whether the deprived happen to be white or brown or black. There may be other ways to reorient our perspective as well. A racially insensitive comment is wrong, not only because it conveys a degrading insult based on race, but also, on a more basic level, because it wounds another human being. Quite apart from their offensive racial content, such statements are intrinsically indefensible, under any system of morality, and objections can be raised on moral, though race-neutral, grounds.

I am not so foolish as to think that race will not remain a part of American life. The development of an ecumenical perspective on our problems will, however, help to preserve a national outlook in the face of the specter of separatism. One may encourage liberals to look beyond the crude duality of white oppression and black victimization. One may remind conservatives, as Glenn Loury has, that "when gazing upon Americans who are welfare mothers, juvenile felons, or the cognitively deficient, we should see human beings with problems, not races of people plagued by pathology." Separatism is so much in our eyes; it is the who and what we see.

In an age of separatism, we know above all how to flee. The "primary response" to the terrifying problems of the inner city, observes Karl Zinsmeister of the *American Enterprise*, is "defensive flight. Not 'indifference.' Not 'hubris.' Not 'dour insensitivity' . . . but horrified, high-speed, flight—individuals fleeing from geographic killing zones. Thinkers fleeing from the governmental, sexual, political, and moral principles that contributed to (or at least refused to declare war on) this depraved, disloyal, responsibility-free underclass culture."

So there is white flight, black flight—on all fronts the racial trumpets sound retreat. There is only one problem. We cannot flee America. As we seek the shrinking islands of racial security, it is well to remember that the larger national destiny still does matter, that the perspectives that have become so racially imprisoned may divide and doom us all.

Part Three

CIVIL RIGHTS AT THE CROSSROADS

— 5 —

Separatist Politics

$\mathcal{I}$n the spring of 1970, I took my one fling into elective politics. I was twenty-five at the time and in my second year of law school at the University of Virginia. At the urging of Republican governor Linwood Holton, I decided to challenge a three-term Democratic congressman. The results were, in a word, disastrous. "Send Satterfield back to Congress, and Wilkinson back to school," my opponent's billboards read. Sixty-seven percent of the electorate took up that suggestion.

The district in which I ran comprised the city of Richmond, Virginia, and two large surrounding suburban counties of Henrico and Chesterfield. The city had a substantial black community, and the suburban counties were overwhelmingly white. Governor Holton was attempting to build a Republican party in Virginia which could attract the support of black voters. As a Holton Republican, I spent some time attending black social functions, church services, and political events.

The Crusade for Voters was the largest black political organization in the district. At the head of it was a podiatrist by the name of William S. Thornton. To have a chance at the Crusade endorsement, a candidate had to visit Dr. Thornton. Most interest groups in the district had pressed hard for my position on this or that issue, and I expected something of the sort when I drove up to Dr. Thornton's residence. To my surprise, Dr. Thornton wanted nothing more than to chat; it was clear he was less interested in this or that specific issue than with an overall level of personal comfort. The one thought that plainly upset him was that any member of Congress would refuse to hire black staff members or visit black gatherings out of a fear of offending white constituents. Let me see some black faces around you, he said.

I received the Crusade endorsement. But no candidate who receives 33 percent of the vote should try to pose as any expert on politics. I remember only that I learned things from running in that district that I otherwise would not. As a white candidate attending a black political rally or church gathering, I had the experience of being a racial minority of one. The self-consciousness would fade and return, but like a speaker's butterflies, time took care of it.

The biracial coalition I tried to build didn't work. Maybe it was impossible to combine the Crusade endorsement with suburban backing in a year when busing students to achieve racial integration was the burning issue in the district. The biracial composition of that district was a good thing, however. I knew when I spoke to white audiences at Lee-Davis Country Club in Highland Springs that what I said might filter back to the district's black precincts. And when I addressed black audiences, I was also aware of that huge suburban vote. All this tempered what I had to say. I left politics persuaded that multiracial districts promote interracial progress—that they encourage solutions in which diverse constituencies can share.

To be appointed to the federal bench, one must often spend years in politics. But once on the bench, a judge is expected to become apolitical. This apparent oddity is not that odd, if the goal is to have judges appreciate the realities of the political process without involving themselves in it. Impartiality is important, because suits challenging legislative districts are among the most politically charged of all litigation. Unfortunately for many jurisdictions, these suits have become interminable affairs as well. State legislatures must draw up the plans in the first instance; the United States Department of Justice must sign off on many of them; and the courts must pronounce the final say on a challenged plan's legality. No sooner is litigation under one census concluded than redistricting under the next census must begin.

The issues underlying voting rights law are complicated, and many people understandably don't have time to think about them. It is important to think about them, however, because they threaten national unity in the most serious way. The crucial question is how the boundaries of legislative districts should be drawn. This question doesn't affect the United States Senate, of course, because its members run statewide. But it vitally affects the United States House of Representatives, as well as every state legislature and many local governing bodies and school boards. Time was when legislators were left alone to draw the districts in which they ran for reelection, and redistricting sessions revealed political rough-and-tumble at its best and worst. Then, in the early 1960s, the Supreme Court required that legislative districts be roughly equal to one another in population.

This slogan of One person, one vote (or One man, one vote as it was called at the time) was a clear and simple guidepost which legislators could understand. Like "no taxation without representation," the one person, one vote principle was something that bound us all. It transcended race, sex, religion, national origin, business/labor, urban/rural, and every other schism of our politics. In short, One person, one vote seems as American as apple pie.

This principle, however, was not left to stand alone. Like so many of our other unifying standards, it now has a heavy overlay of race. The Voting Rights Act of 1965, whose noble purpose was to ensure that all Americans were free to cast their ballots, has been allowed by courts to become a runaway train of racial separatism.

I look at the law today and I wonder what has happened. The prevalent theory of redistricting today is so far removed from my own experience as a congressional candidate. Absolutely everything in legislative redistricting these days seems to revolve around race. Legislatures now labor under a blizzard of contradictory prescriptions on racial redistricting. Concentrating minority voting power in a district runs constitutional risks. Diluting it among several districts may run afoul of the Voting Rights Act. Ignoring race is no panacea either. The Supreme Court has disapproved of race-conscious districting even as it has required it. No matter which way a legislature now turns, a lawsuit over the politics of race awaits. Legislators themselves are in limbo as litigants consume years climbing up and down the ladder of the federal courts.

Two types of racial separatism emerge in the area of voting rights. The first type involves a redistricting plan which produces simple racial imbalance. A multiracial electorate is thus coupled with a one-race governing body, be it a school board, municipal council, county board of supervisors, or state legislature. Excluding racial minorities from the halls of governance risks the creation of a system of caste rule. Any form of one-race rule is antithetical to our basic democratic premise of inclusion and invites resort to extralegal means of redressing perceived injustice.

The critical question, however, is how racial imbalance comes about. If racial imbalance in governing bodies results from the unfettered choice of voters, then it requires no corrective. If, however, racial imbalance is not random, but the result of racially manipulated rules of electoral competition, then redress should indeed come through the Voting Rights Act. Vote dilution claims under section 2 of that act reflect the fact that elected leaders may choose to deliberately minimize the influence of minorities by concentrating minority voters overwhelmingly in a single district or by distributing them in small numbers among many districts. The act operates to prevent the weakening of minority voting power through such packing or fragmentation. It remains true, of course, that racial manipulation in redistricting schemes is not always easy to detect. The difficulty of detection, however, fails to mitigate the invidious nature of deliberate vote dilution. Elected officials should not be permitted to stack the deck in an election in favor of their own race.

The second type of racial separatism in the area of voting rights has arisen largely as a result of attempts to remedy the first. The second scenario positively endorses race-based representation, and presumes public officials will represent race-based interests and constituencies. Voters under this scenario will presumably vote for members of their own race and will regard the race of their elected official as the sine qua non of effective representation. The unstated premise is of course that each race is an interest group, with its own distinct set of views and priorities, much as farmers or city dwellers or labor union members or business executives are. Under such a system, warned Justice William O. Douglas, "antagonisms that relate to race . . . rather than to political issues are generated."

The tragedy is that race-based representation serves those who already enjoy political influence. It allows incumbents of all races relatively safe racially allocated seats, and it spares them the need to assemble divergent factions into broad electoral coalitions, or to engage in any meaningful interracial dialogue. In fact, the Bush administration merrily deployed the 1990 census to create as many safe minority seats as possible, on the theory that the remaining white districts would be solidly Republican and hasten party realignment in the South. The fact that race-based representation serves the needs of this race or that party, however, does not mean that it serves the interests of the republic, which might benefit if districts were drawn with an eye to integration of the races rather than to the enforced separation of them. The Supreme Court, however, has placed states and localities in a dilemma: if they attempt to achieve some greater ideal of integration, they run the risk of unlawfully diluting minority votes.

Race-based separatism in American politics is largely implemented through a device known as proportionality. By this, the Supreme Court has meant that the proportion of majority-minority districts (ones in which there is a majority of minority voters) must closely approximate the percentage of the minority race in the population as a whole. At bottom, this proportionality principle requires that we look at American voters not as individuals, but as members of racial voting blocs.

The Supreme Court has tried to convince us that it has not adopted a principle of racial proportionality in redistricting. In *Johnson v. De Grandy*, the Court rejected the view that the Voting Rights Act required states or localities to achieve the *maximum* possible number of majority-minority electoral districts for a given minority race. It held that reapportionment plans such as Florida's would be judged by a totality of the circumstances test: proportionality would neither condemn nor immunize the plan as a matter of voting rights law. Justice

Sandra Day O'Connor in a concurring opinion emphasized that proportionality is never dispositive in a voting rights claim under section 2. Justice Anthony Kennedy wrote to underscore the fact that explicit race-based districting would be more vulnerable on constitutional than statutory grounds. In a dissenting opinion, Justices Clarence Thomas and Antonin Scalia contended that the plaintiffs failed altogether to state a claim under the Voting Rights Act. They referred back to Justice Thomas's earlier opinion in *Holder v. Hall*, where he deplored the fact that "proportional allocation of political power according to race" was the driving principle of the Supreme Court's vote dilution jurisprudence.

Notwithstanding the Supreme Court's disclaimers, it seems clear that the proportional resemblance of majority-minority districts in the Florida plan to the various minority shares of the voting population was what saved it in the end. Indeed, the majority stressed the plan's racial proportionality in the opinion's opening paragraph. The Court went on to emphasize that Hispanics had majorities in 42.9 percent of the contested districts in which they constituted 44.8 percent of the voting age population. Blacks had majorities in 14.3 percent of the districts in which they constituted 15.8 percent of the overall voting age population. The Court stated repeatedly that a plan providing both Hispanics and blacks "political effectiveness in proportion to [their] voting-age numbers" could hardly be said to deny "equal political opportunity." It then listed in a lengthy footnote a number of other factors that might prove relevant to a voting rights claim, but allowed those factors to fade into insignificance before the proportionality principle.

The proportionality principle, however, leaves race-based districting, which balkanizes contiguous communities, as the foundation of the American political order. So long as courts use racial proportionality as a measure of a redistricting plan's validity, a numerical safe harbor will exist, with which every redistricting plan will try to conform. The justices seemed anxious, to varying degrees, about the implications of their decision in *De Grandy*, but the refuge of this numerical haven was ultimately too tempting to pass up.

Just how tempting it was becomes evident upon reflection. In the context of Dade County, Florida, the Court used the proportionality principle to sidestep the case's most volatile question. Both black and Hispanic groups were eager to maximize their own representation, but the maximization of electoral clout for one of these racial minority groups would have come at the other's expense. Tensions between the groups ran high. The Court recognized that applying a maximum representation theory to minority groups would only encourage further conflict and would require excruciating trade-offs among minorities when maximum representation for all racial interests was impossible. Proportional, rather than maximum, representation seemed a nifty way out, because it reduced the total number of seats that any single minority could claim.

This solution solved the Supreme Court's immediate problem, but it enhanced racial divisions within the electorate, and it did nothing to combat the trends of racial bloc voting so ensconced in the American political landscape. For example, the Court failed to encourage Hispanic voters to give the slightest consideration to African or Anglo American candidates, or vice versa. The prospects for a politics of interracial overture were snuffed. In short, the unifying force of *De Grandy* was minimal, and its separatist potential very high. The decision brought us one step closer to remedies such as cumulative voting and nondistrict representation, the purpose of which is to encourage racial allegiances in electoral behavior.

The proportionality principle is also a dangerous prescription for New America. Suppose, for example, that an electoral district contains substantial numbers of African, Anglo, Asian, and Hispanic American voters. Does one combine the minorities' percentages in order to constitute a majority-minority election district? Or does one combine only compatible minority interests for that purpose? Is the judiciary to be left the unenviable task of subjectively determining which minority interests are in agreement (and thus subject to aggregation) and which minority interests are antithetical (and thus nonaggregable)? Moreover, the proportionality principle does not tell judges how broad or narrow the definition of a minority should be. Is it fair to speak of Asian Americans as a single minority interest, or must we divide that category in turn into Korean Americans, Vietnamese Americans, Chinese Americans, Japanese Americans, Filipino Americans, and the like? Similarly, is it fair to speak broadly of Hispanic Americans, or must we acknowledge the divergent interests of the Mexican American, Puerto Rican American, and Cuban American communities? To the extent that the proportionality principle requires that we view minority groups as monolithic, it does a profound disservice to the disparate communities involved. And if we recognize real differences, we may never assemble the majority-minority district that the proportionality principle assumes is necessary for a safe racial seat. Multiculturalism has made the Supreme Court's experiment in proportionality the most dangerous of undertakings, though its *De Grandy* decision fails even to acknowledge the degree of potential harm.

The harm is there, however. The Sixth Circuit Court of Appeals recognized the difficulty of applying the Voting

Rights Act to multiracial districts in its 1996 decision *Nixon v. Kent County*:

> If district lines are drawn pursuant to a plan to enhance the political impact of minorities separately, the plan faces potential challenge by a coalition of minorities claiming that greater influence could have been achieved had the minorities been "lumped" together. If, on the other hand, the lines are drawn to accommodate all minorities together, the plan faces potential challenge by an individual minority group on the ground that its influence could have been enhanced had it been treated separately. In both situations, courts and legislatures would be forced to "choose" between protected groups when drawing district lines.

At issue in *Nixon* was whether the Voting Rights Act authorized a coalition of minority groups to complain when, individually, no group had sufficient numbers to constitute a majority in a single member district. The black and Hispanic plaintiffs in *Nixon* contended that the Board of Commissioners in Kent County, Michigan, should have created an additional majority-minority district by combining their adjacent populations, which together amounted to a majority. While other courts had tacitly approved of such coalitions, the Sixth Circuit concluded in a 10 to 5 decision that "the language of the Voting Rights Act does not support a conclusion that coalition suits are part of Congress' remedial purpose and there are compelling reasons to believe that they are not." One such reason is that coalition suits "transform[] the Voting Rights Act from a statute that levels the playing field for all races to one that forcibly advances contrived interest-group coalitions [of] racial or ethnic minorities."

Yet the Sixth Circuit failed to take this sound argument to its logical conclusion: namely that courts which set out to create minority coalition districts assume that the interests of minorities in America are both mutually compatible and equally antagonistic to that of the majority. A more separatist assumption is difficult to imagine.

Coalitions, of course, are the grist of the political mill. When racial minorities in America coalesce, however, they should do so "for the same reason that any two groups coalesce, i.e., to further their mutual political goals." Judges should be the last ones to add or subtract minorities in the course of redrawing district lines. In New America, with so many minority groups to account for, it will be increasingly difficult to convince each group that a court's racial building blocks constitute a "fair" allocation of political power. Some group someplace will feel slighted by being included or excluded from the court-created coalition, and, ultimately, we will all suffer from the cumulative resentment of such unabashedly racial judgments. Better that we as judges leave the surreal task of matching up racial minorities in American politics alone. As the Sixth Circuit noted, however, almost all of the other courts addressing minority coalition claims under the Voting Rights Act "have simply assumed that they are permissible." That in itself is a sad commentary on how inextricably federal judges have immersed themselves in the politics of race consciousness.

★   ★   ★

The problem of race-conscious politics does not end with the Voting Rights Act. It also remains to be seen whether the proportional allocation of political power according to race can be squared with the Constitution. One year after the Supreme Court in *De Grandy* endorsed racial proportionality in redistricting under the Voting Rights Act, it appeared to disapprove it under the Constitution.

In *Miller v. Johnson* the Supreme Court held by a 5 to 4 vote that Georgia's congressional redistricting plan violated the Fourteenth Amendment. The plan had created majority-minority districts in proportion to the state's African American population. Twenty-seven percent of the state's population was black, and three of the eleven congressional districts in the new plan (27 percent) were majority-minority districts, the other eight going Republican. Because Georgia had utilized race as the "predominant, overriding factor" over "traditional race-neutral districting principles, including but not limited to compactness, contiguity, [and] respect for political subdivisions or communities defined by actual shared interests," the constitutionality of its redistricting plan was judged suspect. The Supreme Court found that Georgia had gone too far in its creation of the third majority-minority district, the Eleventh, dubbed "Sherman's March" because "it traces the 100 mile wide swath the Union general cut from Atlanta to the sea in 1864." Further, the Court recognized that the Eleventh connected black communities in metropolitan Atlanta and coastal Chatham County that were "worlds apart in culture. In short, the social, political and economic makeup of the Eleventh District tells a tale of disparity, not community."

The aftermath of the *Miller* decision was intriguing. Representative Cynthia McKinney, the black incumbent in the rejected Eleventh District, was forced into a Democratic primary against two white moderates in a district where only 33 percent of the voting age population was black. Georgia State Representative Billy McKinney, who is Cynthia McKinney's father, denounced *Miller* as "a day of infamy for us, for black people in the South . . . I'm saying that four racist white people and one Uncle Tom made this decision." At McKinney's visit to the Victory Baptist Church in Stone Mountain, Georgia, a supportive pastor likened the *Miller* decision to "Pontius Pilate's conviction of Jesus." From a more secular perspective, the ground rules of politics had certainly changed. Deprived by the Court of a predominately black electorate, McKinney had "to appeal to a larger number of white voters than she has had to in the past," noted Merle Black, a political scientist at Emory University in Atlanta. All three of the primary candidates had to make a broad appeal, in fact, and all three boasted of their ability as racial coalition builders. Indeed, the primary rhetoric was of three candidates heading, more or less, to the racially conciliatory center. Representative McKinney won the primary with 67 percent of the vote, carrying many majority white precincts in the process. "We put together the kind of campaign that transcends race," she said.

Georgia is not the only state to have bent over backward to draw congressional district lines on the basis of race. North Carolina fashioned a district "approximately 160 miles long and, for much of its length, no wider than the [Interstate]-85 corridor. It winds in snake-like fashion through tobacco country, financial centers, and manufacturing areas 'until it gobbles in enough enclaves of black neighborhoods.' "

Not to be outdone, the Texas legislature employed a computer program called REDAPPL to help draw its congressional district boundaries. Technology, it seemed, had transformed racial redistricting from an art form into a highly exact science. Indeed, REDAPPL broke down racial data on a city block by city block level, allowing ever more minute manipulations of district lines to achieve racial objectives. With each new experimental movement of district lines, REDAPPL displayed new racial composition statistics for each affected district. "In numerous instances," noted the Supreme Court, "the correlation between race and district boundaries is nearly perfect. . . . The borders of Districts 18, 29, and 30 change from block to block, from one side of the street to the other, and traverse streets, bodies of water, and commercially developed areas in seemingly arbitrary fashion until one realizes that those corridors connect minority populations."

REDAPPL's most amazing creation, however, was the Houston area's District 29, with a 61 percent Hispanic and 10 percent African American population. It resembled, noted two political observers, nothing so much as "a sacred Mayan bird, with its body running eastward along the Ship Channel from downtown Houston until the tail terminates in Baytown. Spindly legs reach south to Hobby Airport, while the plumed head rises northward almost to Intercontinental. In the western extremity of the district, an open beak appears to be searching for worms in Spring Branch. Here and there, ruffled feathers jut out at odd angles."

Campaigning in such a district is quite a feat. In order to identify their constituents, the candidates had to carry a map, because the district's border shifted from block to block. Often the voters didn't know the candidate running for office, because they "did not know which district they lived in." Apart from such practical difficulties, these contorted districts illustrate the lengths to which American politics now goes to encourage the cultivation of racial followings. Six Texas voters challenged District 29 as unconstitutional racial gerrymandering in violation of the Fourteenth Amendment. One plurality opinion, two concurring opinions, one opinion concurring in the judgment, and two dissenting opinions later, the Supreme Court, by a vote of 5 to 4, struck it (and two other Texas districts) down.

One gazes at these bizarre configurations in astonishment. The tortured trails of these congressional district boundaries reveal a politics where race is the be-all and end-all and a country that is losing its way. Practically speaking, the Supreme Court's *Miller* standard will invalidate misshapen mon-strosities of districts drawn with an eye to representation based on race. Practically speaking also, the jurisprudence of voting rights has become even more of a mess. *Miller*'s rejec-tion of race as a predominant principle of redistricting is hard to square with *De Grandy*'s tacit endorsement of it. *Miller* also represents a collision between the Justice Department's en-forcement of the Voting Rights Act and the Supreme Court's more color-blind interpretation of the Fourteenth Amend-ment. The Court in *Miller* had strong words for the Justice Department's interpretation of the Voting Rights Act, which it summarized as requiring "states to create majority-minority districts wherever possible," explaining:

> It takes a shortsighted and unauthorized view of the Voting Rights Act to invoke that statute, which has played a decisive role in redressing some of our worst forms of discrimination, to demand the very racial stereotyping the Fourteenth Amend-ment forbids.

State legislatures now find themselves between the Scylla of the Justice Department's enforcement of the Voting Rights Act and the Charybdis of the Fourteenth Amendment. States cannot ignore race because the Voting Rights Act requires that the racial composition of a district be a factor in redis-tricting. Conversely, *Miller* prohibits race from being the pre-dominant factor. The Supreme Court's prohibition of race as a predominant factor in redistricting is a good first step. Prohibiting race as a predominant factor implies, however, permitting it as a secondary one. To say that one may make "limited" use of race is akin to saying one may take a little poison. The "limited use of race" standard invites two things: first, racial politics in redistricting; and second, endless litiga-tion over what is "limited."

Rejecting race-conscious districting will not return America to rule by racial caste. The demise of the proportionality principle is unlikely to usher in a regime in which members of racial minorities hold few offices. This is so for several reasons. First, black politicians of both major parties have been successful in a number of nonblack venues. Congressman J. C. Watts of Oklahoma and former congressman Gary Franks of Connecticut have been elected from mostly white Republican districts. Senator Carol Moseley-Braun and former governor Douglas Wilder, both Democrats, have won statewide races in Illinois and Virginia. A Latino teacher, Victor Morales, won a hotly contested 1996 Democratic Senate primary in Texas, and Gary Locke, the son of Chinese immigrants, rose to become governor of Washington State and the first Asian American chief executive outside of Hawaii. In Indiana, Julia M. Carson won a very tight race for the U.S. House stressing local issues that transcended race. "I am not your African-American candidate," she said, "I am the Democratic candidate for Congress."

Second, even if race is no longer used to create districts, many communities, particularly in urban areas, will be comprised primarily of minorities, and accordingly, majority-minority districts will continue to exist. The happenstance creation of such districts is no more wrong than the happenstance creation of primarily white districts based on traditional redistricting principles. Given residential patterns in America, the principles of compactness and contiguity will operate to produce majority-minority districts. That again is constitutionally acceptable. Finally, a constitutional prohibition on the use of race as a redistricting factor cuts both ways, and will protect minority communities from majoritarian attempts at racial dispersion.

Meanwhile, the story in Georgia is worth following. Under Georgia's new plan, Representative Cynthia McKinney won reelection in her new majority white district. To do so, she had to disavow separatist rhetoric from her father, Billy McKinney, who called her opponent a "racist Jew." Two other black congressmen, John Lewis and Sanford Bishop, also won reelection in Georgia, the latter in a majority white district. Representative Bishop not only voted for a balanced budget amendment and welfare reform. He worked hard on a race-neutral issue—protecting peanut subsidies in the new farm bill. "We've gotten to a point where people are being evaluated as individuals," Representative Bishop told supporters. "It's not about where the lines are drawn. It's about the quality of service rendered."

★　★　★

*O*ne need only look at the sharp divisions and close votes on the Supreme Court to know that the issue of race-based redistricting is far from settled. Such redistricting may be a fact of modern politics, but the pursuit of power along purely racial lines is a deeply disturbing trend. Racial gerrymandering is cutting out the middle from American politics. It is pushing representative bodies toward the extremes and is resulting in the polarization of the deliberative process. Texas commentator Dave McNeely explains:

> The result in Texas and several other states has been districts created to elect members of a particular ethnicity and packing of Democrats in some districts and Republicans in others. That in turn has resulted in selection of members of Congress increasingly from the poles of the Republican and Democratic parties—with the result that the moderates have been left behind, or left out.

There is also the real risk that racial gerrymandering will serve to "freeze rather than thaw the previous system of racial politics." As Abigail Thernstrom explains:

> The heightened sense of group membership works against that of common citizenship. . . . [E]thnic boundaries, by diminishing the sense of common citizenship, may "ultimately smother democratic choice and threaten democratic institutions."

She uses the example of V. S. Naipaul's account of Trinidad's multiracial politics in *The Suffrage of Elvira*. Indeed, Trinidad's population is "the most heterogeneous in the Caribbean," comprised of individuals from Spanish, African, East Indian, Syrian, French, English, Chinese, and Lebanese ancestry. In the novel, Hindu politicians work with Muslims, black politicians unite with Hindus, and Muslim and Hindu campaigners pursue Spanish and black votes. Thernstrom notes:

> Only the candidate who successfully reached across religious and ethnic lines could hope to win in that small multiethnic election district in Trinidad. Democratic politics (only four years old) was thus working to ameliorate interethnic conflict. . . . [Such] political necessity brings groups together.

The recognition that political interaction fosters unity in multicultural societies is nothing new. In 508–507 B.C., Athenian citizens, including recent immigrants, were enrolled in their neighborhood or "deme"; groups of these demes were then randomly assigned to one of ten larger political districts or "tribes" so that "men from different parts of the polis were therefore intermingled." Republican Rome similarly mixed citizens of different ethnic backgrounds. For example, with the end of the Social War in 89 B.C., the newly enfranchised Italians were distributed among thirty-one of Rome's thirty-five voting districts. While the motives behind such policies were admittedly complex, and neither Greek nor Roman societies were ever completely free of separatist tendencies, such examples do illustrate the use of political assimilation in ancient societies.

Indeed, though again the point should not be oversimplified, there is evidence that ancient societies did not prosper when separatist tendencies were followed. An Athenian law in 451–450 B.C., which excluded from citizenship all those who were not "born of such parents as were both Athenians," weakened Athens, as perhaps a quarter of the city's population was sold into slavery. Later, the Romans remembered the mistakes of the Greeks. In the first century A.D., the Emperor Claudius proclaimed:

> What was the ruin of Sparta and Athens, but this, that mighty as they were in war, they spurned from them as aliens those whom they had conquered? Our founder Romulus, on the other hand, was so wise that he fought as enemies and then hailed as fellow-citizens several nations on the very same day.

Today, in American politics, the integrative ideal has been abandoned. Race-based districting is a far cry from the dream of *Brown*. State-sponsored electoral enclaves seem a species of segregation, which has more in common with *Brown*'s predecessor, *Plessy*. It is wrong for legislators to arrive in office as representatives of races rather than as champions of American citizens. In bestowing upon elected officials a racial power base, the law encourages political leaders to accentuate the role of racial differences in America and to maintain the racial solidarity of their followings. Thus, it is a separatist political future that we face.

It is legitimate to ask where the road of race-based politics will end. New America has given rise to more interest groups based upon race and ethnicity. For example, the League of United Latin American Citizens, the Mexican American Legal Defense and Education Fund, and the National Council of La Raza represent the interests of many Hispanic Americans, just as the NAACP, the National Urban League, and the Southern Christian Leadership Conference have traditionally represented the interests of many American blacks. The Leadership Conference of Civil Rights, an umbrella coalition of civil rights groups, includes many with racial, ethnic, or religious constituencies such as the Organization of Chinese Americans, the NAACP, and the Anti-Defamation League of B'nai B'rith.

Whereas the organization, lobbying efforts, fund-raising, and endorsements of interest groups have often borne a close relationship to race, ethnicity, or national origin, American political parties have not sought to define themselves primarily in racial terms. True, the major parties in America have appealed to minority communities by endorsing civil rights laws and by appearing sensitive to minority concerns. Presidents have appointed cabinet members and Supreme Court justices to send a message of inclusion to a minority religion or race. Political parties have distributed patronage, nominated candidates, designed ads, and arranged political conventions with an eye to their ethnic appeal. But they have not taken the final step. We do not—not yet, anyway—have black, Hispanic, Asian, or Anglo American political parties within the United States. As race-based districting becomes the norm, as race-based constituencies become more prevalent, and as race-based caucuses in representative bodies grow in influence, one has to wonder where we are headed. America's two-party system has traditionally sought to mute racial politics and to encourage the creation of multiracial coalitions. However, deep public disillusionment with politics as usual has brought that system under assault. If race-based representation becomes ingrained, a new political culture and reconstituted political parties will have race as their rallying cry and their focal point.

The longer we travel down this road of race-based politics, the more difficult and divisive it becomes to turn back. When the Supreme Court limited the use of racial redistricting in *Miller*, the respected commentator Carl T. Rowan boldly proclaimed that "this court propels America toward a race war." Such a comment only demonstrates how strongly many have come to rely on a system of racial shares and how the principle of racial districting can establish a truly dangerous legal baseline. Regardless of whether a legal baseline is right or wrong, society tends to conform itself to the baseline and to rely upon the existing system. The longer the racial regime is in place, the more entrenched such reliance becomes, and the more intensely its beneficiaries feel about any modification. If we do not move now to remove racially contrived redistricting from our midst, it will become more entrenched and more costly to change, and the racial strife that Mr. Rowan predicts could indeed become the tragic American reality.

— 6 —

Separatist Entitlements

$\mathcal{S}$eparatist entitlements present some of the same dilemmas as separatist politics. On the one hand, it is neither socially healthy nor morally right to limit membership in the learned professions, the upper echelons of corporate management, or the faculties and student bodies of the nation's elite universities to members of a single race. The prospects for interracial understanding would greatly diminish, and such a system would take on all the appearances of a racially segregated ruling caste. As a practical matter, a society permeated with de facto exclusions would be hard-pressed to prove to young minority students that the best opportunities in America were truly open to them. Racial exclusivity, however it arises, can deprive the social order of any appearance of fairness and of any incentive for personal improvement. Minority groups often "notic[e] the color-coded aspects of privilege, and . . . end up raising questions about fundamental issues of rights and the distribution of benefits." The existence of racial exclusivity in the upper reaches of business, academia, government, and the professions would surely cause those excluded to doubt that a society is genuinely governed by color-blind rules.

Affirmative action efforts in education and employment were devised to end such exclusivity. Many of the plans embodied the noblest of integrative intentions, but many managed to perpetuate the discrimination they purported to eradicate. For example, at the University of California at Berkeley, black and Hispanic applicants were twenty times as likely to be accepted as Asian students with the same academic qualifications. Ultimately, the plans, like the discrimination they sought to overcome, valued racial characteristics over individual attributes.

Much has been written in defense of and in opposition to affirmative action. While this debate is an interesting one, it overlooks the overriding question—what is affirmative action doing to America? It is this question that people on both sides of the great affirmative action divide must consider.

★ ★ ★

*I*n counting, sorting, and categorizing American citizens by race, affirmative action ensures our separation. Behind all the racial statistics are not just blacks or Hispanics or Asians or whites, but honest-to-goodness human beings. Consider the celebrated case of Cheryl Hopwood, a 1992 applicant to the University of Texas School of Law. One way to look at Ms. Hopwood is how Texas did: as a *white* woman with an eighty-third-percentile score on the Law School Admissions Test (LSAT) and a 3.8 grade point average. Hopwood's application, like all of the others, was "sorted in folders color-coded by [the applicant's] race." After arranging the folders of Texas residents into racially coded groups—white, black, and brown—the University of Texas determined each folder's Texas Index (TI)—the applicant's GPA multiplied by ten, plus his or her LSAT score. This TI determined whether a folder would be presumptively admitted, presumptively denied, or placed in a discretionary review zone.

In 1992, white folders were presumptively admitted with a 199 TI and presumptively denied with a 192 TI, while black and brown folders were presumptively admitted with a 189 TI and presumptively denied with a 179 TI. Thus, all black and all brown folders with TIs of 189, 190, 191, and 192 were presumptively admitted while all white folders with identical scores were presumptively denied admission. Cheryl Hopwood's TI score was 199, just within the category of presumptive admission for white folders. Despite being within the presumptive admission zone, Hopwood was not offered admission to Texas because her two undergraduate institutions were deemed insufficiently competitive. Yet while Hopwood was never offered admission, forty black folders and fifty-two brown folders with TI scores below hers were admitted. Moreover, *all* black folders with a TI of 186 or higher (*thirteen* points below Hopwood) and *all* brown folders with a TI of 193 or higher (*six* points below Hopwood) were offered admission. Thus, there is little doubt that if Cheryl Hopwood's folder had been a different color, she would have been admitted to the University of Texas School of Law.

There is another way to look at Cheryl Hopwood, however—one that has nothing to do with her race. The color-coded file masked a moving human story of struggle and determination. Hopwood was born the daughter of a Vietnam veteran who died while she was a child. Thereafter, her mother worked as many as three jobs to support her. This life continued until Hopwood's mother remarried some years later, when Cheryl was in high school. Cheryl's stepfather, however, refused to contribute to her support, and as a result, Hopwood supported herself with after-school jobs.

Despite these hardships, Hopwood managed to realize her dream: admission to Princeton University. While she anticipated F. Scott Fitzgerald's "towers and spires of Princeton," the tuition posed a serious problem. On the one hand, Hopwood was excluded from need-based aid by virtue of her stepfather's income. On the other, she had no parental source of support to secure her tuition. Thus, while Princeton expected Hopwood's stepfather to pay her tuition and/or guarantee student loans, that money was never forthcoming.

In the end, Hopwood's dream of attending Princeton went unrealized. She could earn only enough money to afford tuition at Montgomery County Community College. In May of 1984, she received an associate's degree in accounting from that institution, and four years later, she completed her bachelor's degree in accounting at California State University in Sacramento. While attaining these degrees, she worked twenty to thirty hours a week and was active in her local Big Brothers and Big Sisters chapter. Following graduation, Hopwood became a certified public accountant and practiced in that field. She eventually married an air force captain, and in 1991, they had their first child, Tara. Tara was born with a rare muscle disease, and until Tara's death from heart failure in late 1995, Hopwood had to balance her professional career with caring for her daughter.

In 1992, Hopwood applied to law school at the University of Texas. Unfortunately, the university never saw the individual behind the racial statistic, an individual whose record reflected character and life experience that would have contributed to that institution's diversity. In the end, Hopwood was reduced to a white folder, her 199 TI, and the fact that she attended California State University at Sacramento and Montgomery County Community College rather than, say, Princeton. The circumstances of rejection were, as they often are in affirmative action plans, rife with the potential for racial resentment. As Hopwood explained, " 'They dinged Sac State. . . . They dinged me for the same thing that they credited blacks for'—lack of access to the best undergraduate education."

Cheryl Hopwood and three white male applicants subsequently challenged the University of Texas's color-coded affirmative action plan in federal court. Though the district court found certain aspects of the university's affirmative action program unconstitutional, the court upheld the university's use of race to obtain diversity and awarded Hopwood only one dollar in damages and the opportunity to apply to the University of Texas once again.

Hopwood and her coplaintiffs then appealed to the United States Court of Appeals for the Fifth Circuit. That court agreed with Hopwood and unequivocally held that

> the University of Texas School of Law may not use race as a factor in deciding which applicants to admit in order to achieve a diverse student body, to combat the perceived effects of a hostile environment at the law school, to alleviate the law school's poor reputation in the minority community, or to eliminate any present effects of past discrimination by actors other than the law school.

The court explained that "the use of race to achieve diversity undercuts the ultimate goal of the Fourteenth Amendment: the end of racially-motivated state action." The use of racial preferences, said the court (quoting Judge Richard Posner), "exemplifies, encourages, and legitimizes the mode of thought and behavior that underlies most prejudice and bigotry in modern America." Indeed, Cheryl Hopwood's case demonstrates the dehumanization that results from viewing unique people as mere representatives of racial groups. It also illustrates the degree to which a program initiated under the very best of intentions became nothing less than racialism with a vengeance.

★   ★   ★

The effects of racial admissions policies such as those at Berkeley and Texas do not end with a letter of acceptance or rejection. They establish a dangerous baseline of racial judgment that encourages racial preoccupations to persist long after those admitted have enrolled. Troy Duster, a sociologist at Berkeley, concluded that "students from different backgrounds came to college thinking of themselves as 'individuals' or 'Americans' but, once at Berkeley, began to think of themselves as 'African American, Asian American or whatever.'" Minority students have taken the lesson of affirmative action and applied it elsewhere, demanding separate dormitories and specialized racial curriculums. And minorities are hardly alone in this impulse toward separatism. White students at Temple and Florida State have established white student unions to oppose affirmative action programs at their institutions.

The whole furor seems the very antithesis of education. Universities symbolize, or used to symbolize, the common search for knowledge, but affirmative action has brought a change upon them. As Professor Gertrude Himmelfarb of the City University of New York explains:

> The traditional ideal of the university, as a community where professors and students are united in a common enterprise for a common purpose, has been replaced by the idea of a loose, almost amorphous, federation made up of distinct groups pursuing their special interests and agendas (and, often, voluntarily segregating themselves in dorms, dining rooms, and lecture halls).

At the University of Virginia, where forty-five years ago official segregation was broken, self-segregation is now the rule: "There are black and Asian dormitories; white and black fraternities; black, white and Asian parties; even a 'black bus stop.' "

Education, by definition, must be a shared experience—it is, after all, the idea that matters, not the race of the person who happens to advance it. By indulging race-conscious policies of their own, universities stripped themselves of the moral authority to combat the separatism in their midst. Race-based policies also burdened even the most brilliant minority students with unnecessary baggage. Errol Smith, a black entrepreneur from Los Angeles, was incensed:

> I'm offended by [the] underlying assumption that you and I as minorities don't have what it takes . . . that we are so bereft of resources, intelligence and innovation that we can't make it without some quota or some preference.

When Smith attempted to convey his position to students at California State University, Hayward, he "was taunted by cries of 'Tom' and other racial epithets" from affirmative action supporters. Minority students argued that racial entitlements were their "right," even their "dignity."

The confrontation between Smith and the minority students illustrates how racial entitlements contribute to separatism and how separatism in turn requires racial solidarity. The student group's position was: You are either with us (your race) or against us (your race) on the basis of a single-issue, race-based affirmative action. When the lines of public policy are drawn along race, the beneficiaries of preferences generally become cohesive in an effort to preserve their position, thus creating race-based political organizations, and where possible, self-segregated arrangements.

Dormitories provide the obvious example. When members of an embattled group live together, peer pressure intimidates those who have a tendency to jump the fence (for example, labeling opponents of entitlements "Toms"). Such self-policing via isolation helps to preserve the political strength of the racial group. Further, other races, whose members may oppose the racial entitlement, loom as the opposition, thus decreasing the likelihood of interracial cooperation. The result is a tension that engenders suspicion both within racial factions and between them.

One can pay too much attention to headlines that play up racial discord and overlook examples of racial cooperation. Still, too many educational environments are awash in claims of racial entitlement and patterns of racial thought. Historical events spur present-day hostilities. White students have shoved the Confederate battle flag and the strains of "Dixie" at minority students with in-your-face contempt. Efforts are now under way to discredit important moments of American history as "Anglo," or at least to cancel their celebration.

A telling example occurred in March of 1995 at the University of Texas at Austin. Hispanic groups there, after four years of protesting, succeeded in cancelling the traditional Texas Independence Day celebration. The event was an important one for many Texans, including some of Hispanic descent, whose ancestors fought for freedom from autocratic rule and for democracy. Ethnic Mexicans who participated on the Texas side were called "Tejanos." Lorenzo de Zavala, architect of the Mexican Federal Constitution of 1824, helped frame the Texas Constitution and became the first vice president of Texas. Antonio Navarro and Francisco Ruiz signed the Texas Declaration of Independence.

The protestors, however, argued that the holiday represented:

a tradition of exclusionary and distorted history [that ignores] the bitter legacy of violence and oppression against the Native American, African American and Mexican American peoples. . . . We can't celebrate the conquering of one people over another.

Despite the University's action, the Young Conservatives of Texas organized a last-minute celebration that drew several hundred supporters, as well as fifty Hispanic protesters who held signs reading "Forget the Alamo" and "The Lies of Texas Are Upon Us." It may be, of course, that all this racial rancor was destined to occur no matter what. Public policies that make incessant use of race, however, have added immeasurably to the difficulty of achieving a nonracial outlook on any aspect of American history or any practice of American society. As the Texas protest showed, these policies have also contributed to making self-flagellation an American preoccupation.

Race-conscious policies have also finally succeeded in making every last segment of American society believe itself a victim. Listen as Paul Craig Roberts and Lawrence M. Stratton introduce their book, *The New Color Line*, by expressing the angst of the Angry White Male:

In the United States today, white males don't have to read Lillian Smith and John Griffin to understand the affront of racial discrimination. As white males, many experience "reverse discrimination" in university admissions, law and medical school admissions, test scoring, employment, promotions, and access to training programs. The expansion of quotas has deprived white males of the protection of the Civil Rights Act. Preferment is replacing merit, and the institutions of liberal society are slowly giving way to a new feudalism based on race and gender estates. In pursuit of a moral cause, we let the ends justify the means and lost our way. We are in the process of losing our society along with the presumption of goodwill that is the basis of a democratic society in which law flows from a legislature accountable to the people.

Some may say, Who cares? White males have had it so good for so long, this view holds, that it is high time they experience the sort of adversity they have visited upon others. Whatever one may think of a racial eye for an eye, it is worth noting that affirmative action has managed to do away with every conceivable class of "nonvictim" in the United States. Indeed, race-conscious policies are designed to right wrongs to old classes of victims by creating new classes of victims. Even those who have little sympathy for white males might acknowledge the danger to a society whose sense of victimization, past and present, runs this high. In truth, there are ever fewer Americans around who do not feel America has done them in. With race-based preferences there is no part of society without a chip on its shoulder, no group whose racial resentments cannot be skillfully stoked by those with a mind to do so. As for America—the question becomes not what we may give to the whole, but what each race might claim for its part. As for Americans, the only thing we may have in common anymore is that we all feel shortchanged.

★   ★   ★

*I*t is extraordinary that a country that has experienced the pernicious effects of racial classifications would resort to them with such alacrity. Justice Blackmun's paradoxical assertion that "to get beyond racism, we must first take account of race" actually endorses race-based means as a first choice, not as an alternative of last resort.

Race-based means have always seemed to involve an infatuation with numbers. In adopting race-based criteria, judges were prone to worship at the altar of the almighty statistic. The success of school desegregation plans was never assessed by any qualitative interaction or achievement, but only by the percentages of each race that were enrolled together in school. As the district court explained in *Swann v. Charlotte-Mecklenburg Board of Education* (1969), "efforts should be made to reach a 71–29 ratio in the various schools so that there will be no basis for contending that one school is racially different from the others." Counting by race also became an accepted practice for employers who were looking to get the federal bureaucracy off their backs and to stay out of court. In *Griggs v. Duke Power Co.* (1971), the Supreme Court cast a long shadow over employment tests that had a negative numerical impact on minority hiring. In *United Steelworkers of America v. Weber* (1979), the Court said that the maintenance of racial balance in an employer's craft training program could override claims of workplace seniority or personal merit. When the Court began to pull back from these two decisions in *Wards Cove Packing Co. v. Atonio* (1989), Congress rebuked it in the Civil Rights Act of 1991. For businesses averse both to prolonged litigation and unpleasant public controversy, the message was clear: "'they are safer in hiring and promoting by numbers reflecting the percentages [of racial minorities] in the surrounding community than by risking disparate impact lawsuits they are likely to lose.'"

One can understand the practical pressures driving some employers to race-by-the-numbers. But why have so many other people of goodwill opted for race-conscious means of achieving diversity rather than race-neutral ones? Several reasons are typically advanced. One is that of old-fashioned guilt. Inasmuch as our past discrimination was based on race, the reparations must also be. Other advocates of race consciousness claim that race-neutral plans ignore unconscious racial discrimination. Race-conscious policy makers also seem to believe that race can be used as a visible, convenient proxy for social or economic disadvantage. Race makes it all so easy: it is easier to determine who belongs in the preferred categories, and it is easier to set the numeric goals or targets by which "progress" can be assessed.

Most of all, though, people fear that a colorblind society will be a "white" society, with minorities being effectively shut out of the best colleges and jobs. The prospect of a "white" (or Asian) American upper class, they claim, is the real separatist threat. Perhaps this was the fear that led to the University of Texas School of Law program. But as Terry Eastland points out:

> The black and Mexican-American applicants admitted under affirmative action were not *un*qualified to practice law; their academic qualifications were good enough to win admission under non-affirmative action standards at fully two-thirds of the nation's law schools. Affirmative action thus stigmatizes beneficiaries who could succeed—and be seen to succeed—without it.

The fear of a white society itself underscores the existence of a pervasive racial baseline: the presupposition that racial proportionality must become the nation's great sine qua non. It also overlooks the fact that racial imbalances can, and do, result from self-selection—random combinations of personal preferences, family traditions, and expressions of individual aptitudes and talent. If racial imbalance results from racial discrimination, law can and must remedy that. The danger, however, is that we will find ourselves perpetuating racial discrimination to "fix" proportional imbalances that are driven by a host of causes and choices unrelated to race.

Abandoning race by the numbers need not mean that we evaluate applicants solely by another set of numbers such as college board scores. Many admissions offices are already accustomed to evaluating people on criteria that are other than strictly numerical; some colleges no longer require applicants even to submit their SAT scores. A college director of admissions might find, for example, that numbers—college board scores no less than racial goals and guideposts— only obscure personal expression and demean individual accomplishment. Numbers may be the cautious, convenient, and "correct" way to assemble a student body, but standing alone, what ultimately do they show?

Indeed, the personal qualities of human beings emerge only when one looks beyond the numbers. Musical success might show "hard work and cultivated taste"; adeptness in sports, discipline and teamwork. Personal interviews and literary essays, job experiences and teacher recommendations should continue to be part of a nonnumerical admissions mix. As the Fifth Circuit explained in *Hopwood*: "A university may properly favor one applicant over another because of his ability to play the cello, make a downfield tackle, or understand chaos theory." One's geographic and economic background might count too. Disadvantage in all its permutations might be plugged in as a legitimate, nonracial, nonnumerical factor by which applicants can be judged. Although some complain that such systems may be too subjective, the real problem, I suspect, is that individualized assessments of disadvantaged applicants consume too much time and result in unpredictable "imbalances." Thus the temptation to ground entitlements on a simple, controllable, numerical criterion such as race.

The ubiquitous setting of numerical goals and the pervasive keeping of racial statistics ensures the perpetuation of race-based perspectives. The racial number has the unique potential to dehumanize, and it confers a sense of racial entitlement. Numbers herd American citizens, like cattle, into so many separate pens of race. The most separate future one can imagine for America is a numerical one.

★   ★   ★

*T*he social costs of installing race-based entitlements have been significant. "In practice," writes Michael Lind in *The Next American Nation; The New Nationalism and the Fourth American Revolution*, "racial preference means categorical representation *within* each class: upper-middle-class blacks in upper-middle-class professions, and working-class blacks in working-class occupations." Even within a class, however, relative hardships may be unrelated to race. Some kids have learning disabilities to overcome; others do not. An upper-middle-class black child may be born to loving parents, while an upper-middle-class white child may experience domestic indifference from day one.

Race-based devices not only lose sight of individual differences within classes; they discriminate among classes as well. In the search for racial balance, the upper-middle-class Anglo and the upper-middle-class African American fare well enough, while the poor of both races face a further constriction of their opportunities. As Cheryl Hopwood's case shows, the losers in race-based decisions are frequently disadvantaged members of disfavored racial groups. The losers also have little recourse—they cannot vote the company personnel officer or the university admissions dean out of office at the next election. The class implications of affirmative action are reminiscent of the school desegregation decrees in the 1970s. Court-ordered student busing was implemented largely with "hard-hat" pupils, while those who could afford suburban residences or private schooling were left unaffected.

This whole series of events has infused many American conservatives with populist zeal. The new populism surfaced in many places, among them the California Civil Rights Initiative of 1996, a ballot measure aimed at checking racial preference and discrimination in America's most populous state. Opposing affirmative action meant standing up for the little guy, the deserving individual who was being cuffed around by public bureaucracies, big corporations, special interest groups in Congress, and the United States Supreme Court. Opponents of racial preferences were quick to point out that life's hard knocks could stagger individual Americans of every race. Yet quotas assume that we can attribute all the obstacles and hardships of life to race. The only losers in the affirmative action process, wrote Justice Scalia, are those in this country for whom civil rights law "has not been merely repealed but actually inverted. The irony is that these individuals—predominately unknown, unaffluent, unorganized—suffer this injustice at the hands of a Court fond of thinking itself the champion of the politically impotent."

Why has the class-based separatism of affirmative action not attracted more attention? Why should not efforts based on a race-neutral concept of disadvantage attract greater support? Disadvantaged Americans who have overcome socioeconomic obstacles merit consideration not because of their race but because of, among other things, their determination and perseverance. An approach which concerns itself with disadvantaged *individuals* does not suffer the drawbacks of traditional race-based action such as injustice to dispreferred groups, stigmatization of preferred ones, and flagrant race consciousness. Race-blind measures such as the Head Start program and need-based loans and scholarships are successful examples of such nonracial preferences. Some have even applied the label "affirmative action" to government assistance based on need. " 'Affirmative' because government authority must be employed to remove the obstacles to upward mobility and human advancement. 'Action' because democratic societies must act positively and create real equality of opportunity— without promising equality of reward." This policy would obviate constitutional obstacles too. "There appears to be a societal consensus—from Douglas to Scalia—that kids from poor backgrounds deserve a leg up."

Class friction is only part of the social division spawned by explicit racial preferences. Race-based goals and targets, whether in employment or education, have infiltrated society with a race consciousness which may be impossible to root out. At every turn, Americans are asked to identify themselves by race. One college application, that of Tufts University in Medford, Massachusetts, requests that applicants identify themselves by both a primary race as well as by a subgroup within the race:

BLACK/AFRICAN AMERICAN
Other Black/African Descent
Black West Indian

HISPANIC/LATINO NON-CAUCASIAN
Cuban American
Mexican American/Chicano
Puerto Rican–Mainland
Puerto Rican–Commonwealth
South or Central American

ASIAN AMERICAN
Chinese American
Filipino American
South Asian
Japanese American

Korean American
Pacific Islander
Southeast Asian
Vietnamese American
Asian Indian

NATIVE AMERICAN
Tribal Affiliation
Alaskan Native

WHITE/CAUCASIAN

OTHER

The purpose of such questions is not lost on applicants: numerically underrepresented groups may rate a preference; overrepresented ones will not.

To be sure, thoughtful advocates of preferences often maintain that the measures are only temporary. They do not, however, explain why we should assume that racial entitlements, once conferred, will be easily withdrawn. At least student leaders like Marc Lopes of California State University, Hayward, aren't persuaded that racial entitlements are provisional: "If affirmative action is abolished, all the social gains our ancestors fought for will be wiped out."

There may of course be a provision in a narrowly tailored court decree that goals will be phased out once they are met. Many preferential systems, however, do not embody such provisions. Even where they are included, employers and educational institutions have an incentive to maintain indefinitely court-ordered minority preference levels in order to avoid unseemly publicity over their repeal and in order to forestall further litigation.

In a more profound sense the widespread use of racial preference has ensured that race will remain a natural and instinctive part of national thought. The categories used by government to count by race accentuate race-consciousness as people identify themselves as part of whatever racial designation stands to benefit. "Before the affirmative action age," contends Linda Chavez in her book *Out of the Barrio*, "there were no *Hispanics*, only Mexicans, Puerto Ricans, Cubans, and so on. Indeed, few efforts were made to forge an alliance among the various Hispanic subgroups until the 1970s, when competition with blacks for college admissions, jobs, and other rewards of affirmative action made it advantageous for Hispanics to join forces in order to demand a larger share of the pie."

The racial categories of affirmative action are thus to a considerable extent artifacts of law. They contain gross stereotypical assumptions that diverse communities are, simply by virtue of the designation "Asian" or "Hispanic," all the same. Affirmative action policies have not only helped to create a Pan-Hispanic and Pan-Asian identity within the American polity. They have used race to muddle the message that opportunity in America beckons those with the grit and the savvy to seize it. An individual whose fortunes have been advanced or retarded on account of race will naturally come to perceive race as *the* great social determinant. Those who have been preferred may develop a stake in racially oriented perspectives, whereas those who have been rejected on account of race may develop a smoldering resentment of them. Either way, race becomes the focal point. When the decisions of public institutions turn on race, race consciousness becomes legitimized throughout society. Every issue begins to assume racial overtones, with all the attendant poisonous effects.

Brown, of course, held out quite a different vision: that it was what individuals did that mattered, not the race to which they happened to belong. After that decision, "many Americans seemed to have accepted the idea that skin color and ethnicity ought not to be relevant in any public or private consideration of the worth of an individual." Individual rights, not group entitlements, were to be the norm. The reemergence of racial status through the use of race-based preferences has risked the reincarnation of the very racial ste-reotypes that the *Brown* decision had condemned. In the end, the resort to racial preferences will create rationales for more such preferences. Advocates of those preferences will point to the very race consciousness that race-based means have helped instill to explain both why a color-blind society has not arrived and to justify the indefinite perpetuation of race-based relief.

Perhaps the best evidence of the degree to which racial modes of thought have taken over social discourse lies in the connotations of the word "diversity." The word has come to mean exclusively racial or ethnic diversity, though it is not clear why the meaning should be so narrow. Campus diversity might sensibly be defined in many ways, including broad-based racial pluralism. Diversity could mean that many differ-ent philosophical points of view are represented on a campus, that students come from a wide variety of socioeconomic or geographical backgrounds, or that students in a professional school bring a variety of skills and career objectives to their studies. It may be that these forms of diversity are indeed reflected in a given educational environment, but they are very seldom discussed. Diversity, like many other terms, has come to be defined exclusively by race. Its narrow meaning stands as evidence of the degree to which race-based distinc-tions have come to permeate our thinking.

★ ★ ★

*W*hile the dangers of racial separatism are significant in the bipolar context of black-white relations, those dangers prolif-erate in a multiracial context. The apparent commonality of interests among minorities during the period when whites were the dominant demographic force will fade as minority populations increase in number. In San Francisco, as Chinese Americans grew as a percentage of the school population, so did the pressures to contain their enrollment, which was capped by a 1983 consent decree at 45 percent for neighborhood schools and 40 percent for magnet schools. Distressingly, many Chinese American students became the victims of their own strong academic performance. In order to maintain racial balance at certain San Francisco schools, Chinese American students had to present stronger credentials than applicants of other races to be admitted. Patrick Wong, fourteen, believed he was denied admission to the school district's prestigious Lowell High School because of his Chinese ancestry. So Wong became a class action plaintiff. His suit alleges that Chinese Americans had to score 66 out of 69 points on an exam to enter Lowell, while whites and other Asians gained admittance with a 59 and blacks and Hispanics with a 56.

One commentator sadly observed that "forty years after *Brown v. Board of Education*, American children are still being locked out of public schools on account of race." That the lines of conflict are no longer strictly black-white is of no comfort. In the multiracial setting, no less than in the bipolar one, individual children seeking the best education have found themselves pawns on another ugly battleground of race.

The justification used for the San Francisco standards was not remediation, but rather "diversity." Diversity has a good meaning—namely that citizens will always be welcome in America for who they are. As we have noted, however, the word "diversity" is one that must be closely watched. Racial entitlement in the name of diversity is, if anything, more deficient than racial entitlement on reparational rationales. Diversity implies the allocation of government benefits for reasons of race alone. Under a regime of diversity, it matters not that Chinese Americans had themselves suffered invidious past discrimination, only that the government had determined what constituted an appropriately diverse percentage of Chinese, white, black, and Hispanic students in any given school. To the number crunchers, Patrick Wong's sin was belonging to an overrepresented race.

Asian Americans have the growing perception that diversity in education is being achieved at their expense. Indeed, the phrase "Angry Yellow Men" is now used to describe the opposition of Asian Americans to the uniquely high academic standards imposed upon them by some affirmative action plans. Treatment of Asian Americans recalls the deplorable efforts to limit enrollment of Jewish students whose academic success threatened the diversity of America's elite educational institutions. Ironically, schools imposed quotas on Jewish admissions to preserve a "diversity" that was almost all-white. If achieving diversity qualifies as a compelling state interest under the law, it would seem that almost any racial entitlement program could now pass constitutional muster. As Justice O'Connor has noted:

> Like the vague assertion of societal discrimination, a claim of insufficiently diverse . . . viewpoints might be used to justify equally unconstrained racial preferences, linked to nothing other than proportional representation of various races.

All a school or employer need do is proffer data showing that its existing racial composition was somehow out of line with local, state, or national averages—that is, that it was insufficiently diverse. And so long as a program moves racial representation toward some local or national statistical average, any racial entitlement program based on diversity would qualify as narrowly tailored under equal protection principles. "Diversity" in this sense means nothing more than an absorption in the arithmetic of race. The result of such absorption can be absurdity, penalizing racial groups for both over- and underrepresentation. In Montgomery County, Maryland, Eleanor Glewwe and Hana Maruyama were prevented from enrolling in a French-language immersion campus because their transfer would have diminished the "Asian head count" at their initial school. School officials were ironically unmoved by the argument that their transfer would boost the tiny Asian enrollment at their new school, which stood at 4 percent.

Proponents of racial preferences refuse to recognize just what a quagmire the use of race in New America will turn out to be. It becomes difficult in a multiracial context to devise criteria by which racial groups should receive preferential treatment. In forming an affirmative action plan, should priorities among the races be set according to the historical discrimination suffered by each group? How then do we define the racial group? How do we assess the quantum of historical discrimination suffered? How do we weigh the amount of racial reparations due? While the reparational focus of the law of affirmative action seemed plausible enough in a biracial setting, a multiracial fight for scarce public resources tends to resemble less an act of social atonement than a simple racial spoils system.

Should priorities then be based on the disparity between a minority's enrollment in a particular school or workplace and the minority's percentage in the relevant population pool? Disparity approaches may be, if anything, more dangerous than racial reparations. "For the past five years," writes *The New Republic*'s Jeffrey Rosen, "many states and cities have

been commissioning what are now called 'disparity studies.'
. . . So far, more than 100 studies have been completed at an
estimated cost to taxpayers of $45 million. . . . The studies
have proved to be so unreliable that they have failed to convince any court to uphold a set-aside program." The studies
seek to collect, among other things, anecdotal evidence of racial grievances. But the prospect of spending more millions of
taxpayer dollars "to encourage citizens in every state to enu-
merate their racial and sexual discontents," warns Rosen,
"could ignite the most toxic elements in our civil culture."

The disparity approach to affirmative action also returns us
to all the drawbacks of numerical proportionality. In a multiracial environment, setting numerical racial preferences will
become even more volatile and provocative than in the traditional bipolar context. Here, a preference for one racial minority may mean the loss of opportunity for another. America
could not cultivate a more fertile terrain for interracial conflict
than to encourage multiple racial groups to chase limited
public resources. Every position becomes a potential racial
plum: blacks threatened to recall San Francisco's Board of
Education when the board selected a Hispanic from New
York to head the school district (over an African American
candidate from California). When racial factions are pitted
against one another for preference and entitlement, they
begin to view their relationships with other groups as a zero-
sum game.

An entitlement should spring from the concept of citizenship, not from some racial subset of the same. Indeed, it becomes difficult in a multiethnic culture to determine who is a
member of what group. There are now more than three million interracial married couples in the United States, more
than a fourfold increase from 1970. Intermarriage is frequently identified as a phenomenon that may soften the

edges of ethnic division in America. Yet how to classify the children of such marriages has become an issue. Interracial couples anxious to find an official home for their children have pressed the Census Bureau to designate a Multiracial category for the form used in the 2000 census. Opponents of the new category question what it really means. "The child of a black and white relationship would not have a lot in common with the child of a Korean and Japanese relationship," contends Lawrence Hirschfeld, a University of Michigan associate professor who advised the Census Bureau on its research. Even under the best of circumstances, an issue of this sort is likely to be contentious. But when the dispensation of government benefits, the drawing of electoral districts, and the design of affirmative action plans and school desegregation remedies all come to depend on the racial classification of citizens, the controversy can only be expected to intensify. Unfortunately, this intensification will come at a moment when the "correct" racial classifications of Americans are becoming less clear.

The Eleventh Circuit confronted the classification problem in *Peightal v. Metropolitan Dade County*, in which Alan Peightal brought an individual reverse discrimination claim against the Dade County Fire Department because under its affirmative action plan it had hired minority applicants who scored lower than he on the applicant examination. Peightal challenged, among other things, the fire department's definition of "Hispanic," which included "all persons of Mexican, Puerto Rican, Cuban, Central or South American, or other Spanish culture or origin, regardless of race." The Eleventh Circuit upheld this definition of the preferred group in part because the Dade County Fire Department had adopted Equal Employment Opportunity Commission guidelines requiring that an individual's claim of Hispanic identification present "strong visible indication that the person *culturally* and *linguistically* identifies with the group." The court appeared to accept the Hispanic affiliation of two categories of applicants: "Hispanic female applicants [who] had married non-Hispanic men, thereby taking non-Hispanic surnames," as well as those "applicants who had Anglo surnames but were actually born in Spanish-speaking countries." The court appeared to disapprove as overbroad, however, the automatic inclusion in the preferred group of "Spanish-surnamed individuals . . . who have married someone of Spanish ancestry but who themselves lack Spanish heritage," as well as those "of Caucasian ancestry who have simply chosen to [become fluent in] a second language."

It ill behooves one to quibble with this or that aspect of the above definition. As a general matter, individuals should be deemed to belong to the racial or ethnic group to which they wish to belong, unless of course the search for employment or educational benefits makes the choice patently fraudulent. To concentrate, however, on the fine points of racial or ethnic definition is to miss the larger issue. It is astonishing, really, that employers should devote small bureaucracies to determining which individuals qualify for membership in which racial group. Such a practice, notes Deroy Murdock of the *Washington Times*, "already boosts costs and headaches for American industry. Many firms that work with public agencies must keep records on the ethnic composition of their staffs. These tasks only will grow more bothersome and expensive if companies must plug their workers into a profusion of new racial pigeonholes." The historical antecedents of such close racial calibrations seem too ominous to dismiss. That American institutions should be parsing so finely the racial characteristics of American citizens should make us shudder. I do not doubt that those engaged in the parsing go about their task with the best of intentions. The task itself, however, is uncomfortably akin to that performed by the most vulgar apostles of apartheid.

★ ★ ★

In the end, affirmative action rests on the perception of America as an oppressor nation. The list of beneficiaries in an affirmative action program is meant to read like a litany of victims. There are indeed historical villainies—slavery, segregation, and the subjugation of Native Americans being worst among them. Other groups have historical grievances also. There is the notorious internment of Japanese Americans during World War II, and the mistreatment of Chinese Americans in California. Irish Americans and Italian Americans met with discrimination as they tried to make their way in WASP society. Mexican Americans faced displacement and condescension as America expanded into Texas and the Southwest. Cuban Americans and Filipino Americans can point to American imperial designs on those islands around the turn of the twentieth century. Affirmative action demands that groups highlight racial oppression at the hands of America in order to bolster their present claims for preferential treatment.

This oppressionist view of American history is as wrong as the old uncritical one, symbolized by the slaughter of Native Americans by blue and yellow cavalry charges in those early western movies. That popular view of American history was virtually mythological, and the affirmative action movement has provided a useful correction. It is time, however, to bring the American heritage back into balance. No nation can maintain its self-esteem if its faults are forever paraded and its accomplishments ignored.

It is time to refresh our recollection of America's gifts to human liberty, and to recognize that no country has meant more. For centuries, the American Revolution has stood as a central rebuke to colonial regimes around the world. Its example is the very opposite of oppression. So too is the Bill of Rights, with its guarantees against government tyranny, the right to trial by jury and the freedom to speak one's political mind foremost among them. Popular sovereignty and representative government and democratic checks and balances are not oppressive notions, and America was founded upon them. America contributed mightily to the defeat of the planet's two most oppressive ideologies—fascism and communism—and it deserves everlasting credit in the eyes of its citizens for that. It is important not to forget the injustices of the American story. However, a prevailing national creed of perpetual atonement makes the American identity one of wrongdoing writ large. It is time to say, yes, much has been wrong about America, but much more has been right.

It is time too to rethink our approach to racial preferences and racial entitlements. Increasing upward mobility for underprivileged citizens is an American imperative. Rooting for the underdog is an American thing to do. But rooting for one's race is neither right, American, nor for that matter constitutional. The problems that inhere in the design and implementation of race-based preferences in multicultural settings will suffocate our national spirit. Claims to racial entitlements in employment and education will grow, not shrink, as demographic diversity in New America increases. Soon, these racial conflicts may become truly insoluble under the traditional systems of affirmative action. It would be a happy irony if our nation's increasing ethnic diversity forced us to reexamine the validity of race-based approaches and to reaffirm the principle that our dignity lies in our humanity, not in our race.

Questions dealing with race are probably the most difficult and sensitive in all of law. As a judge, I did not come casually to the view that affirmative action programs have profound separatist tendencies. In quiet moments, I still turn it over in my mind. One of the saddest chapters in all of judicial history has been the setback dealt by the Supreme Court to racial progress in the nineteenth and early twentieth centuries. It happened not once, but twice. In *Dred Scott v. Sanford*, the Court held, among other things, that "neither black slaves nor their descendants could be considered citizens of the United States or persons who received any individual rights under the Constitution." That holding helped to precipitate the Civil War. In *Plessy v. Ferguson*, the Court upheld the constitutionality of separate facilities for black and white citizens and helped to legitimize Jim Crow. Those are only the most notorious cases. No judge today wants the late twentieth century to resemble the late nineteenth, when the denial of racial justice to generations of black Americans could fairly be laid at the feet of the courts. So, I ask myself: In opposing the broad use of race-based remedies, am I a party to another historical travesty? Are the courts blocking, for yet a third time, the path of African Americans to racial justice in the United States?

Two brief quotations are of great comfort to me in answering this question. The first is from Justice John Marshall Harlan's famous dissent in the *Plessy* decision: "Our Constitution is color-blind, and neither knows nor tolerates classes among citizens." The second quotation is from Martin Luther King's celebrated speech: "I Have a Dream" that "my four little children will one day live in a nation where they will not be judged by the color of their skin but by the content of their character."

When I served in the Civil Rights Division of the Department of Justice under President Ronald Reagan, we often used these two quotations to explain why it was that we opposed the award of preferences on the basis of race. Both President Reagan and Attorney General William French Smith were opposed to racial quotas. Both also knew it was going to be difficult to translate that opposition into a litigating principle unless we convinced the public that our opposition to preferences had everything to do with individual dignity and nothing to do with any prejudice based on race. In speech after speech, we used these quotations to show that race by the numbers was incompatible with the liberal vision of racial justice in America.

We faced much opposition, the reasons for which were not hard to surmise. How dare the Reagan administration expropriate such estimable icons as John Marshall Harlan and Martin Luther King to suit its purposes? How could the Reagan administration use King's summons to rise above race when there remained so much racial inequality and injustice? Didn't we know that Harlan and King were prophets, as far ahead of their time as the Reagan Department of Justice was behind?

I respect those misgivings, but we never intended the use of the Harlan and King quotations to be inflammatory. We tried in our work to follow Harlan's principle and to move toward King's goal. Their words are neither ahead of nor behind the times. Rather, they are timeless. Discrimination can be conquered only if we condemn it whenever and against whomever it occurs. Racial equality can be grounded for the long haul only in the indivisibility of human worth. Only when the human core in each of us becomes the object of respect from all of us can America come together. If this sounds idealistic, then so be it. Harlan and King spoke to the better angels of our nature, in the hope that a nation freed from its ancient nemesis of race might soar.

— 7 —

Separatist Education

$\mathcal{S}$eparatist education presents every bit the threat to national community that separatist politics and separatist entitlements do. The values of *Brown* are most poignantly implicated here, because society has traditionally relied upon public schools to lay the bedrock for integration. Our schools not only prepare students for the challenges and opportunities of American life; they also serve as melting pots where interracial friendships can counteract prejudice at an early age. Separatist educational arrangements threaten both of these traditional goals. The issues surrounding separatist education are complex. Here, too, however, the integrative ideal of *Brown* is under siege in New America.

Separatist schooling has caught the fancy of many different ethnic groups. Whites flocked to segregated private academies in the South in the wake of *Brown*. Although many of the academies now proclaim a willingness to admit black students, tuition remains steep, and blacks "remember what the intent was when that school was started." Some black activists have pushed Afrocentric curricula as a means of enhancing the self-esteem of minority pupils. But this movement, Arthur M. Schlesinger Jr. has claimed, transforms history into boosterism and elevates an "obsession with differences" over the idea of an American identity. Controversy centers also on the role of historically black colleges and universities. Do these institutions open doors for poor blacks into mainstream American life or do they perpetuate the most insular and debilitating aspects of segregated school systems? Though the educational settings may differ, the basic question stays the same: Are our schools now locking into place lifetimes of separatist practices and preferences?

This debate has raged most prominently over the issue of bilingual education. While there are many methods of teaching students with limited English skills, the approaches can be simplified as: (1) "bilingual instruction," or "native language instruction," in which core academic subjects are taught primarily in the students' native language with the eventual goal of bringing the students into the mainstream; and (2) "English as a Second Language," or "immersion," in which classes are taught primarily in English from the outset. The first approach seeks to prevent students from falling behind in other classes while they learn English and to "avoid the confusion of 'semilingualism,' or the imperfect learning of two languages." The second approach posits that students will be better off in all subjects if they learn English as soon as possible.

The second approach also has a firm foundation in American history. America has assimilated wave upon wave of non-English-speaking immigrants who quickly learned English. The new immigrants soon sensed it was in their interest to do so. This historic pattern is now changing. At Los Angeles's Eastman Avenue School, the originator of a native-language instruction program adopted across the nation, only 8 of 1,135 native-language students tested out of the elementary school's bilingual program in 1993 and 1994. Although Massachusetts state law recommends that bilingual students leave that program within three years, 46 percent of Hispanic students in Boston middle schools had been in the bilingual program since kindergarten or first grade. A New York study comparing students in native-language bilingual programs with students enrolled in English as a Second Language (ESL), where instruction occurs in English, found a startling disparity: while 80 percent of ESL students entered mainstream classes within two to three years, the figure was only 51 percent for native-language students.

It is treacherous to generalize about the assimilation of language-minority pupils in the United States. The pace at which they learn English may depend on where they live, on the length of time their family has been in America, and on the educational policies adopted by their particular school districts. There is a good deal of evidence, however, that something is amiss. Delaine Eastin, California Superintendent of Public Instruction, believes that the current means of providing government support for bilingual education creates the wrong incentives for school districts. In California, the state provides schools with a yearly stipend based on the number of LEP (limited English proficiency) students: the more LEP students, the more state funding. This money may well serve as a disincentive for schools to mainstream their bilingual students. "We have built a system that's backward," Eastin says. "We reward districts whose students don't progress." Indeed, there are suggestions that whether or not Hispanic parents prefer bilingual education for their children, and whether or not the children are proficient in English, young Hispanics are placed in such programs on the basis of their ethnicity. The *Washington Post* reports that in Rhode Island, a "Puerto Rican boy, bewildered by his referral to bilingual classes, told [his] counselor in flawless English that he had grown up and gone to school in Lawrence, Mass."

The data raises questions about how well bilingual programs actually transmit English. It even raises doubts about the degree to which bilingual education has instruction in English as a goal. Former Secretary of Education Lauro F. Cavazos explained:

> At the same time that we are teaching our children English, we must do all we can to help them maintain their native language and culture.

Having the state oversee the preservation of particular cultural norms is a tricky proposition, however. Surely, the primary responsibility for that task should rest with the family. Some Chinese, Jewish, and Greek communities, for example, have after-school and/or weekend programs that convey cultural traditions to their children. Schools have the obligation to educate children about the society around them, but bureaucratic efforts at cultural inculcation create problems. Whose culture, after all, is most deserving of protection? How can a single Spanish class simultaneously seek to preserve the cultures of the Guatemalan Cakchiquel Indian and the Spanish Argentinean?

Native-language instruction also faces practical obstacles in a multicultural society. According to a 1994 report by the General Accounting Office, more than 2.3 million students with limited English skills live in the United States. The report evaluated bilingual education programs in five school districts where students spoke eighty-five, sixty-seven, fifty-nine, forty, and thirteen different languages. In 1992, 28 percent of the students in the district with eighty-five languages were classified as LEP (limited English proficiency). Just ten years earlier, LEP students comprised only 7 percent of the district's population. Further, by 1992, the district's population could not have been more linguistically diverse: 7,857 Spanish-speaking students, 7,471 Hmong, 2,619 Laotian, 1,673 Khmer, 346 Vietnamese, and 971 students speaking at least eighty other languages reflecting every corner of Africa, Asia, and Europe.

No school district can provide native instruction in all of these different languages, much less instruction in every one of the represented cultures. And the practical obstacles facing bilingual education do not end there. A nationwide shortage of bilingual teachers exists, and in Houston, Texas, it was discovered that "90 teachers in the city's 'bilingual' program speak little or no English." The philosophic questions are as perplexing as the practical difficulties. Is it fair for the school district to provide native-language instruction only for some ethnic groups merely because they are more numerous? Is it right for a district to provide native-language instruction only for Hispanics because Spanish teachers are abundant, while Hmong, Laotian, Khmer, and Vietnamese teachers are unavailable? To answer such questions, schools must decide which native languages and which native cultures government resources will be spent to preserve. Requiring government to make any such decision will result in the appearance of racial favoritism—such partiality will engender divisiveness among the haves and the have-nots of the bilingual entitlement.

The only way such divisiveness can be avoided is by a policy of linguistic and cultural neutrality toward language minorities. All children with limited English proficiency should receive the same English-language teaching, and all children should be brought into mainstream English classes as quickly as possible. Such a policy is important in providing a common

language for so many new immigrants. As the language background of American children becomes more diverse, the importance of English as a medium of common understanding
rises. If four American children claim Russian, Laotian, Spanish, and Somali as their native tongues, the practical path toward mutual understanding for these four children lies once
again in the teaching of English.

★ ★ ★

$\mathscr{B}$ilingual programs were originally conceived as *transitional*
programs for non-English-speaking students. Congress initially
promoted such programs to prevent Spanish-speaking students
from falling behind in their coursework on account of linguistic
barriers. With this laudable goal in mind, Congress passed the
1967 Bilingual Education Act. Recodified in 1988, the act
provides funds for a variety of state and local bilingual programs, including "*transitional* bilingual education," "special alternative instructional programs," "family English literacy
programs," data collection and research efforts, and training
and technical assistance. In its statement of policy, the act
notes not only that "large numbers of children of limited English proficiency have educational needs which can be met by
the use of bilingual educational methods," but also that "the
segregation of many groups of limited English proficient students remains a serious problem." In other words, Congress
carefully tempered the provision of special educational help
for linguistic minorities with assurances that such programs
would not become a segregated backwater. In particular, the
act provided that "in order to prevent the segregation of children . . . a program of bilingual education may include the
participation of children whose language is English."

Courts initially maintained this careful focus on the *integrative* and *transitional* purposes of bilingual programs. The

Supreme Court's 1974 decision in *Lau v. Nichols*, for example, supported bilingual programs that would end the exclusion of linguistic minorities from the educational mainstream. Lower courts have applied similar standards. Most court decisions on bilingual education have distinguished between programs that "provide for the transition of [language-minority] children to the English language," and plans that impose unwarranted segregation in the name of bilingual instruction. Courts have invalidated those bilingual programs that failed to "provide a method for transferring students out of the program when the necessary level of English proficiency is reached." The goal of the programs, said one, is not to "isolate children into racially or ethnically identifiable classes, but [to] encourage contact between non-English and English speaking children."

More recently, however, there has been a perceptible shift in the approach of some bilingual programs. Minority groups that originally sought these programs in order to gain access to the educational mainstream are increasingly using them to pursue a separatist agenda. In many schools, separate bilingual instruction has become less a temporary and transitional concept than permanent programming geared toward fostering cultural pride and ethnic identity in minority schoolchildren. "The promotion of cultural differences has to be recognized as a valid and legitimate educational goal," contended Tomas Arciniega, an educator at California State University at Fresno. In Los Angeles, recently adopted bilingual programs expanded teaching in native languages, despite widespread teacher opposition and evidence of dubious educational merit. And in New York, the bilingual program was expanded to include language-minority students who scored below the fortieth percentile on a standardized English test, where previously the threshold had been the twenty-third percentile. New Jersey even allowed students to take a standardized high school graduation exam in their native languages, effectively dispensing with an English immersion concept altogether.

It is one thing to talk about trends in bilingual education in the abstract. It is better, however, to visit the classrooms themselves. The typical bilingual education program

> is based on early and extended native-language instruction. . . . In first grade, limited English students are placed in a classroom where a bilingual teacher provides all instruction in the home language . . . —reading, language arts, spelling, mathematics, and social studies. For a small portion of the day—perhaps thirty minutes daily, three times a week—an ESL teacher, that is, one skilled in intensive English-language instruction, gives oral English lessons.

In order to achieve the native-language goals at the classroom level, however, teachers must actually discourage any student who speaks in English. Rosalie Pedalino Porter, a former bilingual kindergarten teacher, explained that during a lesson on colors, she held up a picture of a green box and asked, "*Juan, qué color es este?*" Juan answered, "green." Because the class was being taught exclusively in Spanish, "green" was the wrong answer. Ms. Porter corrected Juan, "*verde.*" Still, Juan maintained that the color in the picture was "green."

The insistence on speaking the child's native language is so great that even the asking of a simple question in English is rebuffed. Ms. Porter notes the response of a teacher in her hometown of Amherst, Massachusetts, when a nine-year-old girl pointed to a picture of a fire and asked, "Is this a *fuego?*" The teacher replied, "*Sí, por favor hable en Español.*" The teacher ordered the child to speak in Spanish when she was but one word, "fire," away from comprehending the picture in English.

Such programs simply have things backward; the cart is placed before the horse. Progress in substantive subjects may mean little without corresponding progress in English, without which children cannot put their substantive skills to use. But that is not all. A study published in October 1994 by the New York City Board of Education showed students who were taught in English from the beginning actually tested better in their other subjects, such as math and reading, than those taught in their native language. Of the language-minority pupils who entered school in kindergarten or first grade, "49 percent of those who had been in ESL classes eventually read at grade level, while only 32 percent of those who had been in bilingual classes performed that well." The results in mathematics were similar. The suggestion that native-language instruction not only delayed the entry of students into mainstream classes, but also was detrimental to their academic achievement, sparked protests from the advocates of bilingual programs and pressures to change the study's methodology, and hence, its conclusions.

The protests were no doubt sincere. They also revealed the vested interests that now surround both the maintenance of funding for bilingual instruction and the manner in which many teachers have become accustomed to teaching their bilingual classes. The prospect of change is as threatening to educational establishments as it is to business and political ones. And there is nothing so unnerving as the questioning of basic educational assumptions. To ride along with the status quo, however, is to bequeath our country a future of linguistic separation. In the short run, it may seem the path of least resistance to conduct class in a child's native language. In the long run, schools that fail to transmit a mastery of English have done their students or the larger society no favor.

★ ★ ★

*L*anguage issues are so difficult, because they are so bound up in cultural and personal self-esteem. It isn't just language—it's language as a proxy for everything else. We can see these emotions at work just north of our border. One need only listen to some of the Quebecers whose grievances with English-speaking Canada run so deep. "I can remember taking the train to Chicoutimi [north of Quebec City] in 1950 and the railway conductors didn't speak a word of French," notes the historian Ghislain Bouchard in recalling a long list of language slights. The sovereignists, as Quebec's French-speaking separatists prefer to be called, use language as a symbol of a distinct political destiny. The argument that Quebec depends mightily on English-speaking Canada for capital and subsidies and markets meets a romantic defiance: "We are not sheep," says Nadile Ostegy, a young student in the separatist heartland of Chicoutimi. "We are capable of developing ourselves. Give us the means, give us the possibilities."

One senses in the Parti Québécois something profoundly ancestral. "*Je me souviens*," reads every Quebec license plate—I remember. Just what they remember is left hauntingly opaque. Perhaps it is the distant days before the English defeated the French on the Plains of Abraham, when the French were equal in North America, not "a fragile island in a vast English-speaking continent." Perhaps, as with some American minorities, it is the turns along the road of poverty and oppression. Perhaps . . . but who knows? "It's a fundamental question of existence," says Marc-Andre Bedard, a longtime separatist leader in the region along Quebec's Saguenay River. "Are we a people or are we not? If we are, we should be sovereign. We should be at the table with the international community. It's a society, it's a way of thinking, it's a history, it's a view of the future. It's not just a language."

What the Quebecers and Hispanic American communities have in common is a determination to preserve a way of life. Dominant languages seem a threat to that, a challenge to family, church, and historical memory, and so they are resisted. I find that I cannot just dismiss those beliefs, however separatist they seem. Suppose the shoe were on the other foot—that I was raising my kids in say, an English-speaking enclave of Tegucigalpa, the capital of Honduras. I'd want my children to learn Spanish, for how else could they expect to get along? But I'd also worry about what they were losing— all the appreciation for American democracy, law, literature, history, and politics that had meant so much to me. So I'd try to preserve what I could against the dominant culture, lest my children grow up strangers to my sight. I'd want my kids to adapt, but I'd also want them to remember—the Quebecer's license plate would resonate with me.

As the number of Hispanic Americans rises, the pressures to learn English may fall. The Spanish language is now so common throughout the United States that it is relatively painless for a member of that community to progress through life without ever learning English. Religious services, from baptism to Sunday worship to last rites, proceed in Spanish. One can vote in Spanish, pay taxes in Spanish, and receive most other government services in Spanish. While Spanish print, radio, television, and film provide a valued service, they also obviate the need for an individual to learn English for either entertainment or news. Within Hispanic communities, one can even conduct most commercial transactions without ever speaking English. As Modesto Maidique, president of Florida International University, said of Miami, "it is possible here to obtain the best of all—to go to the best banks, the best law firms and the best restaurants, and to be attended to in Spanish." Finally, with the advent of native-language instruction in the public school system, individuals can complete their primary and secondary education without achieving English literacy.

This relative self-sufficiency has encouraged some Hispanic Americans both to resist calls for "assimilation" and to reject the need to learn English. "We cannot assimilate—and we won't!" insists Arnold Torres, the former executive director of the League of United Latin American Citizens, a leading Hispanic civil rights organization in the United States. One can again understand the depth of feeling on this subject. Residents of Hispanic American communities reap many of the political and economic benefits of American citizenship without having to forgo their language or their way of life. Because Latin American immigrants "live closer to their countries of origin than do Europeans and Asians," they have been especially reluctant to cut their cultural and linguistic ties. "Many Latinos," notes Gregory Rodriguez, an associate editor at Pacific News Service, "hail from countries that have manipulated anti-Yankee sentiment to promote national unity. In Mexico, becoming 'North American' has been seen as a betrayal of one's culture."

Language allegiances reflect this view. Bilingual education, as one commentator observes, "has become a Hispanic institution, one of the few that is all their own, and all the more precious for that." Anglo Americans who protest that expanded individual opportunity need not erode cultural identity doubtless make themselves immediate objects of mistrust. Parochialism, one must recognize, is something a linguistic *majority* can practice. Hispanic Americans rightly sense that there is a big double standard here—the interest in having Hispanic Americans learn English is not matched, as it certainly should be, by an Anglo American interest in understanding Spanish language and culture.

Brown v. Board of Education never sanctioned any such course of cultural supremacy. It also does not suggest that English is intrinsically superior to other languages. The decision rests instead on the premise that differences are only differences: they should not arouse feelings of superiority of any sort. To the extent that *Brown* speaks to the question of bilingualism, it illuminates a two-way street. Intercultural understanding will greatly improve if young Hispanics master English. It will likewise improve if young Anglo students learn Spanish, with all its attendant cultural and literary insights.

Learning the English language should thus not mean forsaking Spanish, or Russian, or French. The problem is that it is becoming increasingly difficult to persuade young language-minority students that they need to learn English at all. We may be approaching the point in America where attachment to one language is arousing antipathy toward another. This is a tragic development. To the extent that cultural pride becomes identified with monolingualism, language minorities will be the losers. It is true that in New America, greater opportunities exist for non-English-speaking citizens who are members of more populous language groups (such as Hispanics). Opportunity correspondingly decreases with the relative obscurity of a non-English-speaker's native tongue. However, the irony is that, in more populous communities, precisely because the costs of isolation are lower, individuals are more likely to forgo learning English and accept life in the enclave.

Even in the most populous linguistic communities, however, individual opportunity will be limited for non-English speakers. Where one lives, for example, will primarily be determined by the location of native-language enclaves, thus curtailing geographic mobility. While employment opportunities may exist within native-language communities, American higher education and a multitude of the most challenging jobs are generally foreclosed to citizens who cannot speak English. Educators note that students of earlier generations could find well-paying jobs in manufacturing that did not demand fluency in English. "You could still be successful professionally without completing your schooling," notes Virginia Collier, a professor of ESL and bilingual education at Virginia's George Mason University. "We're not in an industrial age anymore. We're in a technology-driven, information-driven age," where good jobs require higher education and sophisticated communication skills. Launching children with ever more deficient English skills into an ever more demanding job market is a prescription for individual frustration and social unrest.

The restrictions on language-minority Americans do not end with the lack of jobs, however. To the extent that enclave members venture outside of their community, they are likely to experience difficulty conducting routine business—and even rank discrimination. Further, the inability to speak English will limit political participation. Outside of their language-minority community, Hispanic Americans will find it more difficult to hold office or to participate in political conventions or other civic activities. News from English-speaking America will necessarily reach language-minority citizens through the filter of native-language media. The result for native-language Americans may be a growing isolation from important events and a growing constriction of individual opportunities.

Individuals who are denied the full measure of this country's opportunity may not return to it the fullest measure of their affection and respect. The child who is content at not having to learn English may be the adult who senses that a chance in life was lost. Linguistic isolation may thus place a permanent lid on personal opportunity. In South Africa during apartheid, blacks were not taught in either English or Afrikaans, the languages in which business was transacted. Instead, the Bantu language was "mandated as the medium of instruction in the primary schools for African children." Language became a tool of control that ensured second-class citizenship for students throughout life.

Wishing that more rather than fewer Americans spoke English is thus consistent with *Brown*'s basic integrative social vision. Hoping that all young children master English simply furthers the basic premise of civil rights law—that America should offer individual opportunity to those whose prospects have been limited in the past. Those who see English as the "language of empowerment" are not cultural imperialists. They hope only that all children in this country will be equipped to go as far as their talents and their industry will take them.

★   ★   ★

*W*hat does the future hold? The response of courts to the question of educational separatism will be critical. The law of civil rights must promote bilingualism's integrative tendencies while suppressing its separatist potential. The justifications for such an approach are legally and pedagogically sound. Educational programs that fail to lead language-minority pupils promptly toward proficient English replay "separate but equal" with even more debilitating outcomes. Whether native-language programs will ever be equal is of course the question. In the days prior to *Brown*, officials shabbily shortchanged black students in terms of educational and physical resources. English-deficient students in separatist programs will probably fare no better with the public fisc. As the school population becomes more demographically diverse, resource allocation becomes even more difficult. Where is the public school district that will provide Chinese American, Japanese American, Mexican American, Brazilian American, Russian American, and Haitian American students extended, full-service educational programs in their own languages?

Americans are asking for *Plessy v. Ferguson* all over again when we conceive of education as a special right to separate cultural and linguistic instruction, rather than as a means of mainstreaming all minority groups equally. Recognizing this principle, one federal court upheld against separatist challenges a Berkeley school district language program aimed at fostering English proficiency among a highly diverse student population speaking "approximately 38 languages other than English." Early English immersion programs simply raise far fewer questions of equal resource allocation. By providing intensive lessons in speaking, reading, and writing English, immersion programs liberate all students from an otherwise separate and unequal educational fate.

Other legal responses to the problem of linguistic separatism will be just as important. For example, some have argued that linguistic minorities in America should constitute a suspect, or specially protected, class under equal protection law. Such a recognition would, however, dispense with one of the criteria that the Supreme Court has traditionally used to determine such status—namely, that the protected class possess an immutable characteristic. Although monolingualism may become increasingly immutable as one moves on in life, it is anything but immutable in school-age children. The conferral of special constitutional status upon linguistic minorities would wrongly convey just such a notion. Indeed, it would encourage linguistic separatism among Americans because it would legitimize the immutability of linguistic barriers rather than attempting to overcome them.

The claims of language minorities in America will increasingly wrench the courts. Some of the hottest battles will involve "English as official language" laws. In 1996, a bill entitled the English Empowerment Act was introduced in the House of Representatives requiring the federal government to conduct official business in English, with narrow exceptions for international relations, public health, language instruction, and some judicial proceedings. Approximately eighteen states have now adopted such laws. In most of them, the designation of English as the official language appears to be mainly symbolic, much like a law naming a state bird or a state song. Most of the laws also do not prohibit the use of languages other than English in state and local government.

Arizona, however, decided to go further. In 1988, its citizens adopted a constitutional amendment that not only declared English to be "the official language of the state of Arizona" but also required state employees to use English in performing their official duties. Article Twenty-eight, as it was called, passed by the slimmest of margins, drawing only 50.5 percent of the vote.

Its passage guaranteed the law would land in court. The plaintiff was Maria-Kelley F. Yniguez, who worked for the Arizona Department of Administration, where she handled medical malpractice claims against the state. Yniguez spoke fluent Spanish and English, and she used her language skills in the way one would expect her to—by communicating in English with English-speaking claimants, in Spanish with Spanish-speaking claimants, and in a combination of the two languages with bilingual claimants. With the passage of

Article Twenty-eight, however, Yniguez claimed she stopped speaking Spanish on the job, out of fear she might be subject to sanctions and discipline.

A six-member majority of the Ninth Circuit Court of Appeals ruled Article Twenty-eight unconstitutional. If one took the law's language literally, said Judge Stephen Reinhardt, then "Arizona state universities would be barred from issuing diplomas in Latin, and judges performing weddings would be prohibited from saying 'Mazel Tov' as part of the official marriage ceremony." All this aside, it seemed harsh to encourage the use of English by having government employees speak to some American citizens in a language they barely understand. Every American deals with state government on so many issues, from taxes to drivers' licenses to unemployment benefits. Language accommodations need to be made for business to be done.

How then could five members of the Ninth Circuit possibly dissent and vote to uphold this Arizona law? The answer is that striking down one small, ill-advised law may give birth to a large, even more troubling principle. As Judge Ferdinand Fernandez noted in dissent, the Ninth Circuit majority had come perilously close to embracing three astonishing propositions: (1) that the state has no right to choose the language in which state business can be conducted; (2) that Yniguez's use of "a language of her choice to perform the State's business cannot be restricted"; and (3) that a member of the general public has "a constitutional right to have the State provide services in [a] particular language." In short, the Ninth Circuit majority had set in motion deeply separatist tendencies.

The Constitution cannot compel government to provide services to every linguistic minority in its own language. Nor should it disable state and local governments from promoting the common linguistic bonds among Americans. Because it has no limiting principle, the Ninth Circuit decision has thrown into question laws more reasonable and steps less drastic than that taken by Arizona. As Judge Alex Kozinski, also in dissent, points out: "What Yniguez says, and in what tongue, is thus no longer a business judgment by her employer; it's a constitutional question." And the newest constitutional right created by the federal courts may be the right to speak for and to hear from government in the language that one pleases.

By going overboard on constitutional rights, the courts can contribute to linguistic separatism in America. The dual agendas of linguistic minorities also stand in stark contrast to one another. When the fight for bilingualism is a fight against discrimination and segregation, the law should look favorably upon such claims. When the goal of bilingual practices is to promote separatist agendas, the law should look askance. In the end, the integrationist perspective will hopefully predominate over the separatist so Americans of all linguistic backgrounds may be able to talk to one another.

★   ★   ★

*W*e must ask, finally, what deep linguistic divisions will mean for America. In a country founded on self-governance, the prospect of a sizable percentage of our population being disconnected from political affairs is disconcerting. While the 1975 amendments to the Voting Rights Act require bilingual ballots where selected foreign-language groups account for 5 percent or more of any voting district, this may not help non-English speakers decide among candidates. Robert Rossier, while a member of the Department of Education's National Advisory and Coordinating Council on Bilingual Education, explained:

> Dependence on the home language tends to isolate the group and make it more manipulable. Immigrants who learn English

move closer culturally to the general society and even become assimilated, making political control difficult.

We can always, of course, make use of interpreters. Judges, for example, have the power to appoint an interpreter to assist the conduct of judicial proceedings and especially the conduct of a criminal defense. We can also issue forms and post signs in public places in several different languages. We can—and probably should—do these things, but they enable us in the end merely to make do, not to speak the same tongue face-to-face. Inability to speak English impairs the capacity of a citizen to digest political speech, to serve on juries, to participate in judicial proceedings, to serve in the armed forces, and to participate in a military mobilization. From the viewpoint of society, the fact that some citizens will escape the obligations and miss the opportunities of America will only enhance the prospect for isolation and ethnic strife.

At a broader level, the question of nationhood is never completely settled. Ethnic groups, often with different languages, have fought one another in search of self-rule or geographic hegemony. We need look no further than the ethnic warfare that has raged throughout the former Yugoslavia, or for an example nearer to home, to Canada. As Frank Lowrey notes in the *Emory Law Journal*:

> The Canadian experience provides dramatic empirical evidence that linguistic differences can divide a population, wrenching apart the fabric which once composed a nation. Nothing in the basic nature of the language conflict is limited to the borders of the Canadian confederation.

Language minorities in any country can feel besieged and skeptical. A job of sincere persuasion with language-minority Americans lies ahead. English should be a sign of welcome and a symbol of opportunity. English should serve to empower individuals, not to displace communities. Like the Statue of Liberty, English should become an American embrace of those who might otherwise feel this country failed to care. But by confining children to "language ghettos in school, we discourage contact with English-speaking youngsters who could facilitate newcomers' socialization into American society." At Juarez High School in Chicago, bilingual students banded together to form a gang called La Raza. The *Chicago Tribune* explained:

> These students are secluded. They move in groups from one bilingual classroom to another, having little contact with the general school population. Teachers theorize that because they felt isolated, outcasts in their own school, some of them banded together to form a gang.

It need not be so. Language has the power to unite or to divide. Alexis de Tocqueville, as early as 1835, noticed that a new, democratic language had developed and was continuing to evolve in America. This language came about primarily to "express the wants of business, the passions of party, or the details of public administration." It was precisely this language that enabled Americans of different origins to share in the ideals upon which our Republic rests. So too can the tie of language bridge differences in New America. While the knowledge of different languages and cultures will always remain an immense asset, a shared command of English enables Americans to interact as one nation rather than as a collectivity of enclaves. To subvert this tie will weaken our Republic's very foundation.

— 8 —

Separatist Speech

As a boy, society let me root for the New York Yankees or the Cincinnati Reds or the Boston Red Sox. This marvelous freedom did not extend, however, to the subject of race. I learned this when I was returning home from the dentist one afternoon on the familiar bus line, the Westhampton 16. Dr. Elam had filled some cavities, and my head was feeling pretty gruesome. The problem on the bus was: Where to sit? There were no laws in Richmond at the time, only the most powerful decree of all, unwritten custom.

The seats in the front—or white—section of the bus were all taken, but there were still a few remaining further back. A black man nodded, almost imperceptibly, as if to say, "Come sit by me." For the first twenty seconds, all those stares made me squirm. For the next thirty minutes, my aching teeth were grateful for the seat.

I won't forget this small event. Why could the black man signal his kind intentions only ever so slightly? And why did I utter no more than a mumbled greeting after sitting down? I was terrified at age twelve of being thought a _____, the most terrible thunderbolt white society could hurl. So we rode in silence.

It is a long way, I think, from the unwritten speech codes of my boyhood to the campus speech codes of the 1990s. And yet it is really not so long at all. America is always devising new ways of keeping Americans of different races from communicating. The speech codes, of course, purport to ban only hurtful or offensive or hateful racial speech. What the new censors fail to realize is that efforts to unite us all by speech codes could not be more separatist.

The hate speech codes on many campuses have shared two characteristics with the other trends of modern separatism: they are benignly motivated, and they risk disastrous results. The codes arose in response to ugly and abhorrent incidents of racial prejudice, and they reflect the understandable impulse to forcefully condemn the racists in our midst. But stifling speech has always been a chancy form of surgery. For every interracial insult that a speech code excises, it may cut short ten worthwhile interracial conversations.

The speech codes have varied considerably in content. Some codes are patently senseless, like the University of Connecticut's now-abandoned proviso that condemned "inappropriate laughter" and "conspicuous exclusion of students from conversations." Others, like that of the University of Michigan, sweepingly sanctioned "any behavior, verbal or physical, that stigmatizes or victimizes an individual on the basis of race," possibly including, said one court, any "serious comments made in the context of classroom discussion." Still others condemned "behavior that subjects an individual to an intimidating, hostile, or offensive . . . environment by . . . using symbols, [epithets] or slogans that infer negative connotations about the individual's racial or ethnic affiliation." Other codes attempted to align themselves with the Supreme Court's "fighting words" doctrine and are thus more modest, requiring, for instance, that the sanctionable speech be "addressed directly to the individual" whom it insults, and "make use of insulting or 'fighting' words or non-verbal symbols."

What a shame that these codes were hatched on college campuses. Education at its best exemplifies unfettered curiosity: "You have to let students say the most outrageous and stupid things. . . . To get people to think and talk, to question their own ideas, you don't regulate their speech." Then too, educational environments present opportunities for multiethnic communication which exist nowhere else. If we permit New America to be isolated at the places that provide our greatest chance for an exchange, then we assure that our future will be a fractured one.

Speech codes, to be sure, are not the only regulation of hate speech. The law of defamation condemns malicious falsehood, and racially prejudiced remarks have long been admissible as evidence of discriminatory treatment in suits brought under Title 7 of the 1964 Civil Rights Act. The libel laws, however, are largely preoccupied with factual error; the civil rights acts focus on actionable adverse behavior, such as a dismissal of someone from their place of employment. The speech codes are broader. They impose punitive sanctions—suspension or expulsion—for speech that is not necessarily tied to conduct and whose basic infirmity is that it insults.

Speech codes are misguided gestures, and they are proof positive that we have lost our way. They will accelerate the forms of separatism we have earlier discussed. After all, we cannot become a less separate nation politically or economically or educationally if we cannot openly communicate. The speech codes do not permit this luxury. They are not content neutral: they can be used to threaten any speaker on race relations with an unpopular point of view. They are manifestly vague and overbroad, employing such cloudy terms as "'demeaning,' 'disparaging,' 'harassing,' 'hostile,' 'insulting,' 'intimidating,' and 'stigmatizing'" to describe the speech that they condemn. The codes grant substantial discretion to the enforcers, whose own biases may themselves be unpredictable. The validity of the speech turns on the reaction of its audience, thus rewarding bland words and penalizing robust dialogue. The term "chilling effect" would appear to have been coined with these hate-speech codes in mind.

The First Amendment has helped to unify America by allowing all Americans to have their say. Courts have understood that this means the misguided have as much right as the enlightened to state their point of view. Advocates of speech codes maintain, however, that the First Amendment should not protect those who voice racially offensive speech. As two defenders of speech codes put it: "[hate speech] contributes to the kind of society most of us say we do not want: one in which persons are assigned stigmas on account of who they are." The traditional truth-seeking function of the First Amendment, to these proponents, is subverted by allowing abhorrent speech to be heard.

Like so many champions of restrictive speech laws in the past, today's censors make precisely the wrong argument. Unity is not enhanced by excising some speech from our collective conversations. Indeed, the First Amendment's marketplace of ideas should have special resonance in New America. The United States should become a speech bazaar, with merchants hawking their talk to all takers. It would be a benefit if multiculturalism brought to America an international court of ideas, much as it has already brought us international courts of food. The medley of New America must not only include material wares. There is no place in a multicultural marketplace for suppression of speech.

Speech codes also divide us in another way. They attempt to make virulent thoughts unspeakable, but if successful, they do no more than push prejudice underground. Censorship thus relieves society of the need to combat intolerance in its midst, for ideas that are suppressed cannot be discredited. The codes somehow assume we can cure racism by making unmentionable the subject of race. But as one civil rights activist has argued: "People . . . believe [in racist ideas] openly and consciously or they believe them quietly, subliminally, covertly. But they do believe them." Community responses to hate speech can be unifying, not divisive. The power to counteract racial division with calls for racial cooperation can itself be a source of community unity, one which can remind us that condemnation of prejudice cuts across all racial boundaries.

Speech codes do much more than deprive society of a chance to denounce abhorrent racial acts and speech. Their effect on the debate of difficult questions divides us more subtly, yet more profoundly. As a society, we can no longer openly and honestly discuss the subject of race. Consider just a few of the stories from today's college campuses. Students at the University of California's Berkeley campus scurry away from reporters asking questions about race-related issues, and demand that their names not be used. One confided that "there are things you wouldn't want to talk about around certain people." Another reported that he does not participate in class discussions about race. Law students at the State University of New York at Buffalo effectively relinquish their First Amendment rights by matriculating; the school's speech code declares that a "student's absolute right to liberty of speech must also become tempered in its exercise by the responsibility to promote equality and justice."

One constitutional law professor at Florida State University received a sharp lesson of his own—after he directed a class discussion on the constitutionality of affirmative action, he was reprimanded. Across the country at the University of Michigan, one minority student inquired at an orientation session about rumors that "minorities had a difficult time in the [dentistry class] and that he had heard that they were not treated fairly." Claiming that this jeopardized her chances for tenure, a minority professor who taught the course filed a charge against the student under the university's hate-speech code. The offending student received a modern reeducation: he was "counseled" about the existence of the university's policy and drafted a letter of apology. And these are not isolated incidents. "On campus after campus," observes the columnist Nat Hentoff, "from Brown to Stanford, I have talked to students who say there are some views they hold—or questions they want to ask—that they no longer bring up in class or in most places outside of class. . . . Questions, for example, about affirmative action."

Each account is a garden-variety illustration of the long-recognized concept of "chilling effect." What should really catch our attention is that this wintry climate leaves each sector of our society talking only to itself. Students have not stopped questioning and debating; they have simply stopped doing so in public, or even in private, with people who do not agree with them. Lecture halls and student unions are no longer sounding boards, but isolated conclaves of college thought. The codes allow people to talk with impunity only to members of their own race. One Native American student reported that the atmosphere on her campus hardly fostered interracial understanding; her peers were so careful around her that she could not even discern what they thought. She concluded, "When it reaches the point where sensitivity stifles communication, it has gone too far."

Who among us has not said at some point something we wish we could take back? Despite our best intentions, we all occasionally goof. "Pick up a nice tan?" I once asked a black friend who had been returning from the beach. It was a terrible remark, one uttered quite inadvertently, first to the embarrassment, but then to the laughter of us both. When I first saw Michael Chang play tennis, I wondered aloud what country he was from, foolishly overlooking the fact that he is one of America's best.

Because my remarks were made among friends, I received the benefit of the doubt. Heaven help me had I been subject to a speech code. I should have weighed and measured every word that came out. How many friendships form when lips remain on guard and thoughts are under seal? The codes may spare the world the occasional insensitivity, but at what cost in that colloquial, spontaneous, teasing, affectionate medium we call speech?

In his book *Showing My Color: Impolite Essays on Race and Identity*, Clarence Page remarks that "the biggest tragedy that has happened between the races since the 1960s is our loss of honest conversation across racial lines." He tells the story of young professionals and postgraduates who every Friday evening "line up at two bars at Seventeenth and L streets [in downtown Washington]. . . . The two crowds are almost identical—young, well dressed, and well-educated—except in one very notable respect: One bar's crowd is white. The other's is black."

Why no interaction? It all depends on who you ask. Many of the young people were simply stressed out by the "integration fatigue" of the workweek and wanted to relax with those who shared their backgrounds and beliefs. Blacks showed exasperation at the complete lack of white interest in getting to know them, and whites said the problem was that interracial conversations posed too great a risk of giving offense.

So the crowds at the bars and the schools and the churches and at most private and informal gatherings in America go their separate ways, seemingly mutually content. An air of inertia and an atmosphere of inevitability settles upon the separate gatherings—it's the way things are, that's all. To believe they could be any different is now to be hopelessly idealistic or ludicrously naive. Separate racial talk is human nature, we are told, an echo of my de jure world of long ago.

I know well that racial separation in some settings invokes our constitutional right to free association. But why do we so often exercise that right so as not to associate, rather than to associate, with someone of a different ethnic background or race? Sometimes I think America is still the Westhampton 16—only now the races choose their separate seating sections on the bus.

The example of speech separatism may even be spreading to the legal profession. The American Bar Association recently put itself on record against any form of "bias" exhibited, in words or conduct, by lawyers based on "race, religion, national origin, disability, age, sexual orientation or socioeconomic status." "Legitimate advocacy" is an exception to the prohibition. But if a lawyer's statements do not qualify as "legitimate" and "advocacy"—two terms as murky as "bias"—they could be scrutinized. The ABA proposal is not yet part of the formal ethical code of conduct that governs lawyer action, but supporters hope it will be.

Why have we decided to adopt these separatist rules in every forum of racial interaction? We have finally made of race a cry of fire in a crowded theater—a subject that society must suppress. We should be doing just the opposite. Achieving multiethnic understanding is a process of trial and error and entails misunderstandings along the way. Indeed, cultural interaction may be analogized to interpersonal communication, whose solidity is seldom enhanced by sweeping every sensitive issue out of sight.

Interracial silence is ill-suited to America's changing demographics. No less than for the visitor to a prison or the backseat passenger in a taxicab, the speech code throws up a glass shield before our words. Conversation is natural, or it is nothing. How odd that a society in the midst of sweeping social change is caught in the middle of a meaningless minuet in which each conversational step must be carefully rehearsed. Our free speech tradition remains our best chance for a successful multicultural future. Americans must talk to one another, and keep talking, until the candles flicker and our eyelids close in sleep.

Part Four

THE FUTURE OF
NEW AMERICA

— *9* —

The Future of New America

So what of the future? Where is separatism leading America? What will happen if we fail to change course? If America is now in its multicultural infancy, what will the adult turn out to be like?

Peering into the twenty-first century is a hazardous business. Still, it is necessary to ponder what the consequences of ethnic separatism are and where it may be taking us. Otherwise, we shall be content to drift.

Futures are seldom perfect replays of the past. It seems improbable, for example, that we shall face a replay of the events of 1861–1865. There probably is not another Fort Sumter in our future, not in the sense that seceding states will signal their defiance of federal authority by unleashing their cannon on a federal installation.

Those who may be tempted to predict the outbreak of another great regional Civil War over race are overlooking several things. In 1860, America was of separate regional minds on the issue of race. The conflict in the 1850s over the admission of "Bleeding Kansas" into the Union as a free or slave state betrayed irreconcilable regional differences on the profound question of human bondage. Our country is badly divided today, but not in the same way as before the Civil War. One of the benefits of modern civil rights laws has been their introduction of greater uniformity into American race relations and, hence, of a lesser likelihood of regional racial conflict. The transportation and communications revolutions have also made regional attitudes on race more difficult to identify.

Similarly, the outright secession of existing states from the United States seems an unlikely possibility. An eventual union of the southwestern United States with Mexico in one Spanish-speaking nation has formidable drawbacks—Mexico, for example, has prodigious problems of its own, and millions of Hispanic Americans have in fact left Mexico for America in search of greater economic opportunity. Moreover, the multi-cultural diversity of the American Southwest and the dangers of perceiving the views of any linguistic minority as mono-lithic make the various scenarios of secession improbable. We are not likely, for instance, to wake up one morning in 2050 and find that New Mexico (the state with the largest percent-age of Hispanic Americans) has simply left the United States of America.

Thus, the most dire predictions about the outcomes of our separatist tendencies strike me as exaggerated. That does not mean, however, that we should take comfort from the course on which we are embarked. Signs of deep trouble lie ahead, even if they are not in the nature of the outbreak of civil war or the outright secession of our present states.

We have allowed into our midst several contagious princi-ples. One is that race is a premier civic credential, to be ranked right alongside the credential of American citizenship. The other is that race should define the boundaries of repre-sentation in our democratic system. Once unleashed, these principles will prove hard to restrain. It is not a long leap from the notion that race should define the boundaries of legislative districts to the notion that race should define the boundaries of statehood.

If we continue to count by race and to legitimize race as a criterion for limitless assortments of public acts, then we lay the groundwork for a fundamental reconstruction of the political order. Demands that the boundaries of our voting districts, the admissions decisions of our colleges, the hiring practices of our employers, the contracting policies of our governments, and the curricular choices of our schools all turn on race serve only to divide, not to unite. The notion that America is not a unified republic, but a federation of ethnic states, may not be far in our future. Demands for reconfiguring the boundaries of statehood to maximize racial pride and influence is one logical outgrowth of the policies we are pursuing now. Demands for a black Congress, or Hispanic Congress, or Asian or Anglo Congress, whereby different racial groups send regional representatives to some central location, such as Dallas or Chicago, may begin to grow. Whether or not such demands are ultimately satisfied, the incessant repetition of them will be a debilitating development for New America.

We must remember that around the world federated arrangements are as common as nationally unified ones. We need only look around at some of those federated countries that might serve as a model for the America of the future if we fail to alter our separatist course. What most of the federated arrangements have in common are the factors of (1) economic linkage and (2) political autonomy. The degree of linkage and the extent of the autonomy vary, of course, but the models for a separatist America of the future are already around us and in place.

One example of what may await a confederated America can be found in our northern neighbor's struggle to come to terms with the place of French Canadians and newer minority populations in the Canadian federal state. Francophone Quebecers have long sought recognition for what they view to be a distinct culture. In addition, Canada admits 220,000 new immigrants each year, adding nearly 1 percent annually to its existing population. At the time of its 1991 census, one in seven people in Canada was foreign born; in Vancouver, nearly one in three, and in Toronto, two in five. In its effort to accommodate both French Canadians and other racial, linguistic, and cultural minorities, Canada has expressly rejected the melting pot model and has instead promoted a "cultural mosaic," which aims to celebrate the distinctness of each immigrant group. Unfortunately, the mosaic has not turned out as prettily as the multicultural designers intended.

Prime Minister Pierre Elliott Trudeau founded state-promoted multiculturalism in 1971. The Act for the Preservation and Enhancement of Multiculturalism in Canada later codified the principle, declaring it to be the policy of the federal government to "recognize and promote the understanding that multiculturalism reflects the cultural and racial diversity of Canadian society and acknowledges the freedom of all members of Canadian society to preserve, enhance and share their cultural heritage." This sweet-sounding act spawned a new "multiculturalism" cabinet portfolio with attendant government expenditures, now approaching $30 million annually. Critics argue that the act, and the multiculturalism policy in general, have fostered fragmentation by focusing on differences.

In his recent book criticizing official multiculturalism in Canada, novelist Neil Bissoondath concludes that the policy reduces individuals to simplistic cultural group stereotypes. This, he says, is moving Canada toward a condition of profound intercultural alienation. Bissoondath argues,

Multiculturalism . . . has heightened our differences rather than diminished them; it has preached tolerance rather than encouraging acceptance; and it is leading us into a divisiveness so entrenched that we face a future of multiple solitudes with no central notion to bind us.

The entrenched divisiveness bemoaned by Bissoondath regularly rears its political head in the form of a campaign or referendum promoting Quebec separatism. Within Quebec, no "election in 30 years has been fought without addressing that issue [of Quebec's status] in some way." And the agitation has occupied the attention of much of the rest of Canada as well. While the question of the place of French Canadians in Canada predates confederation, the momentum of separatist forces has increased dramatically during recent decades. When Canada settled other issues in its Constitution Act of 1982 but did not resolve the status of Quebec, the Quebec National Assembly refused to ratify the new constitutional document.

The Meech Lake Accord, hammered out by the prime minister and ten provincial premiers in 1987, was supposed to fill this constitutional void. The accord offered Quebec, and all the other provinces, a veto power over an expanded number of constitutional amendments, a role in Supreme Court appointments, the freedom to administer some programs at the provincial level without federal interference, and increased control over the flow of certain immigrants. Most importantly, the accord granted Quebec's long-standing plea for constitutional recognition as a "distinct society." This concession, however, satisfied no one. English-speaking Canada felt it was being blackmailed by Quebec as the price for keeping Canada one nation. Some Quebecers, in turn, believed that the accord fell short of protecting Quebec's linguistic and cultural differences, compromising its "drive for autonomy and the protection of its culture."

To become part of the Canadian constitution, the Meech Lake Accord had to be ratified by all of Canada's ten provinces. One episode in particular illustrates how difficult this would prove to be. In 1988, Canada's Supreme Court considered the appeals of two shopkeepers who, by posting signs in English outside their establishments, violated Quebec's French-only sign law. The Court held that Quebec's law violated the freedom of expression provisions of the Canadian and Quebec constitutions. Quebecers took to the streets in protest. And the Quebec government invoked a provision of the constitution that permitted its law to remain in effect despite the Supreme Court's decision. The episode reconfirmed the deep divisions between French- and English-speaking Canadians. The former viewed the Court's decision as proof that their distinctive linguistic culture was vulnerable in a federal state; and the latter took Quebec's response as evidence of its willingness to subordinate the rights of English speakers to nationalistic impulses.

After three years of debate, the Meech Lake Accord failed in 1990 when Newfoundland and Manitoba refused to ratify it. While some cheered and others lamented this turn of events, it set the stage for a cascade of commissions and proposals aimed at resolving the Quebec question. The most recent of these, the 1995 referendum by Quebecers on separating from Canada, failed by the narrowest of margins. Quebec's separatists took comfort in the razor-thin margin, and they promised to schedule yet another referendum. The spirit of the day appeared to be: "If at first you don't secede, try, try again." In an attempt to stave off a breakup of the country, the Canadian Parliament tried to give Quebec what it wanted through legislation rather than constitutional reform, but this solution seemed to leave everyone unsatisfied.

This unfolding Canadian drama holds many lessons. Quebec's pressure for recognition as a distinct society has proved contagious. Once French speakers asked for it, others did as well. Canada's western provinces, which have long felt alienated from their eastern counterparts, began to demand more autonomy. British Columbia, for instance, with its tide of Asian immigration, may be nearly as allied with Pacific Rim countries as it is with the rest of Canada; it has been induced by Quebec's efforts to stake its own claim to distinctiveness. And in Saskatchewan, some citizens now talk of German instruction to mimic Quebec's compulsory French instruction. Native Canadians, too, angry that their concerns were left out of the Meech Lake Accord, argue that any acknowledgment of Quebec's unique culture must be accompanied by a similar recognition of their own. In fact, Elijah Harper, the legislator whose vote defeated the Meech Lake Accord in the Manitoba legislature, insisted that if there ever was a group deserving "distinct society" status, it is Native Canadians. And a Muslim group in Toronto contends that if Canada is truly multicultural, its members are entitled to be subject to Islamic law rather than the Canadian judicial system.

We are fooling ourselves if we fail to understand the lessons that Canada's experience holds for us. Racial and linguistic minorities are aggressively asserting their distinctiveness in New America. Even now we may anticipate that the demands of these groups for recognition of that distinctiveness may become requests for some sort of separate polity. Those Quebecers who aspire to sovereign control within their borders, combined with economic relationships with those around them, view such an arrangement as a successful formula for an independent state. That same formula—political self-determination plus economic confederation—will serve as a ready model for this nation's would-be separatists. Given the policies we are pursuing, there is no reason to believe we are immune from that which has afflicted Canada; requests for separate sovereign polities within our own country may come to characterize twenty-first-century America. Indeed, native Hawaiians, who make up one-fifth of Hawaii's population, have already held their first state-funded (and racially exclusive) sovereignty referendum. Canada's experience must teach us that once some ask for such recognition, others will too, and that such requests can tear our country apart.

One cannot leave the subject of Canada—or its lessons for the United States—without considering the proud city of Montreal. Once the financial center and cultural jewel of Canada, the city has fallen on hard times. The symptoms of poverty are spreading—housing construction has fallen for the eighth straight year, roads are deteriorating, unemployment is higher than in any other major Canadian city, and Montreal has fallen far behind Toronto in every major index of financial well-being. "So much office space is vacant," reports Anne Swardson of the *Washington Post*, "that Montrealers are no longer amused by the old saw about the non-French-speaking visitor who asked who 'A. Louer' is because the guy seemed to own every building in town. *A Louer* means For Rent."

After the near victory for Quebec's separatism in the 1995 referendum, many English speakers decided to depart Quebec for other parts of Canada and the United States. In the wake of the referendum, notes Swardson, "one major corporation has announced it will leave Montreal; many that remain are transferring operations elsewhere." Separatism has even reached the point that some Montrealers are saying that if Quebec can separate from Canada by referendum, then Montreal can likewise separate from Quebec and become an independent city-state.

Separatist tensions have the same potential to drive Americans into spiritual despondency and economic decline. If racial, ethnic, or linguistic majorities in a particular American state or city seek to "separate" by referendum in some fashion from the larger community, the effects will be predictable. The minority in that state or city, along with much of its business leadership, will seek to relocate to parts of America where separatist friction is less prevalent. The departures, of course, will only exacerbate the very divisions that led to them, as different areas acquire different reputations, not as parts of America, but as distinctive enclaves. That is what Canada did not avert and that is what America has less and less time to prevent. The Bay Area of California is not Asian; it is American. Detroit, Atlanta, Dallas, and Houston are not black cities—they are American. South Texas and California's Central Valley are not Hispanic—they are American. The Mountain States are not some burgeoning white heartland—they, like all others, are first and foremost American.

The example of Europe, as much as that of Canada, provides reason for concern over the future of America. In designing the European Community (European Union), the European nations have often spoken of becoming the "United States of Europe." Even as they do, there is some question about whether our country is in danger of becoming the "European States of America." I say this because as our social, linguistic, and ethnic divisions multiply, our situation begins to resemble Europe's in more ways than it previously had.

Although the European Community has generally been viewed as a symbol of greater unification, a closer look reveals that many problems beset the road to cooperation among its members. The impulse to unity did enjoy considerable momentum in the early 1990s, particularly on economic fronts. The "Europe 1992" initiative saw the formal unveiling of the single market, which abolished many of the barriers to the free flow of goods, services, and workers across national borders. The Maastricht agreement, signed by European leaders in late 1991, embraced the concept of a single European currency by the end of the twentieth century—the currency, called the Euro, is to be introduced in 1999. While less ambitious in noneconomic areas, Maastricht also advanced measures designed to promote joint action in foreign, defense, and social policy.

These were real achievements. The fanfare attending them, however, caused us to overlook the ways in which parochial pride has dampened the hopes for economic union. This became very apparent in the immediate aftermath of Maastricht. In a startling indication that Europe's citizens were unwilling to relinquish individual interests for the sake of unity, Denmark's population voted against ratifying the Maastricht accord. The "fiercely nationalistic Danes," one observer reports, "feared that Maastricht would destroy their country's independence and perhaps even its national character." France's citizens sounded the same trepidation in their vote—while they ratified the treaty, they did so only by a very close margin, an especially telling message given that France was supposedly among the most fervent champions of broad integration.

Denmark eventually ratified Maastricht in a second referendum, but only after securing a series of "opt-outs" from several of the agreement's central provisions, including the single currency and some of the foreign, defense, and judicial policies. Britain, which had long been suspicious of excessive centralization, likewise insisted that it have the option to retain its own currency and to disregard some of Maastricht's social policies. By 1996, two-thirds of German citizens favored keeping the mark over welcoming the Euro, and most did not want monetary union. The outbreak of such sentiments forced a response from the architects of Maastricht. It took the form of a new concept enshrined into the accord, that of "subsidiarity." Subsidiarity, while deliberately vague, was meant to represent a formal check on the EC's central powers and to reserve a measure of freedom for the entities in the European Community to pursue their own course.

Even the single market, the European Union's "proudest achievement," is being undermined by the instinct of self-interest. Despite an EC directive, Belgium has not implemented measures to recognize higher-education diplomas of other European Community members. Explosives manufacturers in Luxembourg cannot satisfy German standards, even as they fulfill France's and Belgium's. Irish fishermen fear competition in EC waters that were once their own. A British producer of hot-air balloons, the world's largest, can satisfy its own country's standards for aluminum propane fuel tanks but fails Germany's. Danish bacon cannot be sold in EC countries that ban pork from uncastrated pigs. The frustration extends to cash machines (use of a machine in Brussels to withdraw funds from a British account entails a substantial fee), second-hand cars (bureaucratic obstacles at borders), and telephone jacks and electricity plugs (different countries have different types).

The members of the European Union thus appear to be resisting true economic union in important ways, fearing the loss of their distinctive cultural, ethnic, and linguistic heritages. If economic union has traveled a rocky road, the path to union will confront even greater obstacles when the focus shifts to noneconomic arenas. True unity involves "a collective identity and purpose," and a "single market can hardly inspire comparable emotions or the same sense of commitment." The history of war among the countries, the ten different official languages, the distinct religious and cultural traditions, and the widely varying standards of living all stand in the way of social unity. Just over 1 percent of Europeans live (and less than 1 percent work) outside their country of birth. Most citizens identify themselves first as French, Danish, Spanish, and Dutch, and then only secondarily as Europeans. Allegiances to regions also abound, for example among the Scots, Welsh, Bavarians, and Basques. Apprehensions about unity have taken many forms: the head of Poland's Roman Catholic Church warns that joining the European Union would lure the country's citizens into immoral conduct, and France has grown increasingly insecure about its place in an integrated Europe relative to Germany.

From a political perspective, integration is far off. There is no European political process as such. Elections to the European Parliament (EP) do not involve issues of Europe-wide significance; instead, the voting primarily concerns national issues of essentially local interest. There are as yet no European political parties or campaigns, suggesting that Europe "is not a political entity either in fact or in the minds of European voters." The European Parliament, the most democratic of the EC's institutions, has few powers. The European Court of Justice lacks a strong institutional foundation, partly because its authority stems not from a constitution but from a set of treaties. Its rulings go unenforced and unheeded, particularly in the areas of environmental and agricultural policy.

It is tempting for us to shrug off all the troubles that the Europeans are having in getting together. America, we love to say, is unique. The United States is working off of a very different historical tradition from Europe. We've been officially one country for over two hundred years, while the EC has been around for at most two generations. Our common currency has long been in place; we have a common flag; we share one national anthem; the supremacy clause of our Constitution mandates that our federal laws bind the activities of our individual states; our courts have interpreted the commerce clause to maximize the reach of national law and minimize the burden that states may impose on commercial relations. So why worry? Legally, historically, socially, and in every other way, the United States of America goes into the twenty-first century with a stronger concept of union at its heart than Canada or Europe.

This happy insouciance may have been justified twenty years ago, but it is not justified today. The invaluable asset of American nationhood can no longer be taken for granted. As our demographic picture becomes more diverse, as our shared social and cultural traditions become more varied, as our linguistic backgrounds become more diffuse, and as our separatist tendencies become more open and assertive, the concept of One Nation Indivisible is thrown into doubt. We must nurture the aspects of the American experience in order to maintain a sense of togetherness, and not to devolve into a variation of the European or Canadian federations, where emphasis on ethnic differences seems endless and where common aims seem always hostage to the reminders of cultural space.

★   ★   ★

We need look no further than our own yesterdays to illustrate the dangers facing America tomorrow. The mistreatment of Native Americans in our past warns mightily against the creation of separate racial communities in our future. Would separate racial enclaves in America fare better than separate Native American communities do now? Would the majority treat separate racial communities and those who reside in them any better than the majority has treated Native Americans throughout most of our history? Merely to pose those questions demonstrates that we must face our future together—America will remain a child of destiny only so long as our destiny remains a common one.

Our nation's founding was no easy task. As the colonial historian Merrill Jensen has noted:

> The colonies had been founded individually and had developed different traditions and attitudes in spite of a common heritage of language, law, and government. Their relations with one another were often unfriendly, especially after the middle of the eighteenth century, as a result of rival land claims. Actual warfare had been prevented only by the external power of Britain.

The first effort to overcome the differences between the newly independent states was the Articles of Confederation and Perpetual Union, drafted from 1776–1777 and ratified between 1778 and 1781. It enabled the former colonies to enter into "a firm league of *friendship* with each other." The Articles of Confederation, however, was merely the first step in the creation of our national identity, and bears little resemblance to the national Constitution that emerged in 1787. This is particularly evident when one compares how the two documents describe the relationship between the states and the United States:

> Each State retains its sovereignty, freedom, and independence, and every power, jurisdiction and right, which is not by this confederation expressly delegated to the United States, in Congress assembled.
>
> —Articles of Confederation, Article II

The powers not delegated to the United States by the Constitution, nor prohibited by it to the States, are reserved to the States respectively, or to the people.

—Constitution, Amendment X

The first clause of Article II declares that each state retains its "sovereignty, freedom, and independence" while no such guarantee exists in the Tenth Amendment. Merrill Jensen describes the basic distinction between the Articles of Confederation and the Constitution in his book *The Articles of Confederation*:

> The fundamental difference between the Articles of Confederation and the Constitution of 1787 lies in the apportionment of power between the states and the central government. In the first the balance of power was given to the states, and in the second to the central government. The first constitution was one of federal organization; the second was in essence that of a national government, although political realities demanded the retention of federal features.

The Articles of Confederation and the Constitution thus represent two competing images of loyalty—the first, primarily to one's state, the second, primarily to the United States—hence, the debate between the Federalists, perhaps best represented by Alexander Hamilton, and the Anti-Federalists, "most of whom were soon to rally around Jefferson."

Our early history demonstrates an important truth: that union and disunion are not two stark conditions but rather opposite ends of a continuum of national health, measured by the degree to which a nation's people place the national welfare above that of some other interest—sectional, racial, or otherwise. Though a nation may never actually witness disunion, the *quality* of national experience is badly eroded when the welfare of the nation is subordinated to some other interest. This erosion is what constitutes "separatism," and it need not produce actual disunion to detract from the intangible pride and camaraderie of citizenship. The threat to America need not necessarily come from an actual structural breakup as much as from a long, slow, debilitating series of events that sap vitality from the national interest, clarity from the national voice, energy from the national will, and reduce us to the interminable competition of racial and ethnic interests, whereby the good of the faction transcends the welfare of the whole.

Our history warns us of the fragility of nationhood and instructs that the ultimate challenge in a republic is battling back factions that would topple the collective interest. James Madison, arguing for the new Constitution in *The Federalist* No. 10, recognized that the preservation of a republic such as ours depends on:

> a chosen body of citizens, whose wisdom may best discern the true interest of their country, and whose patriotism and love of justice will be least likely to sacrifice it to temporary or partial considerations.

The most threatening "partial consideration" in America today is not regional loyalty but racial loyalty. Whenever citizens take such considerations and place them above the national well-being, the ties with which the founders sought to bind us are strained.

Thus, a similarity underlies the racial divisions of today and the regional divisions of yesterday. Daniel Webster's words from 1850, which condemned both North and South for placing factional interests above the good of the nation, almost describe the condition between the races today:

> In the excited times in which we live, there is found to be a state of crimination and recrimination between the North and

the South. There are lists of grievances produced by each; and those grievances, real or supposed, alienate the minds of one portion of the country from the other, exasperate the feelings, subdue the sense of fraternal connection and patriotic love and mutual regard.

Indeed, replace "the North and the South" with "races" and the words could actually be uttered today.

In the excited times in which we live, there is found to be a state of crimination and recrimination between the [races]. There are lists of grievances produced by each; and those grievances, real or supposed, alienate the minds of one [race] from the other, exasperate the feelings, subdue the sense of fraternal connection and patriotic love and mutual regard.

With the notable exception of the Civil War—the war that Mr. Webster all but predicted, the war that was necessary to remove the terrible stain of slavery from our nation—America has been remarkably successful in mediating political differences. Historically, we have tended to bridge differences among the people by holding endless elections, by countenancing interminable political dialogue, and by requiring ceaseless negotiations among the various branches and levels of government. States and localities have been encouraged to try their own solutions to social problems, subject, of course, to the constraints of federal law and the Constitution.

But American government is better fashioned to mute regional differences than racial ones. While our federal system was designed to accommodate local, state, and regional preferences, it has had difficulty tempering the manifestations of racial pride. Thus the Civil War itself may not be so much an example of the Constitution's failure to mediate between state interests as much as an example of how racial considerations inhibited compromise. In fact, whenever states' rights have been used to assert racial supremacy, as with secession in the nineteenth century or interposition in the twentieth, the result was often violent conflict, not political compromise. It was not surprising that John Brown and the Southern hotbloods at Fort Sumter plunged the nation into civil war, while compromisers such as Henry Clay were relegated to the sidelines.

Time and again, assertions of racial separatism have managed to thwart our mediating apparatus. And there is no basis to suppose things will be any more pleasant when the separatist arguments are made by the John C. Calhouns of 2035. Separatism can thwart the capacity even of American government to control it, because race has the unique ability to fuel raw emotion. This being so, it is all the more important that Americans of 2000 stress their oneness and shunt the happenstance of race aside.

There is much debate these days about what America means. There is also no one answer to this question. To each of us, America means different things. To some, the meaning of America may lie in songs and symbols. To others, America is found in rivers, lakes, and streams. Or maybe the meaning of a nation lies in memory. In the collective memory known as history. In the vision of Thomas Jefferson and the brilliance of James Madison, who devised a politics of democratic freedoms that is second to none. In the struggles of Susan B. Anthony and Martin Luther King, who sought to make Jefferson's and Madison's ideals a reality for all. Maybe America lies in sacred personal recollections—of forebears who came across the waves or who gave their lives for freedom on some foreign shore. Maybe, for those whose ancestors came in slave ships and for those who sacrificed in segregated ranks, the pride in America is mixed with pain. For some, America may be altogether here and now—the shopping mall, the baseball field, the stock market. Or a familiar neighborhood that lets us call this country home. What is America? Many different, worthwhile things.

One can love a country as one does a wayward child, scolding, grieving, pleading for a mend of ways. America will always be that kind of child—a land of distant destiny and unfulfilled promise. Our ideals of individual freedom, human dignity, and the equality of those created equal are proclaimed in such extravagant terms. No nation, even this one, could hope to live up to them. The ideals themselves—freedom and equality—are to some extent contradictory. Thus disillusionment periodically sets in. Measured against its extraordinary aspirations for the human condition, America will always come up short.

Still, we are the better for our ideals. They allow us to stumble and pick ourselves up. Better for presidents such as Lincoln, Wilson, the Roosevelts, Kennedy, and Reagan, who saw the idealism in the American spirit and who tapped it. Better for each citizen who sought to make a fellow citizen part of the American dream. With ideals, one can shoot for the stars, and in falling, land on the clouds. With ideals, a nation can be always less than perfect, but remain more than good.

Americans should fear most the loss of our hope and our ideals. Such things are the sources of our energy and pride. In uncertain times, a country casts about for challenges, the kind that imbue a flagging spirit with new life. In this sense, multiculturalism is a gift. It poses New America a challenge of the most fundamental magnitude—namely, whether a multiracial nation has the resourcefulness to rise above race.

So far, we have not risen to that challenge. Our present course on civil rights is a recipe for racial conflict in the coming multicultural age. We have become timid in asserting the ideals of nationhood and citizenship, and we have allowed racialists and separatists to define us in a most demeaning way. We have embarked on a course of racialism first and nationalism last in every important area of the civil rights debate. This pattern must change. While none of us may agree precisely on what America is, all of us should recognize that a racially obsessed republic is what we do not wish to be. America must remain something more than the sum of its ethnic parts. Nationalism is the antidote to racialism, though only if unity is one in which each individual is the object of respect and one to which citizens of all backgrounds can belong.

It has become fashionable to say that America is too much *pluribus* and not enough *unum*. Such a declaration, however, is too glum. We have always gloried in our pluralism because we have never doubted that a greater unity lay within our capacity to achieve. Historically, the disparate strands of American life have seldom threatened our nationhood. Regional separatism was once the great threat; it led the country into civil war. The lessons of that war should remind us that the task of nation building is never complete.

My father once took me to Times Square as a child. My mother took me on a long trip West to see the Grand Canyon. I remember thinking to myself that the same country couldn't possibly have both things. Dad said it was impossible to stand at any one place and say this is America. It is equally impossible today to look at any one person and say he or she is your typical American. I do not need to define America or reduce it to some symbol or standard. I still need to feel it, however. I need to believe, as I always have believed, that there is something vital there. My parents have bequeathed me this. As much as their love and faith and knowledge and experience, the sense of being an American is their gift to me.

I do not know if I can pass the gift along. Some days, I think America's greatest days passed with my grandparents, who spent their years in a dry-goods store and on a dairy farm. Other days, I see all the variety and diversity in this country, and I envy no one so much as my unborn grandchildren. So much hangs in the balance, I believe. Our decisions will either bring us together as one nation or they will drive us irretrievably apart. Civil rights law has the potential to combine the two great strands of Lincoln's legacy: a unified nation and equality for all Americans under law. Our choices now will determine whether we become that diverse but unified nation that both Lincoln and our grandchildren deserve to see.

Notes

1: *The Medley of America*

3   "The great social adventure . . . ": Walter Lippmann, *A Preface to Politics* (1914), chapter 6, as quoted in *The Columbia Dictionary of Quotations,* ed. Robert Andrews (New York: Columbia University Press, 1993).

3   America is more diverse: Sam Roberts, *Who We Are: A Portrait of America Based on the Latest U.S. Census* (New York: Times Books, 1993), 62–63.

3   Efrian Nava: Nancy Gibbs, "Shades of Difference," *Time,* 18 Nov. 1991, 66.

4   Fresno: Bill Ong Hing, "In the Interest of Racial Harmony: Revisiting the Lawyer's Duty to Work for the Common Good," *Stanford Law Review* 47 (1995): 901, 906 (citing Frank Clifford and Anne C. Roark, "Census Finds Ethnic Boom in Suburbs, Rural Areas," *Los Angeles Times,* 26 Feb. 1991, A1).

4   Nearly one in four Californians: Ronald Brownstein and Richard Simon, "Hospitality Turns into Hostility: California Has a Long History of Welcoming Newcomers for Their Cheap Labor—Until Times Turn Rough," *Los Angeles Times,* 14 Nov. 1993, A1.

4   State experts reported: Dan Walters, "We're Testing Change for U.S.," *Sacramento Bee,* 17 Mar. 1996, A3.

4 The 1990 census: Roberts, *Who We Are*, 64.

4 record number of Asian and Hispanic Americans: U.S. Bureau of the Census, *USA Statistics in Brief 1994: A Statistical Abstract Supplement* (Washington, D.C.: U.S. Department of Commerce).

4 Hispanic Americans may surpass: U.S. Bureau of the Census, *Statistical Abstract of the United States 1994*, 114th ed. (Washington, D.C.: U.S. Department of Commerce, 1994), 13, table 11 (hereinafter, *Statistical Abstract 1994*).

4 By the turn of the century: Roberts, *Who We Are*, 63.

4 27 percent of Americans: Bob Deitel, (Louisville) *Courier-Journal*, 16 Dec. 1993, C1.

4 if present trends continue: *Statistical Abstract 1994*, 13, table 11.

5 An astonishing sixty countries: Philip Q. Yang, *Post-1965 Immigration to the United States: Structural Determinants* (Westport, Conn.: Praeger, 1995), 24–28, table 2.2.

5 Ethiopians in San Francisco: Lawrence H. Fuchs, *The American Kaleidoscope: Race, Ethnicity and the Civic Culture* (Hanover, N.H.: University Press of New England, 1990), 286 (citing Leslie R. Drake, "Ethiopians in California: Aspirations and Reality," *Refugees* (Aug. 1987): 18.

5 Chinese and Filipinos: *Statistical Abstract 1994*, 30, table 30.

5 five other countries: Ibid., 11, table 8.

5 Mexican Americans: Ibid., 30, table 30.

5 at least ten thousand immigrants: Ibid., 11, table 8.

5 Since World War II: Yang, *Post-1965 Immigration*, 1.

5 30 percent of the nation's growth: Roberts, *Who We Are*, 74.

5 The state of California: Leon F. Bouvier, *Peaceful Invasions: Immigration and Changing America* (Lanham, Md.: University Press of America, 1992), 33.

5 Nearly one million new permanent residents: U.S. Office of the President, *Accepting the Immigration Challenge: The President's Report on Immigration* (Washington, D.C.: GPO, 1994), 1.

6   fully 80 percent of these immigrants: Hing, "In the Interest of Racial Harmony," 905.

6   Elected bodies increasingly mirror: *Statistical Abstract 1994*, 281, 284–285 (table 437, Members of Congress—Selected Characteristics: 1981 to 1993; table 443, Black Elected Officials, by Office, 1970 to 1993; table 444, Hispanic Public Officials, by Office, 1985 to 1993, and by State, 1993).

6   Political interest groups: Tim Lopes, "Divided We Fall," *Denver Post*, 16 Apr. 1995, A19 (profiles of three major Hispanic lobbying groups, League of United Latin American Citizens, Mexican-American Legal Defense and Education Fund, and National Council of La Raza); Dick Kirschten, "Ethnics Resurging," *National Journal* (25 Feb. 1995): 484 (power of Central and East European lobbying groups); T. R. Goldman and Daniel Klaidman, "Hispanics Want Blackmun's Seat but Can't Unite," *Texas Lawyer*, 25 Apr. 1994, 8 (describing conflicts within Hispanic community among Hispanic National Bar Association, Puerto Rican Legal Defense Fund and other groups).

6   Groups involved in immigration reform: Dick Kirschten, "Opening the Door," *National Journal*, 18 Aug. 1990: 2002.

6   One contestant for the school board: Steven Lee Myers, "In a Changing School District, Diversity Is an Issue," *New York Times*, 18 Apr. 1993, sec. 1, 39.

6   Washington, D.C.'s, First Ward: Nell Henderson, "Dealing with Diversity in Ward 1," *Washington Post*, 7 July 1994, J1.

6   a statue of Sioux Chief Crazy Horse: Bill Roberts, "Memorial to Crazy Horse Slowly Takes Shape," *Indianapolis News*, 1 Aug. 1995, B1.

6   in shops and on streets: Marcia Coburn, "We Wear the World," *Chicago Tribune*, 23 Nov. 1994, I27.

6   in airports: *Congressional Record* 136 (18 July 1990), 4977 (statement of Congressman Bill Emerson).

6 Spanish-only radio and television: Joe Donnelly, "Where the World Hits the Airwaves," *Washington Post,* 8 Aug. 1994, B1 (Washington, D.C.'s, multicultural radio station); Gene Hoffman, "White Bread Marketing Turns Stale," *Grocery Marketing,* 60 (Jan. 1994): 42 (350 Spanish-language newspapers published in U.S.; 311 Spanish-language radio stations); Jim Cooper, "Low-Power TV Speaks Foreign Languages," *Broadcasting and Cable* (13 Dec. 1993): 96 (low-power foreign language television stations); Josh Friedman, "Direct Foreign Radio: Dishing Up 'Home,' " *Newsday,* 1 Dec. 1993, 15 (subcarrier stations broadcasting foreign radio stations).

7 Black, Asian, and Hispanic dolls: Deitel, (Louisville) *Courier-Journal.*

7 Vendors of ethnic foods: Lavina Melwani, "The Curry Revolution," *Ethnic Newswatch,* 28 Feb. 1993: 10.

7 At Biba in Boston: Florence Fabricant, "Global Village? Just Check the Menu," *New York Times,* 18 May 1994, C1.

7 Birmingham, Alabama: Roberts, *Who We Are,* 82.

7 seventeen hundred arts organizations: U.S. Congress, House of Representatives, *Fiscal Year 1995 Budget: Hearings on Appropriations for Interior and Related Agencies for FY 1995 Before the Subcommittee on Interior and Related Agencies of the House Committee on Appropriations,* 103d Cong., 2d sess. (statement of Jane Alexander, chairwoman, National Endowment for the Arts, 20 Apr. 1994).

7 Along one block in Queens: Myers, "In a Changing School District."

7 New York's ethnic enclaves: Tim Golden, "Changes in Albania Rekindle Pride in Immigrants," *New York Times,* 18 Mar. 1991 (Albanians in Bronx); Jennifer Kingson Bloom, "Neighborhood Report," *New York Times,* 11 Dec. 1994, sec. 13, 6 (Dominicans in Washington Heights); David Gonzales, "Dominican Immigration Alters Hispanic New York," *New York Times,* 1 Sept. 1992 (Dominicans in Spanish Harlem);

John Kifner, "In Central Brooklyn, a Branch of Third World," *New York Times*, 18 May 1990, B1 (Haitians and West Indians in Flatbush).

8 New York's Chinatown: Roberts, *Who We Are*, 79; Richard D. Lyons, "Satellite Chinatowns Burgeon throughout New York," *New York Times*, 14 Sept. 1986, sec. 8, 7.

8 Customers of New York Telephone: Roberts, *Who We Are*, 77.

8 43 percent—of Hispanic Americans: William H. Frey and William P. O'Hare, "Vivan los Suburbios," *American Demographics*, Apr. 1993: 30.

8 Filipino Daly City, Chinese Monterey Park: William P. O'Hare, et al., "Asians in the Suburbs," *American Demographics*, May 1994: 32.

8 Little Saigon of Westminster: Lowell Weiss, "Timing Is Everything: Vietnamese Refugees in the U.S.," *Atlantic Monthly*, Jan. 1994, 32.

8 Franco-Oriental restaurant: "World Flavors Take Root in US," *Nation's Restaurant News*, 1 May 1989, F9.

8 lime-cilantro-jalapeno ice cream: Fuchs, *The American Kaleidoscope*, 310.

8 56 percent of unions among Caucasian Americans: Richard D. Alba, "Assimilation's Quiet Tide," *Public Interest*, 22 Mar. 1995: 3.

8 invalidated antimiscegenation statutes: *Loving v. Virginia*, 388 U. S. 1 (1967).

8 marriages across racial and ethnic boundaries: Alba, "Assimilation's Quiet Tide." (70 percent of U.S.-born Hispanics are married to other Hispanics; two-thirds of U.S.-born Asians marry other Asians).

8 40 percent of native-born American Puerto Ricans: Frey and O'Hare, "Vivan los Suburbios" (reporting on Latino National Political Survey).

9   Arlington, Virginia's, public schools: William Dunn, "Educating Diversity," *American Demographics*, Apr. 1993: 38.

9   teenagers entering the job market: Susan Moffat, "Work Force Diversity," *Los Angeles Times*, 16 May 1994, 15.

9   Police officers in Dallas's: Dan R. Barber, "Diverse Challenges; Immigrant-Filled Area Forces Police to Alter Methods," *Dallas Morning News*, 1 May 1994, 35A.

9   University of California at Berkeley: Gibbs; Sharmila Sohoni, "Young People Are What They Used to Be and More," *San Francisco Examiner*, 4 July 1995, C7 (optimism of high school graduates about racial and ethnic diversity).

10 racial conflict in the high schools: Sharon Bernstein, "Multiculturalism: Building Bridges or Burning Them?" *Los Angeles Times*, 30 Nov. 1992, A1 (describing conflict between African American and Latino students at high schools); Michael Granberry, "10 Suspended in Racial Fracas at High School," *Los Angeles Times*, 19 May 1995, B1.

10 hate crimes: Edward J. Boyer and Timothy Williams, "Hate Crimes against Jews Rise Sharply," *Los Angeles Times*, 16 Feb. 1995, B1.

10 the 'average' American: Sanford J. Ungar, *Fresh Blood: The New American Immigrants* (New York: Simon and Schuster, 1995), 113.

10 attempts to portray the 1950s: David Halberstam, *The Fifties* (New York: Villard Books, 1993), xi.

12 The country Alexis de Tocqueville described: Alexis de Tocqueville, *Democracy in America*, ed. Henry Steele Commager, trans. Henry Reeve (London: Oxford University Press, 1953), 29.

12 "Providence," wrote John Jay: *The Federalist*, Isaac Kramnick, ed. (New York: Penguin Books, 1987), No. 2 (John Jay), 91; see Evarts B. Greene and Virginia D. Harrington, *American Population Before the Federal Census of 1790* (New York: Columbia University Press, 1932), 3–4 (summarizing pre-1727 popu-

lation estimates); Bureau of the Census, U. S. Department of Commerce, *Statistical Abstract of the United States 1993*, 113th ed. (Washington, D.C.: U.S. Department of Commerce, 1993), 14, table 12 (showing that as of 1800 there were 4.3 million white Americans, compared with one million black Americans). (hereinafter *Statistical Abstract 1993*).

12 John Quincy Adams once exhorted: Letter from John Quincy Adams to Baron von Furstenwaerther (4 June 1819) in Moses Rischin, ed., *Immigration and the American Tradition* (1976), 44, 47. (originally reprinted in *Niles Weekly Register*, 29 Apr. 1820, 157).

12 black slaves and Native Americans: Arthur M. Schlesinger, Jr., *The Disuniting of America: Reflections on a Multicultural Society* (New York: Norton, 1992), 14 (describing the marginalization of nonwhite Americans). This assimilation of European immigrants is reflected in early census figures, which divided society into "black" or "white." *Statistical Abstract 1993*, 14, tables 12, 13.

12 Between 1880 and 1920: *Statistical Abstract 1993*, 10, table 5.

12 early "cultural pluralism" theories: See Horace M. Kallen, *Culture and Democracy in the United States: Studies in the Group Psychology of the American Peoples* (New York: Boni and Liveright, 1924), 42–43. (arguing that "cultural growth is founded upon Cultural Pluralism").

12 James Bryce in 1888: James Bryce, *The American Commonwealth* (London: MacMillan, 1888), 328.

12 blacks were excluded: See generally C. Vann Woodward, *The Strange Career of Jim Crow*, 2d ed. (New York: Oxford University Press, 1966) (tracing the history of the Jim Crow laws from the Civil War through the Voting Rights Act of 1965).

13 African Americans began a massive migration: Michael J. Klarman, "*Brown*, Racial Change, and the Civil Rights Movement," *Virginia Law Review* 80 (1994): 7, 21–22, 67–68.

13 This demographic shift: Ibid., 30–32.

13 in 1950 immigration quotas: See, e.g., *Immigration Act of 1924*, Public Law No. 68–139, secs. 11–12, 43 Stat. 153, 159–61 (1924) (setting up quotas based on national origin); Robert A. Divine, *American Immigration Policy, 1924–1952* (New Haven: Yale University Press, 1957), 146 (summarizing the major problems of immigration policy Congress faced in the 1940s and early 1950s).

13 truly worldwide immigration: See *Amendments to the Immigration and Nationality Act*, Public Law No. 89–236, sec. 2, 79 Stat. 911, 911–12 (1965) (codified as amended at *U.S. Code*, Vol. 8, sec. 1152 (1988)) (prohibiting preferences based on "race, sex, nationality, place of birth, or place of residence" but retaining numerical ceilings); Pastora San Juan Cafferty, Barry R. Chiswick, Andrew M. Greeley, and Teresa A. Sullivan, *The Dilemma of American Immigration: Beyond the Golden Door* (New Brunswick, N.J.: Transaction Books, 1983), 53–57 (explaining American immigration policy from 1924 to 1965); Divine, *American Immigration Policy*, 152–54 (describing legislation increasing immigration opportunities).

13 quota system: Yang, *Post-1965 Immigration*, 1.

13 occupational qualifications: Alejandro Portes and Rubén G. Rumbaut, *Immigrant America: A Portrait* (Berkeley: University of California Press, 1990), 62.

13 family-preference policy: Senate Report 748, 89th Cong., 1st sess. 1, reprinted in 1965 U.S.C.C.A.N. 3328–29 (1965).

13 European immigration dwindled: Yang, *Post-1965 Immigration*, 18.

14 ten million people: *Statistical Abstract 1993*, 10, table 8 (listing a total of 7.3 million legal immigrants for the decade); Peter H. Schuck, "The Evolving Civil Rights Movement: Old Civil Rights and New Immigration," *Current* (Jan. 1994): 13, 14 (totaling the number of legal and illegal immigrants at ten million). Immigration totals have continued their increase under the 1986 Immigration Reform and Control Act (IRCA), with 810,000 legal immigrants entering the United States in 1992.

Under the Immigration Act of 1990, the country is poised to admit similar numbers of people in the upcoming years. Ibid.

14 Lawrence Auster alleges: Lawrence Auster, "Avoiding the Issue," *National Review*, 21 Feb. 1994, 48.

14 "American national identity": Lawrence Auster, "Them v. Unz," *Policy Review*, Winter 1995: 88.

15 Peter Brimelow's broadside: Peter Brimelow, *Alien Nation: Common Sense about America's Immigration Disaster* (New York: Random House, 1995), 1–22.

15 "from completely different": Ibid., 56.

15 "the American nation has always": Ibid., 10. See also 19 ("Now, immigrants are overwhelmingly visible minorities from the Third World").

15 "the steady decline of Americans": Auster, "Avoiding the Issue," 48.

15 One statistic roars: Ibid.; Lawrence Auster, "The Forbidden Topic," *National Review*, 27 Apr. 1992, 42; Lawrence Auster, "Immigration Gives Birth to Unfree America," *Atlanta Journal-Constitution*, 15 May 1991, A13; Brimelow, *Alien Nation*, 62–65.

15 percentage of foreign-born Americans: Auster, "Them v. Unz" (foreign-born population considerably higher in 1900 (almost 12 percent) and 1910 (13 percent) than today); *Statistical Abstract 1994*, 52, table 54; Marc Sandalow, "Immigrants Don't Hurt Economy, New Study Says," *San Francisco Chronicle*, 25 May 1994, A3 (percentage of foreign-born Americans half what it was one hundred years ago).

15 what our predecessors saw: John Higham, *Strangers in the Land: Patterns of American Nativism 1860–1925* (1955), 131–57 (development of racial nativism); Rita J. Simon and Susan H. Alexander, *The Ambivalent Welcome: Print Media, Public Opinion and Immigration* (1993), 53. (Henry Cabot Lodge in the 1890s classified Germans, Scandinavians, French, Belgian, and Dutch as "good" immigrants, and Poles, Bohemians, Hungarians, Russians, and Italians as "bad" immigrants).

15   the Know-Nothing movement: Simon and Alexander, *The Ambivalent Welcome*, vii.

16   southern and eastern European immigrants: Ibid.; Higham, *Strangers in the Land*, 65–66 (prejudice against eastern European immigrants). Simon and Alexander, *The Ambivalent Welcome*, 150 (Catholic birthrates) and 198 (Italians' lack of assimilation); Higham, *Strangers in the Land*, 29 (concerns about failure of Irish to assimilate in 1870s) and 77–87 (anti-Catholic ferment of 1890s).

16   previous waves of immigrants: Higham, *Strangers in the Land*, 131; Brownstein and Simon, "Hospitality Turns into Hostility."

16   "Of all the political experiments": Jerry Heaster, "America's Crisis of Confidence," *Kansas City Star*, 21 July 1995, B1.

16   "In an era of crass materialism": Ungar, *Fresh Blood*, 368.

17   economic benefits: See Thomas Muller, "Economic Effects of Immigration," in *Clamor at the Gates: The New American Immigration*, ed. Nathan Glazer (San Francisco: Institute for Contemporary Studies, 1985), 109, 129 (pointing out that while immigration has benefited the nation, there have been "subtle internal distributional effects").

17   new ideas: See David Stewart, "Immigration Laws Are Education Laws Too," *Phi Delta Kappan* 75 (1994): 556, 557 (arguing that America's education system is not taking advantage of the assets diversity offers).

17   "[Immigrants] are strong, adventuresome": A. M. Rosenthal, "Aliens: Let Them Work," *New York Times*, 9 Feb. 1993, A21.

17   "Just as they always have been": Ungar, *Fresh Blood*, 368.

17   contributions of every American: Cafferty et al., *The Dilemma of American Immigration*, 36–37 (pointing out that "while the potential for divisiveness is the unfortunate price of a nonracist immigration policy, American culture and society are enriched").

18 a "loss of courage": Heaster, "America's Crisis of Confidence."

18 aliens should be permitted to vote: Jamin B. Raskin, "Time to Give Aliens the Vote Again," *Nation*, 5 Apr. 1993, 433.

18 "there's no reason whatsoever": Julian L. Simon, *The Economic Consequences of Immigration* (Oxford: Basil Blackwell, 1989), 347–348. Professor Simon said on CNN's *Crossfire* that he was "in favor of more immigrants than anybody else . . . will admit in." *Crossfire*, CNN Television broadcast, 13 Sept. 1991, transcript no. 399.

18 "roughly 1 million legal immigrants": Michael Lind, "Huddled Excesses," *New Republic*, 1 Apr. 1996, 6.

18 "concerns about organized crime": William Branigin, "Unusual Alliance Transformed Immigration Debate," *Washington Post*, 23 Mar. 1996, A8.

19 "Adolph Hitler's posthumous revenge": Brimelow, *Alien Nation*, xv.

19 "self-proclaimed 'real' Americans": Ungar, *Fresh Blood*, 368.

19 " 'There has never been any real basis' ": Ibid., 373.

19 "At pro-187 meetings and rallies": Gregory Rodriguez, "The Browning of California," *New Republic*, 2 Sept. 1996, 18.

20 "The proof of a poet": Quoted in David S. Reynolds, *Walt Whitman's America: A Cultural Biography* (New York: Vintage Books, 1995), 5.

2: Making the Medley Work

24 standoffs at the schoolhouse door: See generally Taylor Branch, *Parting the Waters: America in the King Years 1954–63* (New York: Simon and Schuster, 1988); J. Harvie Wilkinson III, *From Brown to Bakke: The Supreme Court and School Integration: 1954–1978* (New York: Oxford University Press, 1979).

24 the new order of race relations: See Lawrence H. Fuchs, *The American Kaleidoscope: Race, Ethnicity, and the Civic Culture* (Hanover, N.H.: University Press of New England, 1990), 276–277.

24 hostilities between minority races: See Jeffrey Schmalz, "Trial
    Forces Miami to Confront Its Legacy of Racial Tensions," *New
    York Times,* 13 Nov. 1989, A1 (quoting a sociology professor at
    the University of Miami as stating that in Miami there is a
    "sense of 'them' and 'us' between blacks and Hispanic immi-
    grants").

24 African Americans and Korean Americans: Jonathan Rieder,
    "Trouble in Store: Behind the Brooklyn Boycott," *New Repub-
    lic,* 2 July 1990, 16; Elaine H. Kim, "Home Is Where the *Han*
    Is: A Korean American Perspective on the Los Angeles Up-
    heavals," in *Reading Rodney King: Reading Urban Uprising,* ed.
    Robert Gooding-Williams (New York and London: Routledge,
    1993), 215.

24 Hispanic Americans and African Americans: See Alejandro
    Portes and Alex Stepick, *City on the Edge: The Transformation of
    Miami* (Berkeley: University of California Press, 1993), 176–
    202; Bill McAllister, "Postal Official: Too Many Blacks Hired,
    Lack of Hispanics in Big Cities Cited," *Washington Post,* 3 Aug.
    1994, A1; Linda Chavez, "Just Say Latino: A Quota Trap for
    Hispanics," *New Republic,* 22 Mar. 1993, 18; Mike Williams,
    "Miami's Melting Pot Still Boiling," *Atlanta Journal-Constitu-
    tion,* 22 Jan. 1995, A3.

24 politically active Hispanic American: D'Vera Cohn and Evelyn
    Hsu, "Hispanics, Asians Change Face of N. Va.," *Washington
    Post,* 3 Feb. 1991, B1.

25 The 1965 riot in Watts: See Raphael F. Sonenshein, *Politics in
    Black and White: Race and Power in Los Angeles* (Princeton, N.J.:
    Princeton University Press, 1993), 221.

25 The 1992 uprising: See Sumi K. Cho, "Korean Americans vs.
    African Americans: Conflict and Construction," in *Reading
    Rodney King,* 196; "Return of the Nativist," *Economist,* 27 June
    1992, 25; see Harold Meyerson, "Fractured City," *New Repub-
    lic,* 25 May 1992, 23 (describing Chicano anger at Salvadoran
    immigrants for participating in the riot).

25   another videotape of a police beating: See Emily Adams, "Compton to Create Office for Racial Concerns," *Los Angeles Times*, 22 Sept. 1994, B3.

25   substantial Hispanic American communities: U.S. Bureau of the Census, *Statistical Abstract of the United States 1994*, 114th ed. (1994), 44–46, table 46 (Hispanics make up 19.6 percent of Chicago's population, 23.0 percent of Denver's, 31.6 percent of Hartford's, and 16.9 percent of Springfield's).

25   large Asian American communities: See "Asians Lead Virginia's Population Increase," *New York Times*, 23 Jan. 1991, A16; Diana Granat, "Maryland vs. Virginia," *Washingtonian Magazine*, Aug. 1994 (stating that Asians make up almost 9 percent of the population of Fairfax County, Virginia); Anna Borgman, "Area's Asian Americans Step Up Political Activism," *Washington Post*, 1 Nov. 1994, A1 (citing statistics that the Asian population in the Washington, D.C., metropolitan area increased by 136 percent between 1980 and 1990, and that Koreans own 60 percent of the small businesses in the District).

26   Washington metropolitan area: See Borgman, "Area's Asian Americans"; Liz Spayd and D'Vera Cohn, "Montgomery Blooms in a Rainbow Cast," *Washington Post*, 24 Feb. 1991, A19 (mentioning plans to build a large Asian supermarket in Montgomery County); Andrea Stone and William Dunn, "A Slice of Asian Life alongside U.S. Capital," *USA Today*, 27 Feb. 1991, A11 (describing that in Fairfax County, "strip malls . . . are jammed with Asian food shops, barbers and cleaners. Churches list Korean services. Thai, Cambodian and Korean restaurants abound").

26   Garden City, Kansas: Deborah Sontag, "New Immigrants Test Nation's Heartland," *New York Times*, 18 Oct. 1993, A1.

26   migration of black Americans: See Nicholas Lemann, *The Promised Land: The Great Black Migration and How It Changed America* (New York: Vintage Books, 1991).

26 "as American as apple pie": Neil Bissoondath, *Selling Illusions: The Cult of Multiculturalism in Canada* (Toronto: Penguin, 1994), 188.

27 A racial ranking system: Richard Herrnstein and Charles Murray, *The Bell Curve: Intelligence and Class Structure in American Life* (New York: The Free Press, 1994).

28 "the evil of a shared national identity": Richard Sennett, "The Identity Myth," *New York Times*, 30 Jan. 1994, sec. 4, 17.

28 "the most intensely race-conscious decade": Studs Terkel, *Race: How Blacks and Whites Think and Feel about the American Obsession* (New York: The New Press, 1992), 217 (interview with Charles Johnson).

28 the role of race in American history: See, e.g., Branch, *Parting the Waters.*

28 racial and ethnic divisions on the international stage: See Daniel Patrick Moynihan, *Pandemonium: Ethnicity in International Politics* (New York: Oxford University Press, 1993).

28 bewildering pace of modern change: See Cynthia Tucker, "Volume Won't Solve Welfare," *Atlanta Journal-Constitution*, 26 Mar. 1995, 5R (remarking that "much of the public anger directed toward [immigrants and other scapegoats] has at its core an economic unease caused by the transition to an economy ruled by technology").

28 the "giant sucking sound": Robert Wright, "Why Perot Is Still Wrong (About the North American Free Trade Agreement)," *Time*, 9 Jan. 1995, 46.

28 "a lightning rod for anger": Frederick W. Mayer, "Both Sides Missing the Real Point about NAFTA," *Houston Chronicle*, 1 Jan. 1996, A31.

28 California's adoption of Proposition 187: Ronald Brownstein and Richard Simon, "Hospitality Turns into Hostility: California Has a Long History of Welcoming Newcomers for Their Cheap Labor—Until Times Turn Rough," *Los Angeles Times*,

14 Nov. 1993, A1; Brett Johnson, "McClintock: Budget Will Be Cut," *News Chronicle*, 30 Mar. 1994, A3.

29   African Americans may blame Hispanic Americans: See Chavez, "Just Say Latino," 18; Linda Chavez, "Rainbow Collision: Relations between African Americans and Hispanic Americans," *New Republic*, 19 Nov. 1990, 14.

29   in Miami, Washington, D.C., and Los Angeles: See McAllister, "Postal Official," A1 (alluding to tension between black and Hispanic communities over access to government jobs and programs); Steven A. Holmes, "The Nation: Miami Melting Pot Proves Explosive," *New York Times*, 9 Dec. 1990, sec. 4, 4 (identifying " 'perception among blacks of loss of jobs as a result of the Latinization of the city' ").

29   Martin Luther King Hospital: Nancy Gibbs, "Shades of Difference," *Time*, 18 Nov. 1991, 66.

29   a San Francisco high school's admissions policy: See Selena Dong, Note, " 'Too Many Asians': The Challenge of Fighting Discrimination against Asian-Americans and Preserving Affirmative Action," *Stanford Law Review* 47 (1995): 1029; Elaine Woo, "Caught on the Wrong Side of the Line?" *Los Angeles Times*, 13 July 1995, A1.

29   West Indian Americans: Malcolm Gladwell, "Black Like Them," *New Yorker*, 29 Apr. and 6 May 1996, 75, 79.

30   politicians of all persuasions: Nancy E. Roman, " 'Colorblind' Policy Unites GOP Hopefuls," *Washington Times*, 21 Feb. 1995, A1.

31   "Self-segregation is in": Juan Williams, "The Seduction of Segregation," *Washington Post*, 16 Jan. 1994, C1 (describing and generally questioning the growing separatist sentiment).

32   "You hardly ever hear the word": Ronald A. Taylor, "Whither Integration?" *Washington Times*, 13 Jan. 1995, G10.

32   segregated preferences: Nanette Asimov, "Students Say Racism Is on the Rise," *San Francisco Chronicle*, 15 May 1992, A1.

32 "In the short run": *Milliken v. Bradley*, 418 U.S. 717, 814–15 (1974) (Marshall, J., dissenting).

32 One recent survey showed: James L. Tyson, "More U.S. Blacks Favor Going a Separate Way," *Christian Science Monitor*, 5 May 1994, 1.

32 "a weary Kansas City": Dennis Farney, "Fading Dream?: Integration Is Faltering in Kansas City Schools as Priorities Change," *Wall Street Journal*, 26 Sept. 1995, A1. The same article quotes from Mr. Newsome and Ms. Parks.

33 The new segregation traverses all regions: James S. Kunen, "The End of Integration," *Time*, 29 Apr. 1996, 39–40.

33 "ambivalence about integration": Glenn Loury, "The Crisis of Color Consciousness," *Washington Post*, 21 July 1996, C3.

33 pure resignation: Kunen, "The End of Integration," 45, quotes both Mr. Shaw and Ms. Bullard.

33 The media regaled us with stories: See, e.g., Ronald J. Hansen and Ian Zack, "Observers Ponder Case's Questions, Lessons," *Charlottesville Daily Progress*, 4 Oct. 1995, A1.

34 polls rushed to confirm: Richard Morin, "Poll Reflects Division over Simpson Case," *Washington Post*, 8 Oct. 1995, A31.

35 "race politics becomes a court of the imagination": Henry Louis Gates Jr., "Thirteen Ways of Looking at a Black Man," *New Yorker*, 23 Oct. 1995, 56, 95.

35 "to straighten their backs": Richard Cohen, "Marching Behind Farrakhan," *Washington Post*, 19 Sept. 1995, A13.

35 a long list of intractable hatreds: "The Indivisible Louis Farrakhan," *Washington Post*, 15 Oct. 1995, C6.

35 Farrakhan's request to stay away: Michael A. Fletcher and Hamil R. Harris, "Black Men Jam Mall for a 'Day of Atonement,' " *Washington Post*, 17 Oct. 1995, A1.

35 "I don't need to be": Michael Kelly, "Segregation Anxiety," *New Yorker*, 20 Nov. 1995, 43, 54.

36 America's "other" minorities: Louis Aguilar, "Latinos, Asians Seek a Voice in Emerging National Discussion on Race," *Washington Post*, 15 Oct. 1995, A24. Aguilar also quotes Mr. Klor de Alva and Mr. Chang.

36 litigation of the pre-Brown era: See *McLaurin v. Oklahoma State Regents*, 339 U.S. 637 (1950); *Sweatt v. Painter*, 339 U.S. 629 (1950); *Missouri ex rel. Gaines v. Canada*, 305 U.S. 337 (1938).

37 "The men who marched on Washington": Kelly, "Segregation Anxiety."

38 "made up of people who have lost faith": Martin Luther King Jr., *Letter from the Birmingham Jail*, repr. (San Francisco: Harper, 1994), 20.

38 "requires true understanding": Bissoondath, *Selling Illusions*, 191.

38 A lack of understanding: See Taylor, "Whither Integration?" (quoting director of Asian Pacific American Legal Center's mediation services as stating, "One reason for the clash [between blacks and Koreans] is that both communities are really ignorant of the other").

38 "When a customer complains": Linda Wheeler, "Korean Merchants Find Opportunity in D.C.," *Washington Post*, 14 Dec. 1986, B1.

39 "The Koreans who have just gotten here": Taylor, "Whither Integration?"

40 "the very worst racists would be all too happy": Juan Williams, "The Seduction of Segregation."

40 sweeping powers to achieve integration: *Albermarle Paper Co. v. Moody*, 422 U.S. 405 (1975); *Swann v. Charlotte-Mecklenburg Bd. of Educ.*, 402 U.S. 1 (1971).

41 "young people deserve the right": Nat Hentoff, "Segregation Forever?" *Washington Post*, 23 Dec. 1995, A17.

42 The cities of America: See Fuchs, *The American Kaleidoscope*, 296–303.

42 "the history of the populating": *Board of Educ. of Kiryas Joel v. Grumet*, 114 S. Ct. 2481, 2507 (1994) (Scalia, J., dissenting).

42 city-sanctioned ethnic parades: William Murphy, "Parade Rout? Bratton: City Could Reduce Ethnics' Days," *Newsday*, 18 Nov. 1994, A3.

42 Chinese New Year: Phyllis Hanes, "Chinese in U.S. Usher in New Year of the Rooster," *Christian Science Monitor*, 4 Feb. 1993, Food sec., 10.

42 San Francisco parade: Sue Adolphson, "SF Parade on World Route," *San Francisco Chronicle*, 4 Feb. 1990, Datebook sec., 31.

42 Cinco de Mayo: Sam Diaz, "Festival of Mexican Culture Begins," *Fresno Bee*, 3 May 1994, B2.

43 *Wisconsin v. Yoder: Wisconsin v. Yoder*, 406 U.S. 205–224 (1972).

45 *Board of Education of Kiryas Joel v. Grumet: Board of Educ. of Kiryas Joel v. Grumet*, 114 S. Ct. 2481–2491 (1994). Justice Kennedy's concurring opinion, Ibid., 2501–2504.

45 "The Satmars' way of life": Ibid.

46 But Justice Souter's: Ibid.

46 "political boundaries": Ibid.

46 "the danger of stigma": Ibid.

46 Justice Scalia's dissenting opinion: Ibid., 2506.

47 profound nationalist and separatist implications: See generally Arthur M. Schlesinger Jr., *The Disuniting of America: Reflections on a Multicultural Society* (New York: Norton, 1992).

48 "the inventions [will be] excellent": Ralph Waldo Emerson, *The Conduct of Life* VII (1860), as quoted in *A New Dictionary of Quotations on Historical Principles from Ancient and Modern Sources*, ed. H. L. Mencken (New York: Alfred A. Knopf, 1957), 36.

48 Independence Day 1995: Independence Day Exercises, Monticello, 4 July 1995.

50 Affirmative action programs: See Paul Brest and Miranda Oshige, "Affirmative Action for Whom?" *Stanford Law Review* 47 (1995): 855, 862–872.

50 "no other group compares to African Americans": Ibid., 900.

50 "the vast number of groups and subgroups": Ibid.

51 "the debate over affirmative action": Harry P. Pachon, "Invisible Latinos: Excluded from Discussions of Inclusion," in *The Affirmative Action Debate*, ed. George E. Curry (Reading, Mass.: Addison-Wesley, 1996), 184, 186–188, 190.

52 "are depicted as champion entrepreneurs": Theodore Hsien Wang and Frank H. Wu, "Beyond the Model Minority Myth," in *The Affirmative Action Debate*, 192, 195–197.

53 "Asian and Pacific Islander ethnicities": Brest and Oshige, "Affirmative Action," 856.

53 "immigrants arriving at different times": Ibid., 896.

53 "third generation Chinese and Japanese Americans": Ibid., 896, n. 274.

54 Washington, D.C.: Chavez, "Just Say Latino."

54 Miami: Mike Williams, "Miami's Melting Pot."

54 Compton, California: See Emily Adams, "Black, Latino Tension to Be Summit Topic," *Los Angeles Times*, 28 Apr. 1994, J3.

55 "Under these standards, Paul Revere": See Gil Klein, "History: A Study in Political Correctness?" *Charlottesville Daily Progress*, 27 May 1996, A1 and A5.

55 "a gloomy manifestation": George Will, "National History Standards Put Us on a Common Ground of Learning," *Charlottesville Daily Progress*, 7 Apr. 1996, A10.

55 glorious moments of American history: See Schlesinger, *The Disuniting of America*, 92.

56 visit of Nelson Mandela: See generally Liz Sly, "Mandela Snubbed in Miami," *Chicago Tribune*, 29 June 1990, C3.

56 Our postage stamps: See "13 New Afro-American Stamps," *Stamps* (7 Jan. 1995): 10 (announcing that for the second successive year African Americans will be specially recognized by the Postal Service's commemorative stamp collections).

57 *Miller v. Johnson: Miller v. Johnson,* 115 S. Ct. 2475 (1995).

57 *Adarand Constructors v. Peña: Adarand Constructors v. Peña,* 115 S. Ct. 2097 (1995).

57 *Missouri v. Jenkins: Missouri v. Jenkins,* 115 S. Ct. 2038, 2049 (1995).

58 Color-Blind Court: Jeffrey Rosen, "The Color-Blind Court," *New Republic,* 31 July 1995, 19.

58 The majorities for race neutrality: *Miller v. Johnson,* 115 S. Ct. 2497 (O'Connor, J., concurring) ("Application of the Court's standard does not throw into doubt the vast majority of the Nation's 435 congressional districts, where presumably the States have drawn the boundaries in accordance with their customary districting principles. That is so even though race may well have been considered in the redistricting process." Citation omitted).

58 "just one race here": *Adarand Constructors v. Peña,* 115 S. Ct. 2119 (Scalia, J., concurring).

3: The Integrative Ideal

61 *Plessy v. Ferguson: Plessy v. Ferguson,* 163 U.S. 537 (1896).

61 legacies of Abraham Lincoln: See Bruce Ackerman, *We the People: Foundations* (Cambridge, Mass.: Harvard University Press, 1991), 44–46.

61 Thurgood Marshall and Earl Warren: *Brown v. Board of Educ.,* 347 U.S. 483 (1954).

62 The premise of *Brown* was simple: Ibid., 490, 493–95.

62 First, the justices hoped: Ibid.

62 "separate educational facilities": Ibid.

62 "I am watching the comings and goings": Willie Morris, *Yazoo: Integration in a Deep-Southern Town* (New York: Harper's Magazine Press, 1971), 149.

63 moral content: Cf. Robin West, "The Meaning of Equality and the Interpretive Turn," Chi.-Kent L. Rev. 66 (1990): 451, 470–71 (finding *Brown* representative of a substantive vision of equal protection where "legislators must use law to insure that no social group . . . wrongfully subordinates another").

63 landmark civil rights cases: See, e.g., *Peterson v. City of Greenville*, 373 U.S. 244, 247–48 (1963) (reversing the convictions of ten black citizens who challenged local ordinances segregating restaurants); *Edwards v. South Carolina*, 372 U.S. 229, 235–38 (1963) (reversing breach of the peace convictions of blacks who protested in front of the South Carolina State House); *Gayle v. Browder*, 352 U.S. 903, 903 (1956) (per curiam) (affirming lower court's decision finding the statutes and ordinances segregating the Montgomery, Alabama, buses unconstitutional).

63 the innate equality of human worth: See, e.g., Martin Luther King, Jr., *Letter from the Birmingham Jail*, repr. (San Francisco: Harper, 1994).

63 the conscience of the entire country: See Anthony Lewis, *Portrait of a Decade: The Second American Revolution* (New York: Bantam Books, 1964), 74–75. (describing the national attention and support King's speech attracted); cf. *Milton Viorst, Fire in the Streets: America in the 1960s* (New York: Simon and Schuster, 1979), 34 (discussing the dilemma King faced "in inspiring his listeners to show courage in behalf of a just cause without engendering in them un-Christian feelings of resentment and hate").

63 The federal judiciary has played a unique role: See generally J. Harvie Wilkinson III, *From* Brown *to* Bakke: *The Supreme Court and School Integration: 1954–1978* (New York: Oxford University Press, 1979).

63 *Unlikely Heros:* Jack Bass, *Unlikely Heroes* (New York: Simon and Schuster, 1981).

63 *Fifty-Eight Lonely Men:* J. W. Peltason, *Fifty-Eight Lonely Men: Southern Federal Judges and School Desegregation* (New York: Harcourt, Brace and World, 1961).

63 Fifth Circuit judges: Bass, *Unlikely Heroes*, 15–16.

63 "Skelly Wright had become": Ibid., 115.

64 black citizens themselves made the greatest contribution: See Jay R. Mandle, *Not Slave, Not Free: The African American Economic Experience since the Civil War* (Durham, N.C.: Duke University Press, 1992), 95–96; cf. Jack Greenberg, *Crusaders in the Courts* (New York: Basic Books, 1994), 268 (relating how, after *Brown*, blacks "spoke up for racial equality in numbers so large and in protests so vigorous that they could not be gainsaid").

64 John Hardy, a black college student: Lewis, *Portrait of a Decade*, 126–128. (Hardy was also arrested on a breach of the peace charge, but the Fifth Circuit enjoined his prosecution). Ibid., 127.

64 extraordinary fortitude: See, e.g., William H. Chafe, *Civilities and Civil Rights: Greensboro, North Carolina, and the Black Struggle for Freedom* (New York: Oxford University Press, 1980), 100–102 (describing the hardships the first black students at Greensboro High School endured); Greenberg, *Crusaders in the Courts*, 271–73 (recounting the ordeals participants in sit-ins faced).

64 Little Rock High School: See Taylor Branch, *Parting the Waters: America in the King Years 1954–1963* (New York: Simon and Schuster, 1988), 222–225.

65 "Yes friend, my feet is real tired": Quoted in Martin Luther King, "The Time for Freedom Has Come," *New York Times Magazine*, 10 Sept. 1961, 25.

65 "massive resistance": Quoted in J. Harvie Wilkinson III, *Harry Byrd and the Changing Face of Virginia Politics, 1945–1966* (Charlottesville, Va.: University Press of Virginia, 1968), 113. The date of the statement is 24 Feb. 1956.

65 "I am not a gradualist": Quoted in William B. Crawley Jr., *Bill Tuck: A Political Life in Harry Byrd's Virginia* (Charlottesville, Va.: University Press of Virginia, 1978), 219. The statement was made in 1956.

66 "We will oppose": Quoted in Benjamin Muse, *Virginia's Massive Resistance* (Bloomington, Ind.: Indiana University Press, 1961), 42.

66 Interposition: See James W. Ely Jr., *The Crisis of Conservative Virginia: The Byrd Organization and the Politics of Massive Resistance* (Knoxville, Tenn.: University of Tennessee Press, 1976), 39–40.

67 "one of the most significant positions": See Earle Dunford, *Richmond Times-Dispatch: The Story of a Newspaper* (Richmond, Va.: Cadmus Publishing, 1995), 299–302, 401–409.

67 In 1943, Roy Wilkins: Ibid.

67 his conservative bosses: Ibid.

67 For Dabney himself: Ibid.

68 "only two of Richmond's 23,000 black children": See John C. Jeffries Jr., *Justice Lewis F. Powell Jr.* (New York: Charles Scribner and Sons, 1994), 140–41.

68 "Powell's years in state and local education": Ibid., 178.

68 debate with James J. Kilpatrick: Ibid., 145–46.

68 visited Senator Byrd: Ibid., 148–49.

68 "massive resistance was the greatest single obstacle": Ibid., 151–53.

68 the right of black leaders to speak: Oliver Hill, "A Tribute to Justice Lewis F. Powell Jr.," *Harvard Law Review* 101 (1987): 414–16.

69 "he always chose education": Jeffries, *Justice Lewis F. Powell*, 176.

69 "with all deliberate speed'": *Brown v. Board of Educ.*, 349 U.S. 294 (1955).

70   the ideal of integration: See generally Arthur M. Schlesinger Jr., *The Disuniting of America: Reflections on a Multicultural Society* (New York: Norton, 1991).

70   controversies over school busing: See Wilkinson, *From* Brown *to* Bakke, 161–192.

70   unravelling of a national civil rights consensus: See Cornel West, *Race Matters* (New York: Vintage Books, 1993), 2–6 (describing the range of political and social views on race within America and the black community).

70   continuing debate over affirmative action: See generally Russell Nieli, ed., *Racial Preference and Racial Justice: The New Affirmative Action Controversy* (Washington, D.C.: Ethics and Public Policy Center, 1991).

70   the gulf in racial understanding: See Andrew Hacker, *Two Nations: Black and White, Separate, Hostile, Unequal* (New York: Charles Scribner and Sons, 1992), 3–4 (arguing that, in modern America, "the separation [of the races] is pervasive and penetrating. As a social and human division, it surpasses all others"); Christopher Herlinger, "Poll: Racial, Religious Lines as Deep as Ever," *San Diego Union-Tribune*, 8 Apr. 1994, E4 (finding that minority groups harbor prejudice toward each other and "bitter feelings" toward whites).

70   The inner city's plight: See, e.g., Anthony Shadid, "Urban Decay Is Brewing Trouble in Milwaukee," *Los Angeles Times*, 10 Mar. 1991, A20 (pointing out the spread to smaller cities of urban problems once unique to large cities).

71   United States marshals and federal troops: See Lewis, *Portrait of a Decade*, 87–90 (relating how federal marshals were sent to Montgomery to escort the freedom riders); Harvard Sitkoff, *The Struggle for Black Equality 1954–1980* (New York: Hill and Wang, 1993), 114–15, 145 (describing instances of federal use of force in Alabama and Mississippi).

72   "we must be able to rise above [race]": Tamar Jacoby, "Does *Brown* Still Matter?" *Nation* 258, 23 May 1994: 725, 726.

72   race is not . . . a relevant characteristic: See *Brown v. Board of Educ.*, 347 U.S. 483, 493 (1954).

4: The Specter of Separatism

75   "Southern strategy" of the Nixon administration: Reg Murphy and Hal Gulliver, *The Southern Strategy* (New York: Charles Scribner's Sons, 1971), 3.

76   "I understand the bitter feeling": Ibid., 139.

76   "I yield to no man": Ibid., 132–33.

77   "federal remedial power may be exercised": *Milliken v. Bradley*, 418 U.S. 717, 738 (1974) (quoting *Swann v. Charlotte-Mecklenburg Board of Educ.*, 402 U.S. 1, 16 [1971]).

78   destructive exercises of racial factionalism: Andrew Hacker, *Two Nations: Black and White, Separate, Hostile, Unequal* (New York: Charles Scribner and Sons 1992), 200–207 (explaining the role race plays in political elections).

78   discrimination remains alive: See, e.g., Derrick Bell, *And We Are Not Saved: The Elusive Quest for Racial Justice* (New York: Basic Books, 1987), 26–50 (tracing blacks' ongoing struggle against discrimination); Ann O'Hanlon, "Hiring Bias Attributed to '86 Immigration Act," *Washington Post*, 6 Aug. 1994, B1 (noting studies by the General Accounting Office and the Urban Institute revealing pervasive discrimination against the foreign-born).

78   "self-segregation": See Julianne Malveaux, "Don't Knock Theme Houses," *USA Today*, 9 Mar. 1994, 12A (defending self-segregated housing options for black college students).

78   interminority friction: See Bill Ong Hing, "Beyond the Rhetoric of Assimilation and Cultural Pluralism: Addressing the Tension of Separatism and Conflict in an Immigration-Driven Multiracial Society," *California Law Review* 81 (1993): 863, 888–94 (discussing the "multitude of causes" of the competition for jobs, education, and access to social programs underlying interminority friction).

79   numerical set-asides in public contracts: See, e.g., *City of Rich-mond v. J.A. Croson Co.*, 488 U.S. 469, 478–80 (1989); *Fullilove v. Klutznick*, 448 U.S. 448, 480–92 (1980); see also Tony Munroe, "SBA to Offer Changes in Programs Affecting Minority-Run Businesses," *Washington Times*, 23 Sept. 1992, C3 (discussing changes in the sec. 8(a) set-aside program); Maureen O. Boyle, "Asian, Hispanic Businesses Want Piece of City Contracts," *Business First-Columbus*, 22 Nov. 1993, 1 (describing conflict between minority groups over Columbus, Ohio, set-asides).

79   allocation of jobs: See *United Steelworkers of America v. Weber*, 443 U.S. 193, 208–09 (1979); see also Lynne Duke, "Cultural Shifts Bring Anxiety for White Men: Growing Diversity Imposing New Dynamic in Workplace," *Washington Post*, 1 Jan. 1991, A1 (describing white males' reactions to the workplace's changing racial landscape); Bill McAllister, "Postal Official: Too Many Blacks Hired," *Washington Post*, 3 Aug. 1994, A1 (describing a Post Office hiring fight as "an example of the tension between blacks and the growing Hispanic community over access to . . . jobs").

79   education admissions process: See *Regents of the Univ. of Cal. v. Bakke*, 438 U.S. 265, 311–18 (1978); *DeFunis v. Odegaard*, 416 U.S 312, 320–27 (1974) (per curiam) (Douglas, J., dissenting); see also Richard Bernstein, "Racial Discrimination or Righting Past Wrongs?" *New York Times*, 13 July 1994, B8 (discussing admissions standards at the University of Texas Law School).

79   redistricting disputes: See *Shaw v. Reno*, 113 S. Ct. 2816, 2823 (1993); See Peter H. Schuck, "The Evolving Civil Rights Movement," *Current* (Jan. 1994): 14–15 (noting the impact of geographic distribution on minority representation).

79   workers' unions: Jonetta Rose Barras and Vincent McCraw, "Moving Up and Moving In: Blacks, Hispanics Vie for Civil-Rights Benefits," *Washington Times*, 9 May 1993, A1 (describing the tensions between blacks and Hispanics in Washington, D.C., hotel workers' union elections).

79 juries: Shannon P. Duffy, "Juries Lacking Hispanics?" *The Legal Intelligencer,* 12 July 1995: 1 (attempt to dismiss indictment based on underrepresentation of Hispanics on grand jury).

79 Brooklyn's West Indian Carnival: "Caribbean New York," *New York Times,* 7 Sept. 1994, A22.

79 The direction that pride separatism will take: See, e.g., Wendy Brown-Scott, "Race Consciousness in Higher Education: Does 'Sound Educational Policy' Support the Continued Existence of Historically Black Colleges?" *Emory Law Journal* 43 (1994): 1, 7, 73–80 (emphasizing preservation of cultural integrity and reparation as justifications for educational separatism).

80 minority groups on college campuses: See Drew S. Days III, "*Brown* Blues: Rethinking the Integrative Ideal," *William and Mary Law Review* 34 (1992): 53, 72 (linking the demand for separate facilities to the increasing number of black students and their concerns about the difficulty of adjustment); Kenneth Lee, "Separate and Unequal: Segregation on Campus," *American Enterprise,* Sept./Oct. 1996: 63.

80 Brown University: Mary Jordan, "College Dorms Reflect Trend of Self-Segregation," *Washington Post,* 6 Mar. 1994, A1.

80 University of Pennsylvania: Ralph Vigoda, "Goals of Diversity Challenged by Separatists' Demands," *Houston Chronicle,* 3 Apr. 1994, A8.

80 Cornell University: Lee, "Separate and Unequal," 63.

80 Georgia Tech: John Head, "Separatist Blacks at Tech, Other Campuses Making Mistake,"*Atlanta Journal-Constitution,* 10 June 1991, A13.

80 "Multicultural curriculum": See Arthur M. Schlesinger Jr., *The Disuniting of America* (New York: Norton, 1992), 73–99 (weighing the dangers of an "Afrocentric" history curriculum); see also John O'Sullivan, "Nationhood: An American Activity," *National Review,* 21 Feb. 1994, 36, 38–44 (arguing that multiculturalism rejects American ideals and is not a viable theory of nationhood).

80   expression of racial pride: See Kenneth J. Cooper, "Coming to Grips with Diversity: At Berkeley, the Future Is Now," *Washington Post*, 26 May 1991, A1 (noting "peer pressures against dissenting on racial matters").

80   *Snapshots of Color:* "Dartmouth Rejects Minority Magazine," *Washington Post*, 17 Aug. 1995, A18 (college denied recognition and student funding to magazine).

80   calls for racial secession: Blake Dickinson, "UNC Professor Advocates Nation of Islam's Way," *Chapel Hill Herald*, 19 Jan. 1995, 1.

80   resegregation of public schools: Wendy R. Brown, "School Desegregation Litigation: Crossroads or Dead End?" *St. Louis University Law Journal* 37 (1993): 923, 928–31 (describing a debate between an integrationist and an advocate of immersion schools); Carol Innerst, "Schools Becoming Less Integrated," *Washington Times*, 14 Dec. 1993, A5 (reporting increased segregation in urban centers and their suburbs); Larry Tye, "U.S. Sounds Retreat in School Integration," *Boston Globe*, 5 Jan. 1992, 1 (noting that the resegregation trend has been most marked in the Northeast).

80   "When the school bell rings": Nanette Asimov, "Students Say Racism Is on the Rise," *San Francisco Chronicle*, 15 May 1992, A1, A8.

81   Language differences: See "Conflict Among People of Color: Cubans' Success Spurs Racial Tensions," *Minority Markets Alert*, July 1993, available in LEXIS, Nexis Library, MMALRT File ("English-speaking blacks are increasingly alienated from Spanish-speaking blacks who identify themselves by their language and cultural heritage instead of race").

81   Petersburg High School: Mike Allen, "The Segregated Reunions of an Integrated School," *New York Times*, 4 Aug. 1996, A24.

81   "perpetuate a caste system": *Adarand Constructors, Inc. v. Peña*, 115 S. Ct. 2097, 2120 (1995) (Stevens, J., dissenting).

82 "permanent structures based on race": Constance Horner, "Reclaiming the Vision: What Should We Do After Affirmative Action?" *Brookings Review*, 22 June, 1995: 6.

82 "traditions are worth teaching": Kwame Anthony Appiah, "Beware of Race-Pride," *American Enterprise*, Sept./Oct. 1995: 50. The following two quotations come from the same article.

82 "Bach *and* James Brown": Henry Louis Gates Jr., "On Honoring Blackness," *American Enterprise*, Sept./Oct. 1995: 49.

83 division in the name of interracial peace: See, e.g., *Riddick v. School Bd.*, 627 F. Supp. 814, 817–18 (E.D. Va. 1984) (school board members supported increasing the number of "racially identifiable" black schools), *aff'd*, 784 F.2d 521, *cert. denied*, 479 U.S. 938 (1986); see also Cooper, "Coming to Grips," A1 (noting campus officials' tolerance of separatism). But see Jordan, "College Dorms," A1 (reporting that Brown officials halted the opening of additional self-segregated dormitories until their effect could be studied).

84 "generates a feeling of inferiority": *Brown v. Board of Educ.*, 374 U.S. 483, 494 (1954).

84 community cohesion and pride: See Hing, "Beyond the Rhetoric," 890–898 (examining separatism as both an ideological and a sociological phenomenon).

84 rise of black power spokesmen: See Milton Viorst, *Fire in the Streets: America in the 1960s* (New York: Simon and Schuster, 1979), 345–347 (arguing that black power grew out of whites' failure to promote the endogenous development of African American self-sufficiency).

84 rise of neighborhood school associations: *Keyes v. School Dist. No. 1*, 413 U.S. 189, 246 (1973) (Powell, J., concurring in part and dissenting in part).

86 African Americans are said not to appreciate the language issues: See Larry Rohter, "As Hispanic Presence Grows, So Does Black Anger," *New York Times*, 20 June 1993, sec. 1

(pointing out that language issues have not been part of the traditional black agenda).

86   Hispanics . . . and . . . slavery and Jim Crow: See Walter Stafford, "When Peoples of Color Conflict," *Newsday*, 28 Oct. 1993, 72 ("New immigrants are often unaware of, or minimize, the historical civil rights struggles of native-born blacks, and the importance of overcoming entrenched racism").

86   supporters of all-black schools: Susan Chira, "Rethinking Deliberately Segregated Schools," *New York Times*, 11 July 1993, sec. 4, 20 (reporting that black parents are "looking to all-black schools to infuse children with racial pride and offer role models of successful and powerful black adults").

86   that nonblack teachers cannot transmit: See Tom Dunkel, "Self-Segregated Schools Seek to Build Self-Esteem," *Washington Times*, 11 Mar. 1991, E1; Jill Nelson, "Is Segregation the Answer? Racist or Realistic?" *USA Weekend*, 19 May 1991, 4 (detailing proposals for immersion and "Africa-centered" schools).

86   "You needed an African-American": Marshall Fine, "Trying to Feel the Poison," Gannet News Service, 12 Nov. 1992, available in LEXIS, Nexis Library, GNS File (quoting Lee).

87   the selection of Jack Greenberg: See Jack Greenberg, *Crusaders in the Courts: How a Dedicated Band of Lawyers Fought for the Civil Rights Revolution* (1994), 502–04.

88   " 'minority views' that must be different: *Miller v. Johnson*, 115 S. Ct. 2475, 2487 (1995) (quoting *Metro Broadcasting, Inc. v. FCC*, 497 U.S. 547, 636 (1990) (Kennedy, J., dissenting)).

88   historically black colleges and immersion schools: See Days, "*Brown* Blues," 60–62, 64–66.

88   African Americans . . . in favor of capital punishment: Tamar Jacoby, "Conservative, African American, Making Waves," *Washington Post*, 20 Aug. 1995, C1, C4.

88   radio talk shows: Ibid.

88 Pacifica radio network: See, e.g., Jeff Jacoby, "A Year of Character-Assassination from the Left," *Boston Globe*, 27 Dec. 1994, 11.

88 Hispanic American groups . . . of . . . (NAFTA): See Adonis Hoffman, "Recognizing NAFTA's Racial Dimensions," *Legal Times*, 8 Nov. 1993, 28.

88 mayoral candidates . . . in Washington, D.C.: Anna Borgman, "Area's Asian Americans Step Up Political Activism," *Washington Post*, 1 Nov. 1994, A1.

89 "radical double agent": Derrick Bell, "A Radical Double Agent," in *Court of Appeal: The Black Community Speaks Out on the Racial and Sexual Politics of Clarence Thomas vs. Anita Hill*, ed. Robert Chrisman and Robert L. Allen (New York: Ballantine Books, 1992), 36 (reprinted from the *New York Times*). See also Charles P. Henry, "Clarence Thomas and the National Black Identity," in *Court of Appeal*, 83 (claiming Clarence Thomas is "hostile to traditional black interests"); Ronald W. Walters, "Clarence Thomas and the Meaning of Blackness," in *Court of Appeal*, 215, 217–218 (maintaining that although Clarence Thomas "shares a 'Blackness' with others of his race," he is "not politically Black").

89 Vincent Chin: K. Connie Kang, "Hate Crimes against Asians in Southland Rose Last Year," *Los Angeles Times*, 2 Aug. 1996, A3.

90 "During the forum": William McGowan, "Reporting by the Numbers," *Wall Street Journal*, 18 Mar. 1996, A18.

91 "in a 90-second meeting": Ibid.

91 "Metro reporter Sandra Evans spent months": Ruth Shalit, "Race in the Newsroom: *The Washington Post* in Black and White," *New Republic*, 2 Oct. 1995, 20, 31–37.

91 "In early 1993": Ibid., 37.

92 "presumes that if therapist and patient": Sally Satel, "Psychiatric Apartheid," *Wall Street Journal*, 8 May 1996, A14.

92   In accord with this theory: Ibid.

92   "The patient is a human being": Ibid.

92   "I believe in my bones": Studs Terkel, *Race: How Blacks and Whites Think and Feel about the American Obsession,* 218 (interview with Charles Johnson).

93   race relations as inherently oppressive: See, e.g., Derrick Bell, *Faces at the Bottom of the Well: The Permanence of Racism* (New York: Basic Books, 1992), 150–153 (arguing that African American empowerment might come at the cost of integration and inclusion).

93   members of Congress who passed . . . civil rights laws: See Viorst, *Fire in the Streets,* 239–241; C. Vann Woodward, *The Strange Career of Jim Crow,* 2d ed. (New York: Oxford University Press, 1966), 27–28, 32–33.

93   strategies of nonviolent protest: See, e.g., David J. Garrow, *Bearing the Cross: Martin Luther King, Jr. and the Southern Christian Leadership Conference* (New York: Vintage Books, 1986), 171–172.

94   *Brown* sought to discourage us from racial stereotypes: See *Brown v. Board of Educ.* 347 U.S. 483, 494 and n. 11 (1954) (stating that modern authority supports the view that segregation retards black children's educational and mental growth). For a description of modern stereotypes, see Jacki Lyden, "Portrait of America—Minority vs. Minority," NPR Transcript no. 1412-9, 5 Mar. 1994, available in LEXIS, Nexis Library, NPR File (describing a recent study of biases by National Opinion Research Center).

94   Leonard Jeffries: Richard Bernstein, "Judge Reinstates Jeffries as Head of Black Studies for City College," *New York Times,* 5 Aug. 1993, A1; Lynne Duke, "Colliding Racial Beliefs Test Speech Limits at CCNY," *Washington Post,* 9 Nov. 1991, A1.

94   Michael Levin: Duke, "Colliding Racial Beliefs"; Alexis Jetter, "Offending Speeches Spark Protests," *Newsday,*

3 May 1990, 5. See generally *Levin v. Harleston*, 770 F. Supp. 895, 899–903 (S.D.N.Y. 1991), *aff'd in part and vacated in part*, 966 F.2d 85 (2d Cir. 1992).

95 objections . . . on moral, though race-neutral, grounds: Cf. *IOTA XI Chapter of Sigma Chi Fraternity v. George Mason Univ.*, 993 F.2d 386, 388, 391 (4th Cir. 1993) (objections to offensive fraternity skit raised on both racial and nonracial grounds); *State v. Wyant*, 64 Ohio St. 3d 566, 579; 597 N.E.2d 450, 459 (1992) ("Conduct motivated by racial . . . bigotry can be constitutionally punished . . . without resort to constructing a thought crime"), *vacated sub nom. Ohio v. Wyant*, 113 S. Ct. 2954 (1993).

96 "when gazing upon Americans": Glenn Loury, "What's Wrong with the . . . Right," *American Enterprise*, Jan./Feb. 1996: 31, 38.

96 "defensive flight": Karl Zinsmeister, "Painful but Productive: Toward Honesty on Race," *American Enterprise*, Jan./Feb. 1996: 4, 5.

5: Separatist Politics

101 legislative districts be roughly equal: *Baker v. Carr*, 369 U.S. 186 (1962); *Reynolds v. Sims*, 377 U.S. 533 (1964).

102 a system of caste rule: This was precisely the problem that the *Voting Rights Act of 1965, U.S. code*, vol. 42, secs. 1971, 1973–1973bb-1 (1988), was meant to address. See Samuel Issacharoff, "Polarized Voting and the Political Process: The Transformation of Voting Rights Jurisprudence," *Michigan Law Review* 90 (1992): 1833, 1838–1853 (tracing the development of voting schemes meant to reward a majority with superordinate representation and racially polarized voting).

103 Voting Rights Act: *U.S. Code*, vol. 42, secs. 1971, 1973–1973bb-1 (1988).

103 packing or fragmentation: See *Voinovich v. Quilter*, 113 S. Ct. 1149, 1155–56 (1993); *Thornburg v. Gingles*, 478 U.S. 30, 55–61 (1986); See Andrew P. Miller and Mark A. Packman, "Amended

Section 2 of the Voting Rights Act: What Is the Intent of the Results Test?," *Emory Law Journal* 36 (1987): 1, 8.

103   racial manipulation . . . is not always easy to detect: It was for this reason that the Voting Rights Act Amendments of 1982 shifted the focus from an intent to a results-based test. Public Law 97–205, sec. 3, 96 Stat. 131, 134 (1982) (codified at *U.S. Code*, vol. 42, sec. 1973(a) [1988]); see Frank R. Parker, "The "Results" Test of Section 2 of the Voting Rights Act: Abandoning the Intent Standard," *Virginia Law Review* 69 (1983): 715, 747–750 (describing congressional debate over the results-based test).

103   "antagonisms that relate to race": *Wright v. Rockefeller,* 376 U.S. 52, 67 (1964) (Douglas, J., dissenting).

104   Bush administration merrily deployed the 1990 census: John E. Yang, "Remapping the Politics of the South: Court Challenges to Minority Districts Are Shifting the Odds for Blacks," *Washington Post,* 16 Apr. 1996, A4.

104   The Supreme Court, . . . has placed states and localities in a dilemma: See *Johnson v. De Grandy,* 114 S. Ct. 2647, 2664 (1994) (O'Connor, J. concurring); and 2666–2667 (Kennedy, J., concurring).

104   The Supreme Court has tried to convince us: Ibid., 2647, 2659, 2661–2662.

105   Justice Sandra Day O'Connor in a concurring opinion: Ibid., 2664 (O'Connor, J., concurring).

105   Justice Anthony Kennedy: Ibid., 2666–2667 (Kennedy, J., concurring).

105   Justices Clarence Thomas and Antonin Scalia: Ibid., 2667 (Thomas, J., dissenting); *Holder v. Hall,* 114 S. Ct. 2581, 2601 (1994) (Thomas, J., concurring).

105   the opinion's opening paragraph: *Johnson v. De Grandy,* 2651 ("No violation of sec. 2 can be found here, where, in spite of continuing discrimination and racial bloc voting, minority voters form effective voting majorities in a number of districts

roughly proportional to the minority voters' respective shares in the voting age population.").

105 "political effectiveness in proportion": Ibid., 2663; 2658.

105 a number of other factors: These factors were:

> The history of voting-related discrimination in the State or political subdivision; the extent to which voting . . . is racially polarized; the extent to which the State or political subdivision has used voting practices or procedures that tend to enhance the opportunity for discrimination against the minority group . . . ; the exclusion of members of the minority group from candidate slating processes; the extent to which minority group members bear the effects of past discrimination in areas such as education, employment, and health, which hinder their ability to participate effectively in the political process; the use of overt or subtle racial appeals in political campaigns; and the extent to which members of the minority group have been elected to public office in the jurisdiction.

Ibid., 2656, n. 9 (quoting *Thornburg v. Gingles*, 478 U.S. 30, 44–45 [1986]). Given the presence of factors other than proportionality, it seems clear that a plan should not be condemned under sec. 2 for failure to satisfy the proportionality principle.

106 to sidestep the case's most volatile question: See Ibid., 2661–2662.

106 come at the other's expense: See *De Grandy v. Wetherell*, 815 F. Supp. 1550, 1578 (N.D. Fla. 1992) (noting that remedies for Hispanics and African Americans were "mutually exclusive"), *aff'd in part, rev'd in part sub nom. Johnson v. De Grandy*, 114 S. Ct. 2647 (1994).

106 Tensions between the groups ran high: Ibid., 1569 (noting a "high degree of tension in Dade County between the African-American population and the Hispanic population"); Larry Rohter, "A Black-Hispanic Struggle over Florida Redistricting," *New York Times*, 30 May 1992, sec. 1, 6 (describing the "ethnic and political tussle between two minority groups of

almost equal size"); see also *Meek v. Metropolitan Dade County*, 985 F.2d 1471, 1481 (11th Cir. 1993) ("The district court found that a 'keen hostility' exists between blacks and hispanics in Dade County").

106   maximum representation . . . would only encourage further conflict: see *Johnson v. De Grandy*, 2663.

106   cumulative voting and nondistrict representation: For a general discussion of such remedies see Lani Guinier, *The Tyranny of the Majority: Fundamental Fairness in Representative Democracy* (New York: Free Press, 1994).

107   a dangerous prescription for New America: Aggregation issues are becoming more important as residential integration creates more multiethnic districts. See T. Alexander Aleinikoff and Samuel Issacharoff, "Race and Redistricting: Drawing Constitutional Lines After *Shaw v. Reno*," *Michigan Law Review* 92 (1993): 588, 635 (describing potential problems of aggregating claims).

107   which minority interests are in agreement: See, e.g., *Latino Political Action Cmte. v. City of Boston*, 784 F.2d 409, 414 (1st Cir. 1986) (noting the difficulty of measuring "cohesiveness" and "polarization" of voters, especially in multicultural communities); *DeBaca v. County of San Diego*, 794 F. Supp. 990, 1000 (S.D. Cal. 1992) (finding insufficient evidence of racially polarized voting in a multicultural setting), *aff'd*, 5 F.3d 535 (9th Cir. 1993).

108   "If district lines are drawn": *Nixon v. Kent County*, 76 F.3d 1381, 1396 (6th Cir. 1996) (en banc).

108   other courts had tacitly approved: See *Bridgeport Coalition for Fair Representation v. City of Bridgeport*, 26 F.3d 271 (2d Cir. 1994); *Badillo v. City of Stockton*, 956 F.2d 884 (9th Cir. 1992); *Concerned Citizens of Hardee County v. Hardee County Bd. of Comm'rs*, 906 F.2d 524 (11th Cir. 1990); *Campos v. City of Baytown*, 840 F.2d 1240 (5th Cir. 1988). Judge Patrick Higgin-

botham wrote a powerful dissent from the denial of rehearing en banc in *Campos. Campos v. City of Baytown*, 849 F.2d 943, 944 (5th Cir. 1988) (Higginbotham, J., dissenting).

108 The Supreme Court has avoided resolving this issue. See *Growe v. Emison*, 507 U.S. 25, 41 (1993).

108 "the language of the Voting Rights Act": *Nixon v. Kent County*, 1393, and 1392 (quoting *League of United Latin Am. Citizens v. Clements*, 999 F.2d 831, 894 (5th Cir. 1993) (Jones, Edith, concurring)). Phrases quoted in the following paragraph come from the same decision.

110 Georgia's congressional redistricting plan: *Miller v. Johnson*, 115 S. Ct. 2475, 2490, 2488 (1995).

110 the Eleventh, dubbed "Sherman's March": Robert A. Branan, "Racial Gerrymandering: How Is It Changing Our Politics?" *Campaigns & Elections*, Apr. 1995.

110 "worlds apart in culture": *Miller v. Johnson*, 2484.

110 "a day of infamy for us": Cal Thomas, "Primaries Show Blacks Can Win without Racial Gerrymandering," *Charlottesville Daily Progress*, 18 July 1996, A6.

111 "Pontius Pilate's conviction of Jesus": Yang, "Remapping the Politics."

111 "to appeal to a larger number": Ibid.

111 "We put together the kind of campaign": Thomas, "Primaries Show Blacks Can Win."

111 North Carolina fashioned a district: *Shaw v. Hunt*, 116 S. Ct. 1894, 1899 (1996) (quoting *Shaw v. Reno*, 509 U.S. 630, 636 [1993]).

111 the Texas legislature employed a computer program: *Bush v. Vera*, 116 S. Ct. 1941, 1953 (1996).

111 "In numerous instances," noted the Supreme Court: Ibid. (quoting *Vera v. Richards*, 861 F. Supp. 1304, 1336 (S.D. Tex. 1994)).

112 "a sacred Mayan bird": Ibid., 1959 (quoting Barone and Ujifusa, *The Almanac of American Politics 1996*, 1335).

112 voters . . . "did not know which district they lived in": Ibid.

112 Six Texas voters challenged District 29: Ibid., 1950–51.

113 "It takes a shortsighted and unauthorized view": *Miller v. Johnson*, 2493–2494.

114 black politicians of both major parties: Such examples demonstrate the capability of Americans to see beyond race even if racial bloc voting continues generally to exist.

114 "I am not your African-American candidate": "New Faces in the House," *New York Times*, 7 Nov. 1996, B3.

115 Representative Bishop not only voted: Yang, "Remapping the Politics."

115 "We've gotten to a point": "Crying Wolf," *Wall Street Journal*, 11 July 1996, A14.

115 Racial gerrymandering is cutting out the middle: See Richard H. Pildes, review of *The Politics of Race: Quiet Revolution in the South*, ed. Chandler Davidson and Bernard Grofman, *Harvard Law Review* 108 (1995): 1359, 1390.

115 "The result in Texas and several other states": Dave McNeely, "Solutions Present Unintended Results," *Austin American-Statesman*, 6 June 1995, A9.

116 "freeze rather than thaw": Abigail M. Thernstrom, *Whose Votes Count?: Affirmative Action and Minority Voting Rights* (Cambridge, Mass.: Harvard University Press, 1987), 242–43 (citing James Blumstein's testimony at the 1982 Senate hearings on the Voting Rights Act Amendments) and (quoting Donald Horowitz's remarks at the 1982 Senate hearings).

116 V. S. Naipaul's account: *Encyclopaedia Britannica*, 15th ed., vol. 29, 721, 784–85.

116 Trinidad's population: V. S. Naipaul, *The Suffrage of Elvira in Three Novels* (New York: Vintage Books, 1982), 173, 186–187, 214–217.

116 "Only the candidate who successfully reached": Thernstrom, *Whose Votes Count?*, 243.

116 Athenian citizens, including recent immigrants: For example, Solon (638–539 B.C.) provided citizenship to those in perpetual exile as well as traders who brought their families to reside in Athens. Plutarch, *The Lives of the Noble Grecians and Romans* (Chicago: Encyclopaedia Britannica, 1952), 73.

116 enrolled in their neighborhood or "deme": Philip Brook Manville, *The Origins of Citizenship in Ancient Athens* (Princeton, N.J.: Princeton University Press, 1990), 188–91. Under Kleisthenes in 508–507 B.C., "the demes . . . were assigned among thirty new *trittyes* based on tripartite division of Attika: city, coast, and inland. Thereafter the *trittyes* were assigned by lot—randomly—to the ten tribes so that each had members from all three areas of Attika." Each tribe contributed fifty members to the Council of 500, which prepared and supervised the business of the Assembly. Ibid., 194.

116 Republican Rome similarly mixed citizens: E. S. Staveley, *Greek and Roman Voting and Elections* (London: Thames and Hudson, 1972), 139; see generally Lily Ross Taylor, *Roman Voting Assemblies: From the Hannibalic War to the Dictatorship of Caesar* (Ann Arbor, Mich.: University of Michigan Press, 1966), 59–83 (describing the history of the thirty-five districts of the *comitia tributa* and the *concilium plebis*).

117 An Athenian law in 451–450 B.C.: Manville, *The Origins of Citizenship*, 24.

117 a quarter of the city's population was sold: Plutarch, *The Lives*, 139–140.

117 "What was the ruin of Sparta and Athens": P. Cornelius Tacitus, *The Annals* (Chicago: Encyclopaedia Britannica, 1952), 106.

118 The Leadership Conference of Civil Rights: Harry A. Ploski and James Williams, *The Negro Almanac: A Reference Work on the African American* (Detroit: Gale Research, 1989), 268.

119 "this court propels America toward a race war": Carl T. Rowan, "The Court Drags Us Toward Race War," *Baltimore Sun*, 3 July 1995, 9A.

119 society tends to conform itself to the baseline: See, e.g., Cass R. Sunstein, "Lochner's Legacy," *Columbia Law Review* 87 (1987): 873. Sunstein argues that if the condition of minorities is seen as an artifact of a previous government baseline of discrimination, then a new baseline, racial assistance, may be necessary to achieve fairness. The pivotal question, however, is normative. We must ask which baseline is best, from a moral and pragmatic standpoint. Perpetuation of a racial baseline, whether or not it seeks to right an imbalance, carries with it so many attendant harms that everyone will be better off under a system in which government neither "discriminates against" nor "favors" particular races.

6: Separatist Entitlements

121 "notic[e] the color-coded aspects": Joel Dreyfuss and Charles Lawrence III, *The Bakke Case: The Politics of Inequality* (New York: Harcourt Brace Jovanovich, 1979), 139–140.

121 racial exclusivity in the upper reaches: See Andrew Hacker, *Two Nations: Black and White, Separate, Hostile, Unequal* (New York: Charles Scribner and Sons 1992), 116–118 (discussing the racial makeup of the private workforce).

122 at the University of California at Berkeley: Dinesh D'Souza, *Illiberal Education: The Politics of Race and Sex on Campus* (New York: Free Press, 1991), 3.

122 the celebrated case of Cheryl Hopwood: David G. Savage, "Bakke II Case Renews Debate on Admissions," *Los Angeles Times*, 30 July 1995.

122 "sorted in folders color-coded": Editorial, "A Color-Blind Constitution," *Wall Street Journal*, 22 Mar. 1996.

122 racially coded groups: The University of Texas grouped all nonpreferred minorities with its white applicants.

122 each folder's Texas Index: *Hopwood v. Texas*, 78 F.3d 932, 935 (5th Cir. 1996).

123 In 1992, white folders were presumptively admitted: *Hopwood v. Texas*, 861 F. Supp. 551, 561–562 (W.D. Tex. 1994).

123 Hopwood was not offered admission: Claire Cooper, "School Integration Faces New Challenges in Court," *San Francisco Examiner*, 1 Aug. 1994, A1. Cheryl Hopwood's case was not alone. Twelve other white folders with TI scores of 200 or more were also denied admission. Savage, "Bakke II Case."

123 forty black folders and fifty-two brown folders: Savage, "Bakke II Case"; *Hopwood v. Texas*, 78 F.3d, 937 n. 9; Plaintiffs' Trial Exhibits from Hopwood.

123 a moving human story of struggle and determination: Savage, "Bakke II Case"; Laurel Shaper Walters, "Lawsuit in Texas Turns Racial Justice on Its Head," *Christian Science Monitor*, 1 Aug. 1994, 1; Cooper, "School Integration."

124 "towers and spires of Princeton": F. Scott Fitzgerald, *This Side of Paradise* (London: Cambridge University Press, 1995), 260.

124 she completed her bachelor's degree: *Hopwood v. Texas*, 861 F. Supp., 564.

124 Tara was born with a rare muscle disease: Terrence Stutz, "UT Minority Enrollment Tested by Suit," *Dallas Morning News*, 14 Oct. 1995, 1A.

124 Hopwood had to balance her professional career: Pedro E. Ponce, "Affirmative Action's Reluctant New Icon," *Legal Times*, 8 Apr. 1996.

125 " 'They dinged Sac State' ": Cooper, "School Integration."

125 the court upheld the university's use of race: *Hopwood v. Texas*, 861 F. Supp., 551–52.

125 "the University of Texas School of Law": *Hopwood v. Texas*, 78 F.3d, 962, 947–48, 946 (quoting Richard A. Posner, "The

DeFunis Case and the Constitutionality of Preferential Treatment of Racial Minorities," *Supreme Court Review* (1974): 12.

126 "students from different backgrounds came to college": D'Souza, *Illiberal Education*, 46–47.

126 separate dormitories: See, e.g., Jordana Shakoor, "Segregated OSU Dorm Is Bad Idea," *Columbus Dispatch*, 24 June 1992, 9A.

126 specialized racial curriculums: See, e.g., Felix Sanchez, "Minorities at A&M Try to Tackle Racial Insensitivity," *Houston Post*, 10 Nov. 1994, A33.

126 white student unions: Robin Wilson, "New White Student Unions on Some Campuses Are Sparking Outrage and Worry," *Chronicle of Higher Education*, 18 Apr. 1990, A1; In Brief, "White Pride Group Recognized by Temple U," *Chronicle of Higher Education*, 14 Dec. 1988, A2.

126 "The traditional ideal of the university:" Gertrude Himmelfarb, "What to Do about Education 1: The Universities," *Commentary*, Oct. 1994, 21.

127 At the University of Virginia: Ian Zack, "UVa's 'Invisible Hand' Builds New Walls as Others Tumble," *Charlottesville Daily Progress*, 31 July 1995, A1.

127 Errol Smith, a black entrepreneur from Los Angeles: Steve Berg, "Simmering Preferences Controversy Nears a Boil," *Star Tribune*, 12 Mar. 1995, 1A.

128 Ethnic Mexicans who participated on the Texas side: See John Knaggs, "Overlooked Origins of Texas Independence," *Austin American-Statesman*, 5 Mar. 1994, A11.

129 "a tradition of exclusionary and distorted history": Scott W. Wright, "Independence Day Draws Supporters, Protesters at UT," *Austin American-Statesman*, 3 Mar. 1995, B1 (quoting Hispanic student group).

129 "In the United States today": Paul Craig Roberts and Lawrence M. Stratton, *The New Color Line* (Washington, D.C.: Regnery, 1995), iii–iv.

130 Justice Blackmun's paradoxical assertion: *Regents of Univ. of Cal. v. Bakke*, 438 U.S. 265, 407 (1978) (Blackmun, J., concurring).

131 "efforts should be made": Quoted in *Swann v. Charlotte-Mecklenburg Board of Education*, 402 U.S. 1, 23 (1971).

131 Supreme Court cast a long shadow: *Griggs v. Duke Power Co.*, 401 U.S. 424.

131 racial balance in an employer's craft training: *United Steelworkers of America v. Weber*, 443 U.S. 193.

131 Court began to pull back: *Wards Cove Packing Co. v. Atonio*, 490 U.S. 642 (1989).

131 " 'they are safer in hiring' ": Roberts and Stratton, *The New Color Line*, 113 (quoting Irving M. Geslewitz).

131 old-fashioned guilt: See T. Alexander Aleinikoff, "A Case for Race-Consciousness," *Columbia Law Review* 91 (1991): 1060, 1108–10 (stating that in many situations "race-consciousness can be part of the struggle against racism").

131 race-neutral plans ignore: e.g., Charles R. Lawrence III, "The Id, the Ego, and Equal Protection: Reckoning with Unconscious Racism," *Stanford Law Review* 39 (1987): 317.

132 "The black and Mexican-American applicants": Terry Eastland, *Ending Affirmative Action: The Case for Colorblind Justice* (New York: Basic Books, 1996), 9.

132 racial imbalances can, and do, result: See, e.g., Linda Chavez, *Out of the Barrio: Toward a New Politics of Hispanic Assimilation* (New York: Basic Books, 1991), 109. For example, "Hispanics are more likely than other Americans to believe that the demands and needs of the family should take precedence over those of the individual. . . . [This] runs counter to the dominant culture of individualism characteristic of American life and may even impede individual success. This perhaps explains why so many young Hispanics drop out of school to take jobs, a decision that has some immediate financial benefits for the family but is detrimental to the individual in the long run."

133 "hard work and cultivated taste": D'Souza, *Illiberal Education*, 53.

133 "A university may properly favor": *Hopwood v. Texas*, 78 F. 3d, 946.

134 "racial preference means categorical representation": Michael Lind, *The Next American Nation: The New Nationalism and the Fourth American Revolution* (New York: Free Press, 1995), 165.

134 losers in race-based decisions: See *Johnson v. Transportation Agency, Santa Clara County*, 480 U.S., 677 (1987) (Scalia, J., dissenting) (arguing that affirmative action in the employment context harms less-advantaged members of nonpreferred groups); see also Herman Belz, *Equality Transformed: A Quarter-Century of Affirmative Action* (New Brunswick, N.J.: Transaction Publishers, 1991), 246 (claiming that affirmative action benefits go to those who need them least).

134 Court-ordered student busing: See U.S. Commission on Civil Rights, *Fulfilling the Letter and Spirit of the Law: Desegregation of the Nation's Public Schools*, (Washington, D.C.: U.S. Commission on Civil Rights, 1976), 66–68, 109–11 (describing the busing experiences of twenty-nine school districts).

135 "has not been merely repealed": *Johnson v. Transportation Agency* 480 U.S. 677 (Scalia, J., dissenting).

135 a race-neutral concept of disadvantage: See, e.g., Don Munro, Note, "The Continuing Evolution of Affirmative Action Under Title VII: New Directions After the Civil Rights Act of 1991," *Virginia Law Review* 81 (1995): 565, 606–608 (proposing affirmative action in employment based on economic status).

136 " 'Affirmative' because government authority": Jack Kemp, "Affirmative Action: The 'Radical Republican' Example," *Washington Post*, 6 Aug. 1995, C9.

136 "There appears to be a societal consensus": Richard Kahlenberg, "Class, Not Race: An Affirmative Action That Works," *New Republic*, 3 Apr. 1995, 21.

137 measures are only temporary: Cf. George A. Rutherglen, "After Affirmative Action: Conditions and Consequences of Ending Preferences in Employment," *University of Illinois Law Review* (1992): 339, 343.

137 "If affirmative action is abolished": Berg, "Simmering Preferences Controversy."

137 goals will be phased out: See, e.g., *Brotherhood of Midwest Guardians v. City of Omaha*, 9 F.3d 677, 678 (8th Cir. 1993) (interpreting a consent decree that was written to expire when its goals were met); *United States v. City of Miami*, 2 F.3d 1497, 1500 (11th Cir. 1993) (setting forth a consent decree's expiration provisions).

137 employers and educational institutions: See *Johnson v. Transportation Agency*, 480 U.S., 676 (Scalia, J., dissenting) ("After today's decision the *failure* to engage in reverse discrimination is economic folly . . . wherever the cost of anticipated Title VII litigation exceeds the cost of hiring less capable . . . workers.").

138 The categories used by government: Lind, *The Next American Nation*, 124–25.

138 "Before the affirmative action age": Chavez, *Out of the Barrio*, 62.

138 a Pan-Hispanic and Pan-Asian identity: Ibid.; Lind, *The Next American Nation*, 124–25.

138 race as *the* great social determinant: See generally Terry Eastland and William J. Bennett, *Counting by Race: Equality from the Founding Fathers to* Bakke *and* Weber (New York: Basic Books, 1979), 165–68 (discussing some of the effects racial preferences have on people who benefit from them).

138 a stake in racially oriented perspectives: See, e.g., Berg, "Simmering Preferences Controversy."

138 When the decisions of public institutions turn on race: See Alexander M. Bickel, *The Morality of Consent* (New Haven: Yale University Press, 1975), 133 (arguing against racial quotas "in a

society desperately striving for an equality that will make race irrelevant").

138 *Brown*, of course, held out quite a different vision: *Brown v. Board of Educ.*, 347 U.S. 483, 493–494 (1954).

138 "many Americans seemed to have accepted": Eastland and Bennett, *Counting by Race*, 10.

139 Advocates of those preferences will point: See Derrick Bell, "The Supreme Court, 1984 Term—Foreword: The Civil Rights Chronicles," *Harvard Law Review* 99 (1985): 4, 7–12 ("The real problem of race in America is the unreconciled contradiction between our commitment to equality and our preservation of the subordinate status of blacks").

139 connotations of the word "diversity": See Sheila Foster, "Difference and Equality: A Critical Assessment of the Concept of 'Diversity,' " *Wisconsin Law Review* (1993): 105, 109–12 (advocating a heterogeneous definition of diversity).

139 The apparent commonality of interests among minorities: See Peter H. Schuck, "The Evolving Civil Rights Movement: Old Civil Rights and New Immigration," *Current*, Jan. 1994, 13–14 (discussing the challenges increasing ethnic diversity poses for civil rights coalitions).

140 In San Francisco, as Chinese Americans grew: Lawrence J. Siskind, "San Francisco's Separate and Unequal Public Schools," *Wall Street Journal* 13 July 1994, A15.

140 Chinese American students had to present stronger credentials: Debra Saunders, "Shameful Injustice in Our Schools: When Will We Stop Clipping Children's Wings in the Name of 'Equality'?," *Atlanta Journal-Constitution*, 22 July 1994, A14; Siskind, "Unequal Public Schools"; Venise Wagner, "S.F. Sued Over School Admissions Quotas," *San Francisco Examiner*, 11 July 1994, A1.

140 Wong became a class action plaintiff: Berg, "Simmering Preferences Controversy."

140   "forty years after *Brown*": Siskind, "Unequal Public Schools."

141   the phrase "Angry Yellow Men": Kenneth Lee, "Angry Yellow Men," *New Republic*, 9 Sept. 1996, 11 ("In California, where Asians represent 10 percent of the population, backers of . . . [the 1996] California Civil Rights Initiative have made special efforts to woo the Angry Yellow Male vote").

141   "Like the vague assertion of societal discrimination": *Metro Broadcasting v. FCC*, 497 U.S. 547, 614 (1990) (O'Connor, J., dissenting).

142   "Asian head count": Dan Beyers, "A Tangle over Diversity: Montgomery Won't Let Two Asian Girls Change Schools," *Washington Post*, 22 Aug. 1995, A1.

142   "For the past five years": Jeffrey Rosen, "The Day the Quotas Died," *New Republic*, 22 Apr. 1996, 26.

143   blacks threatened to recall San Francisco's Board of Education: Louis Freedberg, "Minority vs. Minority in Academia," *San Francisco Chronicle*, 10 Apr. 1992, A1.

143   who is a member of what group: See, e.g. James O'Byrne, "Race Divides, Does Damage," *New Orleans Times-Picayune*, 16 Aug. 1993, A1 (noting the arbitrariness of racial classifications).

143   more than three million interracial married couples: Gary Younger, "Multiracial Citizens Divided on Idea of Separate Census Classification," *Washington Post*, 19 July 1996, A3.

144   "The child of a black and white relationship": Ibid.

144   The Eleventh Circuit confronted the classification problem: *Peightal v. Metropolitan Dade County*, 26 F.3d 1545, 1548–49, 1551–52, 1559–61, n. 25. (11th Cir. 1994).

145   "already boosts costs and headaches for American industry": Deroy Murdock, "The Government Ponders Ways of Counting by Race," *Washington Times*, 7 July 1994, A19.

146   apartheid: For a discussion of South Africa's apartheid-era racial categories, see Johan D. van der Vyver, "Constitutional Options for Post-Apartheid South Africa," *Emory Law Journal* 40 (1991): 745, 746–748.

147   Claims to racial entitlements: See, e.g., Myriam Marquez, "Diversity—and Discrimination—Isn't Just a Black-White Issue," *Orlando Sentinel*, 8 Mar. 1993, A8 (describing "growing friction" between minorities in Florida over job entitlements).

148   *Dred Scott v. Sanford:* 60 U.S. 303 (1857); Ronald D. Rotunda and John E. Nowak, *Treatise on Constitutional Law* (St. Paul, Minn.: West Publishing, 1992), 72.

148   Justice John Marshall Harlan's famous dissent: *Plessy v. Ferguson,* 163 U.S. 537, 559 (1896) (Harlan, J., dissenting).

148   Martin Luther King's celebrated speech: Anthony Lewis, *Portrait of a Decade: The Second American Revolution* (New York: Bantam Books, 1965), 219.

7: Separatist Education

151   Separatist education presents: Issues of separatist education, such as bilingual programs, are in fact closely linked to the questions of affirmative action in education discussed in the preceding chapter. Entitlement issues, however, are primarily manifestations of "power" separatism, whereas the issues discussed in this section include elements of "pride" separatism.

151   interracial friendships: Willie Morris, *Yazoo: Integration in a Deep Southern Town* (New York: Harper's Magazine Press, 1971); J. Harvie Wilkinson III, *From* Brown *to* Bakke: *The Supreme Court and School Integration: 1954–1978* (New York: Oxford University Press, 1979), 42–44.

151   Separatist educational arrangements: See, e.g., Susan Chira, "Rethinking Deliberately Segregated Schools," *New York Times,* 11 July 1983, sec. 4, 20 (listing examples of separatist proposals ranging from all-black schools in Detroit to Hasidic schools in New York).

151 "remember what the intent was": Rene Sanchez, "Academies Are Final Bastions of Separateness," *Washington Post*, 17 July 1996, A1.

152 "obsession with differences": Arthur M. Schlesinger Jr., *The Disuniting of America: Reflections on a Multicultural Society* (New York: Norton, 1992), 74, 93–99.

152 historically black colleges: See *United States v. Fordice*, 112 S. Ct. 2727 (1992).

152 "avoid the confusion": Rosalie Pedalino Porter, *Forked Tongue: The Politics of Bilingual Education* (New York: Basic Books, 1990), 60.

152 America has assimilated: Linda Chavez, *Out of the Barrio: Toward a New Politics of Hispanic Assimilation* (New York: Basic Books, 1991), 87 (citing Joshua Fishman et al., *Language Loyalty in the United States* [The Hague: Mouton, 1966]).

152 At Los Angeles's Eastman Avenue School: Amy Pyle, "Pressure Grows to Reform Bilingual Education in State," *Los Angeles Times*, 22 May 1995, A1.

153 Hispanic students in Boston: Chavez, *Out of the Barrio*, 35.

153 A New York study: Edna Negron, "Will Children Suffer?" *Newsday*, 21 Mar. 1995, A12.

153 "We have built a system": Pyle, "Pressure Grows."

153 young Hispanics are placed: Chavez, *Out of the Barrio*, 29, 37; Mark Zambrano and Jean Latz Griffin, "City Becomes a Babel of Bilingual Education," *Chicago Tribune*, 30 Mar. 1986, C1; Mark Zambrano and Jean Latz Griffin, "Some Schools Can't Translate Bilingual," *Chicago Tribune*, 31 Mar. 1986, C1.

153 "Puerto Rican boy": Cynthia Gorney, "For Teachers, 10 Years of Trial and Error: Bilingual Programs Dismay Advocates, Critics," *Washington Post*, 8 July 1985, A1.

154 "At the same time": Lori Silver, "Education Dept. Shifts, Favors Bilingual Education," *Los Angeles Times*, 26 Aug. 1989, 1.

154   after-school and/or weekend programs: Chavez, *Out of the Barrio*, 164. Chavez also makes the point that follows, that there are many cultural traditions within the Hispanic ethnic group.

154   more than 2.3 million students: U.S. General Accounting Office, *Limited English Proficiency—A Growing and Costly Educational Challenge Facing Many School Districts* (1994) (Rept. # GAO/HEHS-94-38).

155   "90 teachers": Linda Chavez, "Bilingual Education Gobbles Up Kids, Taxes," *USA Today*, 15 June 1994, 15A.

156   Congress initially promoted: But see Rachel F. Moran, "The Politics of Discretion: Federal Intervention in Bilingual Education," *California Law Review* 76 (1988): 1249, 1263 (arguing that the legislative history reveals a debate over whether the Bilingual Education Act of 1968 was intended to "promote assimilation" or to "foster pluralism").

156   1967 Bilingual Education Act: Public Law No. 90–247, secs. 701–703, 81 Stat. 783, 816–20 (current version at *U.S. Code*, vol. 20, secs. 3281–3341 (1988)).

156   Recodified in 1988: *U.S. Code*, vol. 20, sec. 3291(a) (emphasis added); 3301–3307; 3321–3325; 3282(a) (8); 3382(a)(12); 3283(a)(4)(B). See also *U.S. Code*, vol. 20, sec. 3283(a)(4)(C)-(D); see also U.S. House H.R. Rep. No. 1137, 95th Cong., 2d sess. 86 (1978) ("Children of limited English can learn from their peers, and by the same token English-speaking children can benefit from contact with other languages and cultures").

157   Supreme Court's 1974 decision: *Lau v. Nichols*, 414 U.S. 563 (1974). On page 568, the Court quoted federal guidelines: " 'Any ability grouping or tracking system employed by the school system to deal with the special language skill needs of national origin-minority group children must be designed to meet such language skill needs as soon as possible and must not operate as an educational dead end or permanent track' " (quoting 35 Fed. Reg. 11,595 (1970)).

157 similar standards: See, e.g., *De La Cruz v. Tormey*, 582 F.2d 45, 51–52 (9th Cir. 1978), *cert. denied*, 441 U.S. 965 (1979); cf. *New Mexico Ass'n for Retarded Citizens v. New Mexico*, 678 F.2d 847, 853 (10th Cir. 1982); *Lloyd v. Regional Transp. Auth.*, 548 F.2d 1277, 1280–84 (7th Cir. 1977).

157 "provide for the transition": *Keyes v. School Dist. No. 1*, 521 F.2d 465, 482 (10th Cir. 1975), *cert. denied*, 423 U.S. 1066 (1976).

157 plans that impose unwarranted segregation: See, e.g., *Castaneda v. Pickard*, 648 F.2d 989, 998 n. 4 (5th Cir. 1981) (stressing the need for transitional programs with minimization of segregation); *Keyes v. School Dist. No. 1*, 482 (emphasizing that Colorado's policy is to help non-English-speaking children make the transition to English); *People Who Care v. Rockford Bd. of Educ.*, 851 F. Supp. 905, 929 (N.D. Ill. 1994) ("The goal of these types of language remediation programs is to integration Spanish-speaking students into English language classrooms. They should not be used to isolate students") (citation omitted).

157 Courts have invalidated: *Cintron v. Brentwood Union Free Sch. Dist.*, 455 F. Supp. 57, 64 (E.D.N.Y. 1978).

157 permanent programming: See Mary B. W. Tabor, "Closing of Bilingual School Is Denounced in Bronx," *New York Times*, 2 Nov. 1991, sec. 1, 27 (describing Hispanic parents' protests against integrating language-minority children with black students despite continuing bilingual education); see also *Duran v. Center Consol. Sch. Dist.*, No. 85-F-2736, slip op. exh. A at 4-17 (D. Colo. Oct. 2, 1986) (setting out settlement plan designed to maintain permanent bilingual education).

157 "The promotion of cultural differences": William A. Henry III, "Against a Confusion of Tongues," *Time*, 13 June 1983, 30.

157 In Los Angeles: Rosalie Pedalino Porter, "Language Trap: No English, No Future," *Washington Post*, 22 Apr. 1990, B3.

157 in New York: Edna Negron, "Speaking Well of Bilingual Education," *Newsday*, 18 Mar. 1990, 21.

158   New Jersey even allowed: Porter, "Language Trap."

158   "is based on early and extended": Porter, *Forked Tongue*, 25.

158   a lesson on colors: Ibid., 21. The following incident is described on the same page.

159   A study published in October 1994: Barbara Mujica, "To Succeed, Learn in English," *Washington Post*, 20 Sept. 1995, A19.

160   "I can remember taking the train": Anne Swardson, "Quebec's Separatist Heart: Along the Saguenay, Narrow Defeat Presages Victory Next Time," *Washington Post*, 10 Nov. 1995, A31.

160   The argument that Quebec depends: See Anne Swardson, "Money Issues Chip at Quebec Separatist Vote," *Washington Post*, 7 Oct. 1995, A26.

160   "We are not sheep": Swardson, "Quebec's Separatist Heart."

160   "a fragile island": Charles Trueheart, "Sovereignty at Stake, Enduring Grievances Return Quebec to Brink," *Washington Post*, 29 Oct. 1995, A33.

160   "It's a fundamental question": Swardson, "Quebec's Separatist Heart."

161   One can vote in Spanish: Thomas Weyr, *Hispanic U.S.A.: Breaking the Melting Pot* (New York: Harper and Row, 1988), 8.

161   Modesto Maidique: Frank M. Lowrey, IV, Comment, "Through the Looking Glass: Linguistic Separatism and National Unity," *Emory Law Journal* 41 (1992): 223, 310.

162   "We cannot assimilate": Chavez, *Out of the Barrio*, 1.

162   "live closer to their countries of origin": Gregory Rodriguez, "The Browning of California," *New Republic*, 2 Sept. 1996, 18.

162   "manipulated anti-Yankee sentiment": Ibid.

162   "has become a Hispanic institution": Weyr, *Hispanic U.S.A.*, 9.

164   "We're not in an industrial age": Ellen Nakashima, "A First Generation's Second Language," *Washington Post*, 14 May 1996, A1.

165 "mandated as the medium of instruction": Porter, *Forked Tongue*, 162.

165 "language of empowerment": See Porter, "Language Trap."

165 legally and pedagogically sound: See Moran, "The Politics of Discretion," 1259–1262 (discussing the arguments offered by advocacy groups, parents, community leaders, and educators regarding bilingual education and the implementation of the act).

166 a Berkeley school district language program: *Teresa P. v. Berkeley Unified Sch. Dist.*, 724 F. Supp. 698, 700 (N.D. Cal. 1989).

166 a suspect, or specially protected, class: See Note, "'Official English': Federal Limits on Efforts to Curtail Bilingual Services in the States," *Harvard Law Review* 100 (1987): 1345, 1353–56 (examining language minorities as a quasi-suspect class); cf. Mari J. Matsuda, "Voices of America: Accent, Antidiscrimination Law, and a Jurisprudence for the Last Reconstruction," *Yale Law Journal* 100 (1991): 1329, 1398–1400 (discussing the social, civil rights, and equal protection implications of accents).

166 monolingualism may become increasingly immutable: See Antonio J. Califa, "Declaring English the Official Language: Prejudice Spoken Here," *Harvard Civil Rights—Civil Liberties Law Review* 24 (1989): 293, 335 n. 262 ("For immigrants of a certain age, language may in fact be an immutable characteristic").

167 English Empowerment Act: John E. Yang, "House Votes English as Official U.S. Government Language for First Time," *Washington Post*, 2 Aug. 1996, A10.

167 Approximately eighteen states: *Yniguez v. Arizonans for Official English*, 69 F.3d 920, 927, n. 11 (9th Cir. 1995) (en banc).

167 "the official language of the state of Arizona": Ibid., 924.

168 A six-member majority: Ibid., 920. Quotations from the decision that follows appear at 932, 957, 956, 958, and 961.

169 a fight against discrimination: See, e.g., *Diaz v. San Jose Unified Sch. Dist.*, 633 F. Supp. 808, 809, 826–827 (N.D. Cal. 1985).

169 to promote separatist agendas: See, e.g., *Castaneda v. Pickard*, 648 F.2d 989, 1006–1007 (5th Cir. 1981) (rejecting plaintiff's argument that administrative agency's "*Lau* guidelines" measured the sufficiency of the school district's language program); *Guadalupe Org., Inc. v. Tempe Elementary Sch. Dist.*, 587 F.2d 1022, 1030 (9th Cir. 1978) (holding that schools providing transitional bilingual programs are not obligated to offer further separate, permanent bilingual-bicultural education); *Rios v. Read*, 480 F. Supp. 14, 23 (E.D.N.Y. 1978) (concluding that the district is required to establish an adequate transitional program but "is not obligated to offer a program of indefinite duration for instruction in Spanish art and culture"). When bilingual programs have exceeded their transitional purpose, some courts have invalidated them. See *Cintron v. Brentwood Union Free Sch. Dist.*, 455 F. Supp. 57, 63 (E.D.N.Y. 1978).

169 1975 amendments to the Voting Rights Act: James Crawford, *Hold Your Tongue: Bilingualism and the Politics of "English Only"* 192–96 (Reading, Mass.: Addison-Wesley, 1992). A bill entitled the English Empowerment Act of 1996, which passed in the House of Representatives by a vote of 259 to 169, would repeal this requirement. Yang, "House Votes English."

169 "Dependence on the home language": Larry Rohter, "The Politics of Bilingualism," *New York Times*, 10 Nov. 1985, sec. 12, 46.

170 the power to appoint an interpreter: *U.S. Code*, vol. 28, secs. 1827–1828; *U.S. Code*, vol. 18, sec. 3006A(e); *Federal Rules of Civil Procedure* 43(f); *Federal Rules of Criminal Procedure* 28.

170 to serve on juries: A federal judge may disqualify a potential juror who "is unable to speak the English language." *U.S. Code* vol. 18, sec. 1865(b)(3).

170 "The Canadian experience": See Lowrey, 315.

171 "language ghettos in school": Mujica, "To Succeed."

171 Juarez High School in Chicago: Zambrano and Griffin, "Some Schools Can't."

171   "express the wants of business": Alexis de Tocqueville, *Democracy in America* ed. Henry Steele Commager, trans. Henry Reece (London: Oxford University Press, 1953).

8: Separatist Speech

174   "inappropriate laughter": Nat Hentoff, "The Final Nail in the Coffin of College Speech Codes," *San Diego Union-Tribune*, 14 May 1995, G1; Todd Ackerman, "Decision Could Kill College Speech Codes," *Houston Chronicle*, 28 June 1992, A1; Katherine Farrish, "UConn Gives Up on Ban of Hate Words," *The Hartford Courant*, 20 Feb. 1993, B1.

174   "conspicuous exclusion of students": Jerry Adler et al., "Taking Offense," *Newsweek*, 24 Dec. 1990, 48.

174   "any behavior, verbal or physical": *Doe v. University of Mich.*, 721 F. Supp. 852, 856 (E.D. Mich. 1989) (citing the Policy on Discrimination and Discriminatory Harassment of Students in the University Environment of the University of Michigan at Ann Arbor); "Free Speech on Campus," *The Hartford Courant*, 14 Feb. 1994, B8 (discussing Wesleyan University's code, adopted in 1990, that bars "any statement or act that is intended to injure, insult or stigmatize a person or group because of race").

174   "serious comments": *Doe v. University of Mich.*, 866.

174   "behavior that subjects an individual": *Dambrot v. Central Mich. Univ.*, 55 F.3d 1177, 1182 (6th Cir. 1995) (quoting Central Michigan University discriminatory harassment policy) (alteration in original).

174   "addressed directly to the individual": Nadine Strossen, "Regulating Racist Speech on Campus: A Modest Proposal?," *Duke Law Journal* (1990): 484, 524 (quoting Stanford University, Fundamental Standard Interpretation: Free Expression and Discriminatory Harassment (June 1990)).

175   "You have to let students say": Adler, "Taking Offense" (quoting sociologist Howard Ehrlich).

175   malicious falsehood: *New York Times v. Sullivan*, 376 U.S. 254, 279–80 (1964).

175   racially prejudiced remarks: *U.S. Code* vol. 42, sec. 2000e et seq.; *Snell v. Suffolk County*, 611 F. Supp. 521, 524-25 (E.D.N.Y. 1985) (including verbal abuse as part of a "racially hostile environment"), *aff'd*, 782 F.2d 1094 (2d. Cir. 1986).

175   suspension or expulsion: *Doe v. University of Mich.*, 857.

175   Speech codes: An avalanche of commentary debates the pros and cons of speech codes. Dinesh D'Souza, *Illiberal Education: The Politics of Race and Sex on Campus* (New York: Free Press, 1991); Nat Hentoff, *Free Speech for Me—But Not for Thee: How the American Left and Right Relentlessly Censor Each Other* (New York: Harper Perennial, 1992); Catherine A. MacKinnon, *Only Words* (New York: HarperCollins, 1993); Jonathan Rauch, *Kindly Inquisitors: The New Attacks on Free Thought* (Chicago: University of Chicago Press, 1993); William S. Alexander, "Regulating Speech on Campus: A Plea for Tolerance," *Wake Forest Law Review* 26 (1991): 1349; Jeanne M. Craddock, " 'Words that Injure; Laws that Silence:' Campus Hate Speech Codes and the Threat to American Education," *Florida State University Law Review* 22 (1995): 1047; Richard Delgado, "Words that Wound: A Tort Action for Racial Insults, Epithets, and Name Calling," *Harvard Civil Rights—Civil Liberties Law Review* 17 (1982): 133; Charles Lawrence III, "If He Hollers Let Him Go: Regulating Racist Speech on Campus," *Duke Law Journal* (1990): 431; Frederick M. Lawrence, "Resolving the Hate Crimes/Hate Speech Paradox: Punishing Bias Crimes and Protecting Racist Speech," *Notre Dame Law Review* 68 (1993): 673; Mari J. Matsuda, "Public Response to Racist Speech: Considering the Victim's Story," *Michigan Law Review* 87 (1989): 2320.

175   cloudy terms: Strossen, "Regulating Racist Speech," 529.

176   Courts have understood: *Dambrot v. Central Michigan University*, 55 F.3d 1177 (6th Cir. 1995) (Central Michigan University discriminatory harassment policy facially unconstitutional); *UWM*

Post v. Board of Regents, 774 F. Supp. 1163 (E.D. Wis. 1991) (University of Wisconsin hate speech code unconstitutional); *Doe v. Univ. of Mich.*, 721 F. Supp. 852 (E.D. Mich. 1989) (University of Michigan discriminatory harassment policy unconstitutional); see also *Iota Xi Chapter v. George Mason Univ.*, 993 F.2d 386 (4th Cir. 1993) (upholding district court declaratory judgment on First Amendment grounds against George Mason University's sanction of fraternity for contest with racial and sexual overtones); Bill Workman, "Stanford Won't Appeal Ruling on Anti-Hate Speech Rule," *San Francisco Chronicle*, 10 Mar. 1995, A11 (Stanford hate speech code invalidated).

176   "[hate speech] contributes": Richard Delgado and Jean Stefancic, "Controls on Hate Speech Are Not Censorship," *Washington Post*, 13 Nov. 1993, A23.

176   the First Amendment, to these proponents, is subverted: Lawrence, "If He Hollers," 452 ("Racial insults are undeserving of first amendment protection because the perpetrator's intention is not to discover truth or initiate dialogue but to injure the victim") (footnote omitted).

176   restrictive speech laws in the past: See, e.g., *Alien Act of June 25, 1798*, 1 Stat. 570; *Sedition Act of July 14, 1798*, 1 Stat. 596; *Schenck v. United States*, 249 U.S. 47 (1919) (upholding conviction for conspiracy to violate the Espionage Act of 1917); *Abrams v. United States*, 250 U.S. 616 (1919) (same); *Gitlow v. New York*, 268 U.S. 652 (1925) (upholding conviction under New York criminal anarchy statute); *Whitney v. California*, 274 U.S. 357 (1972) (affirming conviction under California Criminal Syndicalism Act).

177   Censorship thus relieves society: See Lawrence, "If He Hollers," 435–436.

177   "People . . . believe [in racist ideas]": Hentoff, *Free Speech*, 102 (quoting Roy Innis of the Congress of Racial Equality).

177   "things you wouldn't want to talk about": Louis Freedberg, "College Controversy: A Campus Fear of Speaking Freely," *San Francisco Chronicle*, 30 Oct. 1991, A1.

177 State University of New York at Buffalo: Hentoff, *Free Speech*, 155–156.

178 law professor at Florida State University: Craddock, "Words that Injure," 1054 n. 44.

178 at the University of Michigan: *Doe v. University of Mich.*, 865–66; Hentoff, *Free Speech*, 178–179.

178 "On campus after campus": Hentoff, *Free Speech*, 153.

179 "When it reaches the point": Freedberg, (quoting Kaydee Culbertson, co-chair of Stanford's Native American Student Association).

179 "the biggest tragedy": Clarence Page, *Showing My Color: Impolite Essays on Race and Identity* (New York: HarperCollins, 1996), 17, 28.

179 "integration fatigue": Ibid., 31–33.

180 The American Bar Association: "ABA Leaders Endorse Affirmative Action but Spin Wheel on Internal Governance," *United States Law Week* (15 Aug. 1995), 2096; Nat Hentoff, "Speech Police for Lawyers," *Washington Post*, 23 Aug. 1995, A23; (reporting that ABA ethics counsel agreed that lawyer who argued in favor of the elimination of welfare because its recipients were lazy would violate the adopted resolution). See also Laura Duncan, "Call for Prohibition on Lawyer Bias, One of Few Hot Issues at ABA Meeting, Put Aside for Year," *Chicago Daily Law Bulletin*, 4 Feb. 1994, 1.

9: The Future of New America

186 (the largest percentage of Hispanic Americans): "Minority Population Growth," *Minority Markets Alert*, July 1991 (Hispanics comprise 38 percent of New Mexico's total population).

187 our northern neighbor's struggle: Roger Gibbins, "The Impact of the American Constitution on Contemporary Canadian Politics," in *The Canadian and American Constitutions in Comparative Perspective*, ed. Marian C. McKenna (Calgary, Canada: University of Calgary Press, 1993), 135.

188 Canada admits 220,000 new immigrants: *Canadian Global Almanac 1996*, (Toronto: Macmillan Canada), 50; *Canada Yearbook 1994* (Ottawa: Census and Statistics Office), 86.

188 The Act for the Preservation and Enhancement of Multiculturalism in Canada: *Revised Statutes of Canada* 1985, c. 24 (4th Supp.), sec. 3(1)(a) (1988).

188 $30 million annually: Neil Bissoondath, *Selling Illusions: The Cult of Multiculturalism in Canada* (Toronto: Penguin, 1994), 7.

189 "Multiculturalism . . . has heightened our differences": Ibid., 192.

189 no "election in 30 years": Michael Rose, "The Canada Vote," *Maclean's*, 25 Sept. 1989, 18.

189 Constitution Act of 1982: Gibbins, "American Constitution," 142; Peter H. Russell, "Can the Canadians Be a Sovereign People?," in *The Canadian and American Constitutions*, 197.

189 The Meech Lake Accord: Gibbins, "American Constitution," 142.

189 The accord offered Quebec: Max Nemni, "Ethnic Nationalism and the Destabilization of the Canadian Federation," in *Evaluating Federal Systems*, ed. Bertus De Villiers, (Dordrecht, Netherlands: Martinus Nijhoff Publishers, 1994), 152; Alain G. Gagnon, "Quebec-Canada Relations: The Engineering of Constitutional Arrangements," in *Canadian Federalism: Past, Present and Future*, ed. Michael Burgess (Leicester, England: Leicester University Press, 1990), 109.

189 "distinct society": Gagnon, "Quebec-Canada Relations," 109.

189 English-speaking Canada felt: Russell, "A Sovereign People?" 199 (Accord seen in English Canada "as a total yielding to the demands of French Quebec.")

189 believed that the accord fell short: Gagnon, "Quebec-Canada Relations," 110.

190 The Court held that Quebec's law: "Judges' Gambit, French Defence," *Economist*, 24 Dec. 1988, 52.

190 the Quebec government invoked a provision: Bruce Wallace and Ross Laver, "War Over Words," *Maclean's*, 2 Jan. 1989, 38.

190 deep divisions between French- and English-speaking Canadians: Lloyd Brown-John, "The Meech Lake Accord in Historical Perspective," in *Canadian Federalism*, 198–199.

190 After three years of debate: Russell, "A Sovereign People?" 199.

190 a cascade of commissions and proposals: Harold M. Waller, "What Lies Ahead for Canada; In the Wake of Charlottetown," *The New Leader*, 2 Nov. 1992, 9 (describing the failure of the referendum on the Charlottetown Accord, which, among other things, included a "distinct society" clause for Quebec, and also granted Quebec greater powers to preserve its character).

190 1995 referendum by Quebecers: Anne Swardson, "Post-Referendum Chill Settles over Canada," *Washington Post*, 5 Nov. 1995, A38 (margin of 50.6 percent against separation and 49.4 percent in favor).

190 "If at first you don't secede": Anthony Wilson-Smith, "Lucien Bouchard Faces a Crucial Choice," *Maclean's*, 13 Nov. 1995, 14.

190 the Canadian Parliament tried: "Canada Politics: Quebec, Provincial Powers, Key Issues," *EIU Viewswire*, 13 Feb. 1996 (discussing House of Commons resolution recognizing Quebec's distinctiveness and proposed legislation to give Quebec and three other regions a veto over future constitutional changes).

191 British Columbia: William Claiborne, "Despite Pact Failure, Precipitous Breakup of Canada Unlikely," *Washington Post*, 26 June 1990, A15 (noting the British Columbia premier's prediction that it would "seek a different type of confederation, perhaps similar to a Quebec-type association within Canada").

191 Saskatchewan: John House, "A Quiet Fury in the West," *Maclean's*, 20 Mar. 1989, 26.

191 Native Canadians: Wilson-Smith, "Lucien Bouchard," 14.

191   Elijah Harper: Barry Cooper and Rainer Knopff, "Canadian Dilemma of Collective Rights," *The Financial Post*, 24 Sept. 1991, 14.

191   Muslim group in Toronto: Bissoondath, *Selling Illusions*, 139.

192   native Hawaiians: Ellen Nakashima, "Hawaii's Aloha Spirit Meets the Spirit of Independence: Vote to Chart Course of Sovereignty Movement," *Washington Post*, 27 Aug. 1996, A1.

192   "So much office space is vacant": Anne Swardson, "O, Montreal, City of Exodus," *Washington Post*, 21 Mar. 1996, A25.

193   the European Community: See generally Louise B. van Tartwijk-Novey, *The European House of Cards: Towards a United States of Europe?* (New York: St. Martin's Press, 1995).

194   The "fiercely nationalistic Danes": Ibid., 11.

194   France's citizens: "France Says Yes to Unity with Europe—by 50.95%," *Toronto Star*, 21 Sept. 1992, A1.

194   a series of "opt-outs": "1996 and All That," *Economist*, 22 Oct. 1994, 19.

195   two-thirds of German citizens: "Getting Cold Feet over the Euro," *Chicago Tribune*, 12 Feb. 1996, 12.

195   "subsidiarity": See Desmond Dinan, *Ever Closer Union?: An Introduction to the European Community* (Boulder, Colo.: L. Rienner Publishers, 1994), 187–90.

195   the European Union's "proudest achievement": "European Union: Is the Single Market Working?," *Economist*, 17 Feb. 1996, 50.

195   Irish fishermen: Lorna Siggins, "Government to Continue Fishing Policy Despite Iberian Access to EU Waters," *Irish Times*, 17 Dec. 1994, 4.

195   A British producer of hot-air balloons: Boris Johnson, "'Single Market Has Been a Singular Disappointment," *Daily Telegraph*, 18 Jan. 1994, 13. The same article describes the examples that follow.

195   even greater obstacles: See Joel Havemann, "Europe on the Road to Unity," *Los Angeles Times*, 21 Sept. 1992, A6.

195   "a collective identity and purpose": Simon Serfaty, *Taking Europe Seriously* (New York: St. Martin's Press, 1992), 99.

196   history of war among the countries: Robert M. Worcester, "Public Opinion and Demographic Pressure in the European Community in the 1990s," in *Political Power and Social Change*, ed. Norman J. Ornstein and Mark Perlman (Washington, D.C.: AEI Press, 1991), 118, 119.

196   Just over 1 percent of Europeans: "European Union."

196   Most citizens identify themselves: "More-or-Less European Union," *Economist*, 26 Aug. 1995, 46.

196   the head of Poland's Roman Catholic Church: Tony Barber, "Cleric Warns Poles of Evils that Lurk in the EU 'Paradise,' " *Independent*, 22 Aug. 1995, 9.

196   France has grown increasingly insecure: Dominique Moisi and Michael Mertes, "Europe's Map, Compass, and Horizon," *Foreign Affairs* (Winter 1995): 122.

196   no European political process: Stanley Hoffman, "The European Union: One Body, Many Voices," *Current* (Sept. 1994): 34.

196   no European political parties: William Pfaff, "'Why a 'United' Europe Is Not in the Cards," *Chicago Tribune*, 19 June 1994, C3.

196   European Court of Justice: Hoffman, "The European Union."

196   rulings go unenforced and unheeded: Dinan, *Ever Closer Union?*, 303–304.

198   "The colonies had been founded": Merrill Jensen, *The Articles of Confederation* (Madison Wis.: The University of Wisconsin Press, 1962), 116–17.

198   "a firm league of *friendship*": Articles of Confederation, Art. III.

199 "sovereignty, freedom, and independence": This key phrase was actually the result of an amendment proposed by Thomas Burke, and was a linchpin of the Articles. "Thus the states retained their sovereign position and the central government was made a subordinate body of severely and strictly delegated powers" (Jensen, *The Articles*, 175).

199 "The fundamental difference": Ibid., 109.

199 the Anti-Federalists: Jackson Turner Main, *The Antifederalists: Critics of the Constitution: 1781–1788* (Chapel Hill, N.C.: The University of North Carolina Press, 1961), 281.

200 "a chosen body of citizens": James Madison, *The Federalist* No. 10, ed. Roy P. Fairfield (Baltimore: Johns Hopkins University Press, 1981).

200 "In the excited times in which we live": Daniel Webster, "A Plea for Harmony and Peace" in *Annals of America* 8 (1976): 24.

204 too much *pluribus* and not enough *unum:* See, e.g., Arthur M. Schlesinger Jr., *The Disuniting of America: Reflections on a Multicultural Society* (New York: Norton, 1992), 133 (asking how "to restore the balance between *unum* and *pluribus*").

Acknowledgments

*N*early everybody has some opinion about what is happening to America. I am grateful to a host of lawyers, judges, journalists, novelists, and scholars in many fields for setting down their views and observations. Even where I did not agree, I learned much from what they had to say.

I am greatly indebted to the editors of the *Stanford Law Review* who first asked me to contribute an article to their symposium, "Race and Remedy In a Multicultural Society." The article was published as "The Law of Civil Rights and the Dangers of Separatism in Multicultural America" in 47 *Stanford Law Review* (1995): 993 © by the Board of Trustees of the Leland Stanford Junior University. Grateful thanks is extended to the *Law Review* and to Fred B. Rothman & Co. of Littleton, Colorado, for permission to include significant passages from the article in this book. I would like to thank in particular Phoebe Yang, the president of the *Review*, as well as Kyle Chadwick, Christopher Davies, Alyse Graham, and Martha Redding of the *Review* board. Their many good suggestions helped me greatly.

One of the real satisfactions of being a federal judge is the continuing seminar that one holds with one's law clerks. Three of them arrive fresh from law school in my chambers each year. They are respectful and reserved at first, but they soon find the most effective ways of letting me know exactly what they think. They have not, thankfully, been quiet on the subject of this book and on the impact of the law upon separatism in America. My special thanks go to Andy Coburn, David Dobbins, Scott Gaille, Kim Hazelwood, Elizabeth Magill, Don Munro, and Sri Srinivasan. As with all of my law clerks, I suspect that in the end I learned more from them than they from me.

My deep appreciation goes to John Bell, my editor at Addison-Wesley. His interest in this subject has been invigorating, and his insight, criticism, and encouragement have helped me at every turn. This book owes a very great deal to his efforts.

Two dear and devoted friends, Professor Laurens Walker of the University of Virginia School of Law and Judge Karen LeCraft Henderson of the District of Columbia Circuit Court of Appeals, have critiqued the manuscript and offered me invaluable advice and suggestions. The responsibility for the book's conclusions and shortcomings remains, of course, solely my own.

My wife, Lossie, spent five years working on a volunteer basis with Alzheimer's patients at the Adult Day Care Center in Charlottesville. All of my royalties from this book will be contributed to the Jefferson Area Board for Aging to assist the construction of a new center, which will help families care for loved ones with this terrible disease.

Index

About the Author

$\mathcal{J}$. Harvie Wilkinson III serves as chief judge of the United States Court of Appeals for the Fourth Circuit. He was appointed to the federal bench by President Ronald Reagan in 1984.

Judge Wilkinson received his B.A. from Yale University in 1967, where he graduated Phi Beta Kappa, magna cum laude, and Scholar of the House with Exceptional Distinction. He received his law degree from the University of Virginia in 1972, where he was a member of the *Law Review* and Order of the Coif. After law school, he clerked two terms for Supreme Court Justice Lewis F. Powell Jr.

Judge Wilkinson was a member of the University of Virginia Law School faculty from 1973 to 1984, where he taught courses in constitutional law, criminal procedure, and federal courts. He served as Deputy Assistant Attorney General in the Civil Rights Division of the U.S. Department of Justice from 1982 to 1983. From 1978 to 1981, he was editor of the *Norfolk Virginian-Pilot*. In 1970 he ran as the Republican nominee for Congress from the Third Congressional District in Virginia. He was appointed the first student member of the University of Virginia Board of Visitors by Governor Linwood Holton that same year.

Judge Wilkinson has written three previous books—*From Brown to* Bakke: *The Supreme Court and School Integration, 1954–1978* (1979); *Serving Justice: A Supreme Court Clerk's View* (1974); and *Harry Byrd and the Changing Face of Virginia Politics, 1945–1966* (1968).

He was married to Lossie Grist Noell on June 30, 1973. They have a son, James Nelson Wilkinson, and a daughter, Porter Noell Wilkinson.